Exploring European Social Policy

This book is dedicated to my wife, Sigrun Skogly, and our sons, Kristoffer and Paul

Exploring European Social Policy

Robert R. Geyer

Polity Press

First published in 2000 by Polity Press
in association with Blackwell Publishers Ltd

Editorial office:
Polity Press
65 Bridge Street
Cambridge CB2 1UR, UK

Marketing and production:
Blackwell Publishers Ltd
108 Cowley Road
Oxford OX4 1JF, UK

Published in the USA by
Blackwell Publishers Inc.
Commerce Place
350 Main Street
Malden, MA 02148, USA

ISBN 0-7456-1930-4
ISBN 0-7456-1931-2 (pbk)

A catalogue record for this book is available from the British Library and has been applied for from the Library of Congress.

Typeset in 10.5 on 12 pt Sabon
by Ace Filmsetting Ltd, Frome, Somerset
Printed in Great Britain by T.J. International, Padstow, Cornwall

This book is printed on acid-free paper.

Contents

Abbreviations

CAP	Common Agricultural Policy
CEDEFOP	European Centre for the Development of Vocational Training
DG	Directorate-General
DGV	Directorate-General V
EAGGF	European Agricultural Guidance and Guarantee Fund
EAPN	European Anti-Poverty Network
EC	European Community
ECJ	European Court of Justice
ECSC	European Coal and Steel Community
ECU	European Currency Unit
EDF	European Disability Forum
EEA	European Economic Area
EEC	European Economic Community
EFTA	European Free Trade Association
EIB	European Investment Bank
EMS	European Monetary System
EPHA	European Public Health Alliance
ERDF	European Regional Development Fund
ERM	Exchange Rate Mechanism
ESC	Economic and Social Committee
ESCB	European System of Central Banks
ESF	European Social Fund
ETUC	European Trade Union Confederation
EU	European Union
EUF	European Union of Federalists

EURES	European Employment Services
EWL	European Women's Lobby
ILO	International Labour Organization
NGO	Non-Governmental Organization
OECD	Organization for Economic Co-operation and Development
OEEC	Organization for European Economic Co-operation
OPEC	Organization of Petroleum Exporting Countries
QMV	Qualified Majority Voting
SAP	Social Action Programme
SEA	Single European Act
UNICE	Union of Industrial and Employers' Confederations in Europe
UV	Unanimous Voting

Chronology

1948   Organization for European Economic Co-operation founded

1949   North Atlantic Treaty Organization founded

1951   European Coal and Steel Community Treaty signed in Paris by Belgium, France, Germany, Italy, Luxembourg and the Netherlands

1957   The Treaties of Rome negotiated (signed 1 January 1958), establishing the European Economic Community

1961   First regulation on the free movement of labour

1962   European Social Fund becomes operational

1965   France begins a boycott of Community institutions to register its opposition to various proposed supranational developments

1966   Foreign Ministers agree to the Luxembourg Compromise; normal Community processes resume

1969   The Hague Summit: agreement to strengthen European Community (EC) institutions, enlarge membership, establish an economic and monetary union by 1980 and support social policy development

1973   Denmark, Ireland and the United Kingdom become EC members

1974   First Social Action Programme created

1974   European Trade Union Confederation created

1979   European Monetary System (EMS) comes into operation

1981   Greece becomes an EC member

1985   The Commission publishes its White Paper on the completion of the internal market; Luxembourg European Council meeting agrees the principles of the Single European Act (SEA); qualified majority voting (QMV) established for health and safety issues

1986 Spain and Portugal become EC members

1987 SEA comes into force

1988 Commission proposes a Social Dimension to the internal market

1989 The Delors Committee presents its report (Delors Report), outlining a scheme for a three-stage progression to EMU; Strasbourg European Council meeting accepts the 1988 Social Charter

1989–90 Implementation of the 1989 Social Action Programme

1991 Maastricht European Council meeting agrees to the Treaty of European Union; the treaty expands QMV for social policy and creates the Social Protocol in order to surmount the British veto

1993 The Maastricht Treaty ratified

1994 First use of the Social Protocol to pass the Works Council Directive

1995 First use of the Social Dialogue to create the Parental Leave Directive

1995 Austria, Finland and Sweden become EU members

1995 1995–7 Medium-Term Social Action Programme launched

1997 The British Conservative government defeated in May; the new Labour government immediately signs up to the Social Protocol

1997 Amsterdam European Council agrees to the Treaty of Amsterdam; the Social Protocol is integrated into the text of the treaties

1998 1998–2000 Social Action Programme launched

1999 Special European Council meeting in Berlin, at which heads of government reach agreement on *Agenda 2000* regarding measures for integrating new East European member-state applicants

Preface

The true foundation of this book project was my failure to find 'socialism' in France in 1984! As a young American university student and social democrat, disgusted with the constraints of American political dialogue in the 1980s, I was determined to find real democratic socialism in the aftermath of the French Socialist Party's victory in 1981. However, by the time I arrived in 1984 for an academic year in Paris, Mitterrand had already abandoned most of the Keynesian reflationary economic strategies that had been put in place in 1981–2 and was beginning to embrace the idea of Europe. Global and European forces, combined with French domestic politics, had overrun the Mitterrand socialist strategy. Two questions were increasingly apparent to me and much of the West European left. Could social democracy exist in any one country? If not, could it reassert itself through the European Community?

Following a year at the University of Essex, I found myself, through a combination of academic interest and fate, working in the last bastion of traditional social democracy in Western Europe in the late 1980s – Scandinavia, specifically Norway. State budgets were still massive, workers' rights incredible, social policy universal and lavish, and hegemonic social democratic parties dominated the political process. Nevertheless, traditional Scandinavian social democracy was increasingly being pressured externally and transformed internally. During the late 1980s in Scandinavia, traditional Keynesian strategies were increasingly abandoned, state expenditure constrained and the expansion of the public sector curtailed. A key element of this transformation was the relationship of Scandinavian social democrats to the European Community. For 'modernizing' social democrats, abandon-

ing traditional strategies and linking to the emerging EC were necessary responses to Europeanization and globalization. Traditional national-level social democracy was dead. The best one could hope for
was some type of Euro-social democracy. Traditional social democrats strongly opposed this thinking and in the early 1990s the two
sides fought each other ferociously over the issue of membership in
the European Union, the Swedes voting to join and the Norwegians to
stay out in 1994.

I was fascinated by this political battle and the interplay between
the 'modernization' of social democratic parties and their relationships to the EU. I spent several years working on this issue while I was
a PhD student at the University of Wisconsin, and subsequently published a number of works on it.[1] In essence, the fate of these battles
hinged on the answers to the questions of the early 1980s. However,
as with most political questions, there was no clear answer. On the
one hand, traditional national-level Keynesian economic controls had
been lost, but national-level welfare states and social policies remained
remarkably resilient to radical change. On the other, European integration had made impressive strides in the late 1980s and early 1990s.
Nevertheless, EU social policy remained limited and secondary. The
welfare states of Western Europe had defended themselves remarkably well, while the European welfare state was little more than a
'nightwatchman state'. The conclusion which I drew from this
conflictual and uncertain state of affairs was that the earlier social
democratic debates on the transition from the national welfare state
to some form of Europeanized welfare state had been misconceived.
The relationship between national-level social policies and the EU level
was much more complicated than those earlier debates assumed. Consequently, analysing this relationship was not just a simple matter of
observing the transference of policy capabilities from the national to
the European level, but a complex one of charting the interplay between the two.

Following the completion of my work on the relationship between
the British and Norwegian Labour Parties and the EU and my acceptance of employment in the Department of Politics at the University of
Liverpool in 1996, I began to explore the development of EU social
policy and its relationship to national-level social policy. Through my
studies and having to teach the subject to inquisitive undergraduate
and graduate students, I quickly made two discoveries: I was unhappy
with the existing works on EU social policy; in order to truly come to
grips with the whole complex area of EU social policy, one had to
pursue a difficult two-step strategy. First, one had to have an accurate
picture or 'map' of EU social policy. Second, with this map, one could
then turn to the particular national arenas and examine how EU social

policy interacted with member states' social policies. The difficulty in the first step lies in the need to focus on European policy developments without ignoring national factors too much, while the difficulty in the second lies in the danger of undue concentration on national dynamics.

I began my 'first step', mapping EU social policy, in 1997. My 'second step' is in the planning stages. As I argue in my final chapter, I am certain that this type of study will be at the centre of the next wave of EU social policy research. In the end, my hope is that these two works will provide students and social policy activists with a thorough understanding of EU social policy and its interrelationship with key national-level social policies. Moreover, as I argue below, I firmly believe that the future of EU social policy lies not with the occasional well-publicized actions of the Commission or Parliament, but with the small-scale, unheralded, daily activities of social policy activists and interest groups. Often operating on minimal budgets and under enormous workloads, these groups quietly struggle to move social policies through the often Byzantine EU policy process. The results of their individual efforts are often minuscule, but the cumulative effect is essential for maintaining the future of the 'human face' of Europe.

Lastly, I would briefly like to express my thanks to a number of institutions and individuals. The University of Liverpool's Research Development Fund provided essential funding for my research. Among my Liverpool colleagues, Andrew Geddes was extremely helpful in helping me obtain funding for the book, in reviewing several chapters and in just being a good friend. Beverly Springer helped to give me the confidence to start this project. Rebecca Harkin at Polity Press was everything a writer could look for in an editor. My father, Bill Geyer, whose 'classical' education far exceeds my own, significantly strengthened my grammatical and stylistic weaknesses. Friends and colleagues in Brussels, especially Ingrid Sogner, Eamonn Noonan, Arnhild Sauer and David Spence, provided me with a place to stay and special insights into the 'real' EU policy process. Special thanks need to be extended to the more than seventy interviewees in the Commission, Parliament, Council and social policy NGOs who freely gave their time and opinions to an often befuddled academic. Most important, I would like to thank my wife, Sigrun Skogly, for her unwavering support and advice. Of course, all errors remain my own.

An interactive website for this book with further EU social policy links, updated material and further information can be found at **www.social-science-forum.org**

Introduction

The phenomenal growth of the European Union (EU) in the period after the Second World War and the remarkable acceleration of that growth in the 1980s and 1990s makes the need to understand the development and impact of EU policy areas on Western (and Eastern) European nation-states essential. This point is obvious in the areas of monetary, trade and economic policy. In other policy areas, particularly social policy, the role of the EU seems much less important, secondary at best, insignificant at worst. A cursory view of the early history of EU social policy would seem to support its subordinate role. The few paragraphs in the founding treaties of the EU, minor policy development in the 1950s and 1960s and the aborted expansion of social policy in the early 1970s characterize the insubstantial nature of early EU social policy development. However, with the revival of European integration in the late 1980s under the Single European Act and in the early 1990s with the Maastricht Treaty, EU social policy experienced a remarkable expansion and growth of influence. Through new documents such as the Social Charter, Social Dimension and Social Protocol, EU policies regarding labour, gender, social inclusion and so on rapidly expanded. This recent expansion raises two key questions. Why did this expansion occur and can it be sustained? Is the growth of EU social policy a positive development?

For the first question, interpretations of traditional European integration theories diverge strongly. For intergovernmentalists, representing the realist view of international relations, EU social policy, like European integration in general, is doomed to move in a Sisyphean[1] cycle of near success, then collapse. For them, deluded Europeanists and social policy supporters have continually tried to create substantial EU social policy through the founding treaties, EU organizations and specific pieces of EU legislation. However, despite their best attempts, EU social policy has always been undercut by resistance from the member states, key interest groups (particularly European capital), by the institutional weakness of the EU, and by the feebleness of social policy within the EU itself. Hence, despite recent successes propelled by key member states, EU social policy is still subject to the will of the member states and is unlikely to make further sustainable advances.

On the other hand, theorists coming out of the functionalist and neo-functionalist tradition would agree that EU social policy has been one of the most laggard areas of policy development. From the onset of the integration strategy, EU social policy has played a secondary role and often stagnated. Even today, it remains unevenly implemented and poorly financed. Key member states and interest groups have continually opposed its development. In spite of this, theorists would point out that due to the development of the EU, to the activities of the Commission and European interest groups and the impact of 'spillover', social policy has grown in scope, importance and influence, paralleling the expanding significance and power of the EU itself. Consequently, social policy has managed to progress and should continue to do so for the foreseeable future.

The answer to the question of whether EU social policy development is positive depends on where one sits on the left–right political spectrum. Generally, for those on the right, particularly free-market liberals, the development of EU social policy has been counterproductive and a potentially dangerous threat. For them, the economic world changed in the 1980s and 1990s. Globalization has stripped Western European nation-states of their ability to control and regulate their economies, and survival in this fiercely competitive environment requires embracing these new forces, reducing national-level controls, deregulating the economy and minimizing social constraints on the functioning of the market. Their support for European integration was based on the free market and deregulatory nature of the common market strategy. As the economies of the EU member states were increasingly forced to open up to each other, European-level market forces would be unleashed, national-level social constraints would crumble and a reinvigorated European economy and society would emerge. EU social policy could undermine all of these potential gains by contradicting the basic deregulatory nature of the new era. It could enable nation-states to maintain existing social policies. It might even introduce new ones at both the national and European level. In short, it represents the growth of the EU state beyond a minimalist, deregulatory, free-market framework.

For others, particularly on the social democratic and Christian left, the growth of EU social policy has been both tardy and frail. They agree with those on the right that growing globalization put increasing constraints on the economic controls and welfare states of the West European nations. As growth and tax revenues declined, unemployment and competition increased, putting a fiscal and political squeeze on national-level social policy. Social democrats had a growing sense that the era of the nationally based Keynesian welfare state had come to an end. As the EU was reinvigorated in the late 1980s and early 1990s, these groups hoped that EU social policy would be capable of protecting Europe's generally high level of social policy and provision from international competition, blunting the excesses ('social dumping') of the free-market-oriented common market strategy, and possibly laying the foundation for some form of new Euro-level welfare state structure as well as the Euro-market.

In this book I argue that neither of the traditional theories adequately explain EU social policy development and the current left–right debate over the impact of EU social policy is misdirected. As is argued in detail in chapters 1 and 2, EU social policy has developed, similar to the EU, due to a variety of factors. Despite its institutional weaknesses and the opposition of the member states, EU social policy has seen significant advances in the 1980s and 1990s. Moreover, due to its increased embeddedness in the EU institutional process, to the growth of EU social policy NGOs and the continued success of the larger integration project, EU social policy is likely to see further development in the foreseeable future. However, as chapters 3–8 demonstrate, this progress has been very uneven both over time and between the various sub-areas of social policy. In essence, no single theory can either fully explain or predict the development of EU social policy. The concluding chapter explores the complex and contingent nature of EU social policy. At present, a number of its key sub-areas appear set for further advances. Further, the larger European and international contexts seem to support further EU social policy developments. However, changes in the larger context and in the dynamic of key sub-areas could easily change. Recognizing this complexity and uncertainty is a key step in moving beyond the traditional debates.

Obviously, this book cannot truly address the second question. The positive or negative nature of EU social policy hinges on the theoretical and moral position one takes towards welfare states and social policy in general. It is beyond the scope of this book to delve into the deep debates and numerous works on the nature and morality of the welfare state. Nevertheless, the left–right debate over EU social policy in the 1980s and early 1990s suffered from two related weaknesses: the debate often lacked detailed knowledge of the policy and its inter-action with national social policy regimes; aggravated by this lack, the debate was premised on the assumption of the imminent collapse of national welfare states and the potential development of an EU wel-fare state. As an increasing number of observers have recognized in the 1990s, national-level welfare states are not collapsing or converg-ing. Moreover, the fears of or hopes for the creation of a European welfare state are both unfounded. Some EU social policy areas, par-ticularly gender policy, have seen significant development and influence. At the same time, others, particularly policy for the elderly, remain inconsequential. The reality of EU social policy is a much more complex mix of success and failure. The aim of this book is to increase the general knowledge of EU social policy and to encourage social policy opponents and proponents to reassess their interpretations of EU social policy and shift away from a rather fruitless debate over the creation of an EU welfare state and towards the complex interaction between EU and member-state social policy regimes. In essence, the new European welfare state is not located at the EU level, but remains predominantly national. However, a new arena of social policy co-operation, co-ordination and struggle has been opened up at the EU level. The more social policy actors are able to take advantage of this level, the more likely symbiotic relationships will develop between the national and EU policy levels. As a proponent of EU social policy, I hope that this shift in debate will allow for the focusing of research and political effort on exploring the potential of this symbiotic rela-tionship.

The strategy of the book

The book's titular objective of exploring EU social policy poses three questions. How do I define EU social policy? Why focus on EU social policy? What do I mean by 'exploring' EU social policy?

Defining social policy is never easy. Richard Titmuss, one of the founders of the study of modern social policy, lamented, 'this tiresome business of defining social policy' (Titmuss, 1974: 28). A brief glance at any basic work on this topic would show the variety of theoretical interpretations and distinctive developments of differing national so-cial policy regimes (Lavalette and Pratt, 1997). Moreover, the EU so-cial policy regime's very distinctive structure and dynamics further complicate the creation of a clear and concise definition. For example, if one were to use T.H. Marshall's classic definition of social policy as the use of 'political power to supersede, supplement or modify operations of the economic system in order to achieve results which the economic system would not achieve on its own' (Marshall, 1975: 15), then one could certainly argue that the most important and substantial European social policy is EU agricultural policy. The Common Agricultural Policy (CAP) is a massive policy area, controlling nearly two-thirds of the EU budget and with its strategies of income support, market direction, education and training could easily be seen as using political power to shape economic outcomes. Lacking a clear theoretical model, I have chosen to use the EU's practical definition of social policy, the activities of the Commission's Directorate-General V (DGV) responsible for employment, industrial relations and social affairs, as my definition of the boundaries of EU social policy. Consequently, all the main areas of DGV activity are reflected in my chapter topics. There are obvious weaknesses in this strategy, one of which is that DGV's activities have varied over time. For example, as this book goes to press it has just been announced that the responsibility for public health policy has been moved from DGV to DGXXIV. Nevertheless, DGV's activities do provide a reasonable and traceable outline of EU social policy.

Regarding the second question, one should ask how one can study EU social policy in isolation from the social policy of the various welfare states of the member states. Clearly, EU social policy is related to the development of these welfare states. EU social policy has generally been built around the institutional structures of existing welfare states as a minimalist floor underneath existing social policy regulations and rules. Throughout most of the history of the EU, member states have maintained strict control over EU social policy though the unanimous voting (UV) procedures in the Council. Moreover, one of the most interesting elements of EU social policy is its relationship and impact on differing welfare state structures. While these are valid points, EU social policy has become so important that it not only deserves specific attention as a policy area in its own right, but it has also become sufficiently substantial as a policy area to fully occupy a book-length manuscript. Further, EU social policy, with the expansion of qualified majority voting (QMV) in the Council, its expanding base in the treaties and the growing activity and influence of social policy NGOs, has increasingly escaped from direct control by member states. As such, it is essential to trace the emergence of this transition not from the perspective of the member states, but from that of the European level. This is not to say that national-level dynamics are unimportant or can be completely ignored. In this book, I often refer to national-level demands and dynamics. However, in order to trace the map of EU social policy, I could mention the national-level influences only briefly. As mentioned in the preface, this book is intended to 'map' the policy contours of EU social policy; my second work will rectify some of the national deficiencies that are inherent in this text.

Third, what do I mean by 'exploring' social policy? There are two parts to my definition of exploration, my desire to explore beyond the limitations of existing works and my methodological approach. Despite its growing importance, academic understanding and debate on EU social policy remain surprisingly limited. The secondary position of EU social policy, the recent focus on economic and monetary integration and EU institutional blockages have combined to constrain the development of and interest in EU social policy. There are a few books that examine EU social policy. These include collections of essays that explore particular elements of EU social policy or bring together excellent published articles on different aspects or implications of that policy[2] and other works which provide some degree of overview to the development and scope of social policy.[3] Unfortunately, none of these works provides a comprehensive and up-to-date examination of the development, scope and theoretical impact of EU social policy. This book is meant to fill that gap.

Exploration is also a good metaphor for my methodological approach. The study of EU social policy lies at the intersection of international relations, regional integration theory and comparative policy studies.[4] What marks this intersection is the reliance on 'historical institutionalism' and the 'comparative approach'. Historical institutionalism, an established theoretical perspective which significantly revived in the 1980s and 1990s,[5] argues that the key nexus for policy development is in the embedded historical policy legacies of central policy institutions. By focusing on the actors and developments within intermediate-level institutions, institutionalism provides the theoretical 'bridge between "men who make history" and the "circumstances" under which they are able to do so' (Rothstein, 1992: 35). Closely linked to historical institutionalism is the comparative approach.[6] As opposed to a more behaviouralist and statistically oriented comparative method, the comparative approach is less scientifically rigorous in that it tries to capture the complexity and interrelatedness of comparative politics and policy studies. As Jean Blondel wrote, the comparative approach is 'a multi-pronged effort designed to come as close as possible to the many facets of the reality of the institutions, people, and countries which constitute the context within which government acts and develops' (Blondel, 1981: 168).

Essentially, this methodology assumes that the primary goal of research is to explore, rather than to prove. Mapping the development of EU social policy requires a knowledge and synthesis of earlier works, extensive analysis of primary documents and a detailed knowledge of the primary actors. Over the past two years, I am confident that I have reviewed all major English language texts on EU social policy, obtained most of the major primary documents (an increasingly easy task due to the internet) and acquired first-hand knowledge through my interviews with EU social policy actors.

Chapter outlines

The choice of chapter topics and overall structure of the book reflect my desire to correct the limitations of the previous literature on EU social policy and lay a foundation for further research into the relationship between EU and national-level social policy regimes. Chapters 1 and 2 provide the fundamental historical and theoretical background for the later policy chapters. Chapter 1 begins with a brief definition and history of social policy and the limited international aspects of its development. It then briefly reviews the three major theories of European integration associated with the period after the Second World War: the federalist 'vision', functionalist 'plan', and neo-functionalist 'spillover', paying special attention to the role of social policy in each. Following this, the chapter explores the foundation of EU social policy in the Treaties of Paris (1951) and Rome (1957), and then turns to the limited developments in social policy during the late 1950s and 1960s and the theory of realism. The role of social policy in realist thinking was of minimal significance and was dependent on the national interests of the various member states. The theory, sceptical of the development of the EU, fit well with the stagnation of the EU in the 1960s.

Chapter 2 begins with a brief examination of the revival of social policy in the early 1970s under the 1974 Social Action Programme and follows the uneven development of social policy throughout the 1970s and early 1980s. During this time, theoretical understanding of European integration and policy development shifted from the starkly pessimistic views of realism to the more cautiously optimistic opinions of confederalism. The chapter then examines the revival of the EU and EU social policy in the late 1980s and early 1990s under the Single European Act and 1992 Project, and explores the development of the Social Dimension, Social Charter, 1989 Social Action Programme and the impact of the EU Commission led by Jacques Delors. During this period, debates focused on the nature of and need for EU social policy.

Generally, free-market conservatives argued against it, and social democrats for it. The final section of chapter 2 discusses the most recent EU social policy developments, the growth of a more pluralist form of EU social policy formation[7] and the theoretical transition from macro- to meso-level theorizing.

Chapters 3 and 4 focus on the crucial areas of EU labour policy. Of the various areas of EU social policy, labour policy is probably the most contentious. It reflects deep philosophical divisions within European politics and society, attracts powerful, committed and determined interest groups (capital and labour) and is obviously extremely important to the functioning of the advanced industrial economies of Western Europe. Chapter 3 explores the less controversial 'core' policies of freedom of movement of labour and health and safety policy. These were built into the earliest EU treaties, both as a strategy for creating a true European market and as a way of reassuring wary workers that their economic and social position would not be eroded by labour market integration. Of primary interest is the way in which these areas were used as 'Trojan horses' to bring in other areas of EU labour and social policy.

Chapter 4 explores the main extensions to EU labour policy that emerged after the 1970s. These included the development of policies in the areas of employment rights and working conditions, worker participation and the social dialogue. These areas emerged in the aftermath of the 1974 Social Action Programme and were justified through direct and indirect reference to the core areas of labour policy. Promoted by DGV in the EU Commission, the Parliament, socialist parties (at the national and European level) and European trade unions, these areas saw some degree of success, particularly during the late 1980s and early 1990s. Although all of them have now become firmly established within the field of EU social policy, their current strength and potential for continued expansion vary substantially.

Chapter 5 concerns the fascinating development of EU gender policy. From its beginning in Article 119 in the Treaty of Rome, ratified on 1 January 1958, through the remarkable European Court of Justice (ECJ) cases of the 1980s to the present 'mainstreaming' of gender issues, EU gender policy has been one of the most impressive areas of social policy development. Spurred on by the growth of 'second wave' feminism in Western Europe, an increasingly effective women's group lobbying organization, as well as the breakdown of the traditional family structure and male-dominated occupational structure, gender policy has made enormous strides since the 1970s. By the 1980s, gender policy had become a well-funded policy area with a significant and growing legal base. In the 1990s it proved to be one of the most important social policy areas and was increasingly 'mainstreamed' into other policy areas.

In chapter 6 I move from the most successful area of EU social policy to the wealthiest, the EU Structural Funds, in particular the European Social Fund (ESF). In the current funding period (1994–9), the structural funds have planned to allocate a total of 138 billion ECU, of which the ESF intend to allocate around 42 billion ECU.[8] In many ways, this is the heart of the European social project. From its very inception in the 1957 Treaty of Rome, the ESF was intended to 'improve employment opportunities for workers', primarily through encouraging mobility, vocational training and unemployment aid. As the EU progressed, the Structural Funds and the ESF expanded and moved into wider policy areas, created a more European orientation and profile, and developed a multitude of distinctive projects and programmes. A key focus of this chapter is the difference between past and present policy roles of the Structural Funds and the ESF. Are they regional or social policies, or are they just bribes for the weaker member states and social groups to keep them committed to the larger integration project?

Chapter 7 looks at three of the most recent areas of EU social policy expansion: those on anti-poverty/social inclusion, anti-race discrimination against racism and on public health. Though anti-poverty policy has its roots in the 1970s, it was not until the late 1980s that these three policy areas begin to develop at the EU level. In the 1990s these policy areas have experienced different levels of success. Anti-poverty policy development looked extremely promising in 1993 with the expanding budget of the Fourth Poverty Programme and the burgeoning concepts of social inclusion/exclusion. However, following the Council's rejection of the programme in 1994, the policy area has stagnated. Anti-discrimination policy against racism has always had a delicate position in the EU system. The EU has been reluctant to accept responsibility for a difficult policy area, while the member states have been unwilling to cede authority over it. Nevertheless, responding to the rise of far right parties in the 1980s and racist crimes in the early 1990s (particularly in Germany and France), the EU began to develop more anti-discrimination legislation against racism and has recently inserted an anti-discrimination Article into the 1997 Amsterdam Treaty. Finally, public health policy emerged out of particular health issues of the 1980s and 1990s: drug dependence; cancer (particularly where linked to smoking); AIDS; health promotion; and information. Emphasizing the importance of member-state co-operation and the information and research orientation of this policy area, the EU has pushed into the field of public health with relative ease. With the continued importance of these health issues and the commitments made by the Amsterdam Treaty to further European public health, this is one EU social policy area which will probably expand.

Chapter 8 examines the emergence of three policy areas linked to specific social groups, the elderly, the disabled and the young. Of these three, the policy for the elderly has been the least successful within the EU policy process. Ignored in the founding treaties, not recognized until the 1974 Social Action Programme and only occasionally referred to in related policy areas of social inclusion and social protection during the 1970s and 1980s, elderly policy did not establish itself until the 1988 Social Charter, the 1989 Social Action Programme and subsequent action programmes. Its failure to gain a firm base in the Maastricht and Amsterdam treaties demonstrates its continued weakness. Similarly, disability policy made no significant appearance in EU social policy until the early 1970s. Following the 1974 Social Action Programme, a series of action programmes were created to improve the condition of the disabled in Europe. By the late 1980s, disability policy had firmly established itself in the programmatic side of EU social policy, but had yet to make significant legislative developments. Though the disabled were ignored by the Maastricht Treaty, the Amsterdam Treaty and subsequent Employment Guidelines did recognize their needs. Finally, some aspects of youth policy have been deeply rooted and very successful in the EU social policy process. Areas such as vocational training, student mobility, and employment promotion for the young have been core elements of EU policy since the Treaty of Rome. These areas of youth policy have substantial roots in the treaties, particularly the Maastricht Treaty, and are supported by substantial funding from the Structural Funds. However, outside these traditional areas, youth policy has seen little or no development.

The final chapter opens with a brief summary of the current 'map' of EU social policy. I then explore how EU social policy is not like national-level social policy, how it has become primarily regulatory, exhibiting a variety of policy dynamics, not significantly replacing or undermining national social policy regimes. I conclude with a discussion of the next wave of EU social policy research and the uncertain future of EU social policy.

1

European Social Policy
1950–1969

[The Commission] cannot conceive that the Community has not got a social purpose.

EEC, Second General Report, 1958[1]

This then is the sum total of social policy measures in the Treaty of Rome: a whiff of society-creating measures in Articles 2, 117 and 118; a gesture towards harmonisation in Articles 119 and 120; and a strong element of functional social policy to encourage the mobility of labour, and the retraining of workers through the ESF.

Hoskyns, Integrating Gender

How is it that such divergent views could be held over the role of social policy in the early years of the EU? Was social policy at the heart of the early treaties of Paris and Rome that laid the foundation for the ECSC and the EEC? Or was social policy an afterthought used to placate the threatened in the integration process? Moreover, what role did social policy play in early integration theory? This chapter attempts to explore these questions. It starts with a review of the key social policy developments at the international level and within the ECSC and EEC member states in the years immediately after the Second World War. I then examine three early integration theories, federalism, functionalism and neo-functionalism as well as their inter-pretation of EU social policy, succeeded by an analysis of the role of social policy in the treaties of Paris and Rome, and a brief overview of major social policy developments. In conclusion I argue that EU social policy has been an uncertain and controversial policy since its crea-tion. It has generally had a secondary role in relation to the larger goal of economic integration, but was expected to become increasingly im-portant as integration progressed.

West European social policy in the early postwar years

The foundations of the European Coal and Steel Community (ECSC) and European Economic Community (EEC) were based on fundamental military and economic bargains between the major member states. These bargains revolved around the answers to such questions as how to rebuild the broken economies of Western Europe, how to deal with the growing threat from the USSR, and what should be done with Germany. Social policy, or concerns over its development, played only a limited role in early integration strategies. The early unimportance of European-level social policy (in marked contrast to national developments) greatly limited its scope, but did not completely eliminate it from the European agenda.

West European social policy has a long and detailed history (Ashford, 1986; Esping-Andersen, 1990; Flora, 1986; Gough, 1979; Marshall, 1975; Pierson, 1991; Titmuss, 1974). Its modern roots easily reach back into the second half of the nineteenth century, when demands for state provisioning of education, health care, unemployment insurance, pensions, labour rights and family support all began to be heard. The variety of these demands was staggering and their various institutional manifestations often reflected the general orientation of early national welfare state structures. For example, early German 'conservative' social policies aimed at co-opting and integrating the working class into a conservative Bismarckian social order. Early French social policies were used to promote a Catholic family structure. Meanwhile, early British social policies, such as the reforming of the Poor Laws in the mid-nineteenth century, reflected the more liberal, market-oriented approach of the British system.

Social policies grew throughout the twentieth century, and expanded rapidly after the Second World War. This postwar expansion was triggered by a number of demands from soldiers who had made tremendous sacrifices during the war, families who had suffered because of the war, and the general population that felt that the state had a growing responsibility to do something about the basic condition of society. In some cases, these policies were undertaken by left-wing governments, particularly in Britain and Scandinavia. In others, they developed under conservative or Christian-democratic regimes such as in Germany and France. Moreover, as the economies of Western Europe began to revive in the late 1940s, the expanding economic capacity and fiscal resources allowed the state to expand social policies and social rights. Despite a great deal of variation between the

European social policy regimes, European welfare states and social policy seemed to be following a similar developmental path.

As T.H. Marshall argued in his seminal work, *Citizenship and Social Class* (1950), West European societies seemed to be going through a similar developmental process in regard to the nature of citizenship and individual and social rights. Marshall saw this as a three-step process involving the creation, expansion and universalization of fundamental civil rights (eighteenth century), the formation of universal political rights (nineteenth century) and the foundation of fundamental social rights (twentieth century). Social rights were the zenith of citizenship rights and had become increasingly universalized, within the various nation-states, in the early postwar period. In the early 1950s social expenditure by West European nation-states varied between 10–20 per cent of GNP. By the mid-1970s it had grown to 25–33 per cent of GNP (Flora, 1986: xxii). Marshall's book was a clear reflection of the public expectations for the development of social rights and policies in the early postwar period. The particular type and level of social policy varied from country to country, but for Marshall (and many others) the trend was towards expansion and universalization of these rights and policies.

At the supranational level, were social policies being discussed and implemented? The answer is: yes, they were discussed; and no, they were not implemented. By 1948 three major international institutions had a substantial social policy component to their work. The oldest was the International Labour Organization (ILO). The ILO was founded in 1919 in the aftermath of the First World War and was oriented towards improving the living standards and rights of working persons. After the Second World War the reputation and influence of the ILO was greatly boosted by a supportive US government and its linkage to the United Nations. Its job was to provide information on labour and working conditions, and promote the creation of full employment, increasing living standards, and basic social and economic rights within the member countries. The ILO did produce a number of documents on basic working, labour and social rights; its power to inform, encourage or embarrass gave it some influence, particularly among smaller nations, but it never had the ability to directly intervene in or substantially influence a national situation (Galenson, 1981). Likewise the UN, founded in 1944, did create a substantial body of basic economic and social rights in its original charter which member states were supposed to fulfil. However, most Western European nations far exceeded the level of these basic rights and the UN lacked the political will and policy capabilities to rigorously implement them. Finally, the Council of Europe, founded in 1948, created a European

Charter of Human Rights in 1953 that included some social rights. Moreover, in 1961 the Council presented its European Social Charter (Gomien et al., 1996). Similar to the principles of the UN and the ILO, this charter was a list of basic social rights which most of the West European countries easily surpassed. Council of Europe members who signed the charter were expected to maintain and improve upon these basic provisions. However, policing and implementing these policies was left up to the member states. The Council of Europe had no money or powers to implement the rights, leaving the charter with little impact on particular social rights other than through its moral force.

Early European integration theory

Before turning to the earliest elements of EU social policy, it is necessary to step back and examine the role of social policy in early European integration theory. During the 1940s and 1950s there were three main theories which attempted to explain and direct the development of European integration: federalism, functionalism and neo-functionalism (Harrison, 1974; Pentland, 1973; Heater, 1992).

Federalism

The theory of federalism has a long and distinguished history both as a type of government and as a theory of governing (Riker, 1964; Wheare, 1953; Heater, 1992). The ancient Greeks established early federalist leagues. Other examples include the Hanseatic League (gradually formed in various north German cities, *c*.1250–1350), the Swiss federation (founded in the fifteenth to sixteenth century), Dutch federal republic (sixteenth century), United States (eighteenth century) and Germany (nineteenth century). As a theory of uniting different regions/states into a diverse yet unified unit, federalism received a substantial boost in Western Europe following the two world wars. These left a desperate desire within many people for the creation of a more unified society that would contain or eliminate such conflicts, at least within Western Europe (Heater, 1992: chapters 6–7). In 1946 the European Union of Federalists (EUF) was established, building on earlier federalist organizations and including a number of former resistance fighters and leading intellectuals (mostly prominently Altiero Spinelli, the future EEC Commissioner).

At its most basic level, postwar European federalism relied upon three main assumptions (Harrison, 1974: chapter 3). First, human society was complex and heterogeneous. Such issues as language, race and culture could not be reduced to one clear and homogeneous social model. Second, society was pluralistic. Different interests had their legitimate place within various cultures and groups and the right to autonomy, protection and influence within general society. Third, since society was diverse and pluralistic (and would continue to be so for the foreseeable future), institutions must be devised to grant not only autonomy and protection, but a voice to these various elements of society while unifying them within a larger framework. The envisioned framework generally included a state structure divided both vertically, between central, regional and local institutions, and horizontally, between distinct central institutions and resting upon a constitutional edifice that balanced the rights and responsibilities of both the central and regional bodies and interests. In theory, the benefits of the federal system included: a barrier against central despotism; the protection of minority interests; the peaceful integration of conflicting interests; and the ability to solve societal problems at the level of government (local, regional, national, supranational) that was most suited to the particular problem.

For the postwar Euro-federalists, their system could resolve the previously irreconcilable differences that had twice torn Western Europe apart. With its combination of local, regional, national and federal governmental structures allowing for a maximum amount of diversity and protection of minority and regional rights within a unifying framework, European federalism would provide the necessary freedom and autonomy for the different European societies at the same time as it would provide for and encourage co-operation and conflict resolution. Pluralistic autonomy would be wedded to a co-operative and integrated federal structure to produce a productive and peaceful West European society that would be a model not only for the rest of Europe, but for the world as well.

The key problem for the federalists was how to go from the existing European structure of antagonistic and competitive nation-states to the formation of a European federation. For moderate federalists, such as Spinelli, the federalist goal could be obtained only through slow moderate reforms that increasingly integrated the differing nation-states into a growing federal structure. For radical federalists, the late 1940s represented a revolutionary moment in West European history. The legacy of two world wars had weakened the traditional hold of nationalism. West European society was sick of war and desperate for a new peaceful political system. Radical federalists hoped to channel this discontent into a political force that would demand the immediate creation of a European federal system.

The role of social policy in both the moderate and radical federal visions was secondary and obscure. The ideas and plans of the federalists were much more grandiose than the petty concerns of social policy. The federalists were trying to establish a new, prosperous and peaceful European order. Their expectation was that if European federalism could be created, then peace would be assured, the economy and society would prosper, and social problems would be alleviated by these broader developments. The creation of European level social rights and social policies would obviously play a role in this development.

What happened to federalist thinking in the 1950s? The radical federalists were doomed to disappointment. In the immediate aftermath of the Second World War, there was a brief upsurge in public opinion against the nation-state and towards some vision of Euro-federalism. However, as war memories faded, the economies of Western Europe revived, and the Cold War heated up, public support for the various nation-states returned and the hopes of creating a political force for federalism turned out to be a mirage. Without the European democratic force, radical federalists were little more than 'voices crying in the wilderness' (Harrison, 1974: 44). Moreover, with the failure of the Council of Europe, the ECSC and EEC to adopt a federal structure and the collapse of the proposed European Defence Community and European Political Community in 1954 (Willis, 1968; Grosser, 1982), the movement lost its internal organization and drive and ceased to play a major role in EU affairs.

On the other hand, the moderate or evolutionary federalists saw the limited successes of the Council of Europe, the ECSC and EEC as laying the basis for some form of future federal structure. As already noted, several of the moderate federalists (Spinelli) moved into prominent positions within the new Euro-institutions. Despite disagreements about the pace of federal transformation, the moderate federalist vision has played a role in the strategies and plans of the EU from its earliest days to the present.

Functionalism

It is rather ironic that the second main theory of early European integration, functionalism, was originally opposed to the creation of regional or continental supranational federations. As David Mitrany argued in the seminal work of the functionalists, *A Working Peace System*: 'There is little promise of peace in the mere change from the rivalry of Powers and alliances to the rivalry of whole continents. . . . Continental unions would have a more real chance than individual states to practise the autarky that makes for division' (Mitrany, 1966: 45). Like early realists in international relations theory, Mitrany and the early functionalists saw the largest threat to peace in Western Europe and elsewhere as the anarchical international system and the self-interested actions of individual states within that anarchical order. Building regional blocs or super-states within that basic order would not change the prospects for peace. For Mitrany, individuals were generally rational, economistic, utilitarian, self-interested and welfare-oriented. Society, mirroring the thinking of classical economics, was little more than a collection of these individuals. In many ways, states were reflections of individuals. They were generally rational and self-interested. However, nation-states, caught in an anarchical world order, continually had to justify their existence to their constituent societies and at the same time defend themselves against attacks from other states. This aggressive-defensive relationship was fundamentally opposed to the basic utilitarian and welfare-oriented nature of individuals. As long as nation-states existed within an anarchical international system, this contradiction would continue, and the basically co-operative and economistic tendencies of society would be suppressed under the potentially violent struggles caused by nation-state competition.

To escape from this trap and to create real peace and prosperity, society had to subvert and eventually eliminate the nation-state. As opposed to international-relations realists, functionalists thought this could be done through a slow, steady process of functional transformation. Individuals and interest groups needed to shift their national orientation and strategies towards the opportunities and benefits of international co-operation. This would not be done at the state level, but on the relatively low level of basic social and economic interactions. Economic groups demanding greater market opportunities, academic groups desiring increased exchange of knowledge, tourist groups yearning to explore different areas, could maximize their own distinctive interests much more effectively outside the constraints of the nation-state. These groups were predominantly 'non-political' for Mitrany in that they were merely pursuing their self-interest rather than the particularist political demands of a given nation-state. Moreover, as these interactions or transactions[2] increased two major transformations would occur. One, individuals and groups would begin to demand the creation of international authorities that would maintain and support these functional links. Sovereignty would begin to transfer away from competing nation-states to non-political co-operative international institutions that would fulfil the functional needs of society. Two, as nation-states became increasingly caught within the growing mesh of functional social relations they would become increasingly constrained and incapable of pursuing their former violent and destructive activities.

The functionalist strategy was relatively straightforward. Ignore the activities of state actors, since state level promises of peace and friendship will come and go. Instead, spend time promoting the low level functional linkages between different societies. As these linkages grow and develop, these individuals and groups will increasingly demand that international institutions 'non-politically' support and enhance these activities. As Mitrany stated, international peace is 'more likely to grow through doing things together in the workshop and market place than by signing pacts in chancelleries' (Mitrany, 1966: 25). Over time, national sovereignty and control would erode in a sea of functionally oriented international institutions.

Following this logic, social policy played an important role for the functionalist. Social policy, like economic policy, was the realm of low politics (as opposed to the high politics of defence and foreign relations). Dealing with unemployment, promoting workers' rights, encouraging labour mobility, taking advantage of larger economies of scale, co-ordinating family, education and health policy and combating poverty were all issues and policy areas that were seen as primarily 'non-political' and best addressed through technically efficient bureaucratic organizations that could promote the fundamental commonality of these issues. Economic factors were clearly at the heart of functionalist thinking, but social factors and policies were important as well.

What happened to functionalist thinking in the 1950s? As mentioned earlier, Mitrany opposed the formation of regional European organizations such as the ECSC and EEC since they would merely form larger units of the same national problem. He and other functionalists strongly supported the creation of the UN and the ILO. For these organizations to be created and to have some impact was a major achievement. However, by no stretch of the imagination could it be argued that they were fulfilling the functionalist dreams of enmeshing nation-states into peaceful co-operation. Ironically, functionalist thinking was central to the creation of the ECSC and EEC. It did not take much of an intellectual leap to take the grandiose global plans of the functionalists and apply them in a constrained yet successful manner at the European level. The ECSC and EEC were designed to promote functional linkages between the various member states. Authority and sovereignty were transferred to an international, functionally oriented, bureaucratic institution that was supposed to maintain and develop these functional linkages. Moreover, the hope was that these growing functional linkages would increase the interdependence and co-operation between the member states; if not end, they would at least reduce the likelihood of violent conflict between them. Unlike federalism, which provided the EU with a proposed goal or vision, functionalism helped to give the ECSC and EEC their actual strategies, concomitantly providing the basis for neo-functionalism.

Neo-functionalism

Ernst Haas's history of the ECSC, *The Uniting of Europe*, published in 1958, remains one of the pre-eminent works of neo-functionalism. It examined in detail the policies of the ECSC and, more importantly, the ECSC-related policies of the major political parties and interest group actors in all six of the member states. For Haas, a marvellous thing had occurred in the early 1950s. Contrary to the expectations of many, after its birth in 1951 the ECSC had not collapsed or stagnated. Not only had the ECSC survived, but the European integration process was about to be greatly expanded with the creation of the Treaty of Rome in 1957. Supranational integration had gone beyond one particular sector (coal and steel) and was embracing the entire economies of the six member states. Haas asked why these countries, which little over ten years earlier had been fighting each other, were now willing to integrate their economies into a common market.

He found the answer in the basic functional needs of individuals and groups and the impact of 'spillover'. Haas's fundamental thinking was quite similar to functionalism. In the past, nation-states had existed in a competitive international system that promoted violent competition and weakened the possibility for economic prosperity. However, as functionalists pointed out, these nation-states were not unified actors, but rather composed of a multitude of individuals and interest groups who were not only rational and self-interested, but could continually evaluate their actions and allegiances in relation to their rational self-interest. As a consequence, national allegiances were not fixed. Interest groups and individuals could reorient their interests and allegiances to an international organization or federal state. The creation of such an organization/state would lead to greater peace and prosperity. Unlike Mitrany, Haas never assumed that the nation-state could, should or would be completely eliminated. A Euro-federalist vision was much closer to what Haas had in mind. Local problems would be dealt with at a local level, regional problems at a regional level, national problems at the national level and European problems at the European level.

In short, not only was there a functional desire/demand for European integration, but once it was created there was an 'expansive logic to integration' (Haas, 1958: 283–317) or 'spillover'. Spillover, though a controversial and shifting concept (Lindberg and Scheingold, 1970) was generally thought to occur in a functional manner within a particular economic or policy sector (intra-spillover) or from one sector to the next (inter-spillover). Haas's notion of intra-spillover was that within a given sector (steel for example), as various nations began to integrate the sector, they would find that the positive effects of integration would grow in proportion to the degree of integration. Steel producers would demand more co-operation. Unions would support it. Political parties would promote it. Ultimately, national governments would see its clear benefits. Hence, for Haas, once a sector began to integrate it had a tendency to continue to integrate until it was fully integrated.

Similarly, in the case of inter-spillover, if one sector integrates, then there is a tendency for the integration dynamic to spill over into other sectors. For example, if steel is integrated then key interest groups in other sectors (automobiles, heavy industry, etc.) begin clamouring for greater integration in their sectors as well. Employer groups and trade unions start pressuring political parties, who pressure governments, who create international agreements, which expand the integration dynamic. In essence, for Haas integration was like an avalanche. Once it started, more and more interests and interest groups got involved, triggering a cascade effect on other interests and interest groups. In the end, Haas expected the democratic nation-states of Western Europe to be swamped by an onslaught of internal interest group demands for greater integration.

The role of social policy in European integration for neo-functionalism was secondary, but still important. The ECSC and EEC were explicitly economic in orientation. Despite some social policy elements that were built into the treaties, both the ECSC and EEC actively avoided major areas of social policy. However, for neo-functionalists, this would clearly be a short-term pattern of avoidance. Once the process of spillover accelerated, particularly inter-spillover, then European social policy would certainly be expected to develop. For example, if coal and steel production were being rationalized in France and Germany, it may make economic sense to reduce production in France and expand it in Germany. This may be opposed by French unions unless unemployment compensation and new jobs were created. Hence, European unemployment, retraining and mobility policies would all need to be developed to deal with the implications of the original integration in the economic sector. Moreover, once these social policies were established, intra-spillover would occur, forcing the development of new social policies, such as gender policies to protect the rights of female employees and family benefit policies to encourage worker mobility. For Haas, social policy was clearly the second step in European integration. It was important and essential, but it was the second step.

In 1957, with the Treaty of Rome being negotiated, the economies of Western Europe prospering, and other nations beginning to consider membership in the emerging EEC, Haas's vision of a neo-functional integration dynamic certainly did not seem far-fetched. The Treaty of Rome was a substantial expansion on the powers of the Treaty of Paris. The ECSC had clearly spilled over into the EEC. By 1960 Britain, Denmark, Ireland and Norway were carrying out membership negotiations. However, by the early to mid-1960s this sense of seemingly unstoppable spillover was already starting to fade. No new members had actually joined the EEC. Economic policy integration was painfully slow and EEC social policy development was virtually non-existent. Moreover, the belief in the power of the integration dynamic was rudely undercut in the mid-1960s by Charles De Gaulle's infamous 'empty chair' policy. Not only did the integration project seem to reach its limits, but individual member states could block or even turn it back. When the French under De Gaulle left their 'empty chair' at the EEC Council chambers, effectively blocking all EEC policy activity, the unstoppable process of spillover became another in a succession of Europeanist mirages. Neo-functionalists were quick to modify and adjust their interpretations. Spillover could now be followed by 'spillback' (Lindberg and Scheingold, 1970) and the process could lurch to a halt as well as move forward. As we shall see, the fortunes of neo-functionalism were closely tied to those of the EU.

EU social policy in the 1950s

During this period, what was actually happening to EU social policy? The first place to look is the 1951 Treaty of Paris of the ECSC.

The Treaty of Paris

The central strategy of the treaty and the common market itself was based on basic neo-classical economic theory.[3] This well-known theory argued that as market structures expand beyond the boundaries of existing nation-states they will, necessarily, lead to greater economic efficiency, production and performance.[4] As Article 2 of the treaty states, as the common market is progressively established, 'the most rational distribution of production at the highest possible level of productivity' will result. Hence, the central goal and focus of the ECSC was the removal of barriers to the creation of this new common market. As such, its central activity would be the dismantling of the previous barriers to that market (Articles 4 and 65). On the social side, the underlying notion was that social benefits would accrue automatically from the creation of the common market.

Despite this neo-classical economic orientation, in many ways the purpose of the ECSC was not the creation of a common free market, but a common regulated market. The ECSC was supposed to play an extensive role in the regulation, co-ordination and development of the common market. The High Authority (predecessor of the Commission) of the ECSC was expected to act as a central planning body for the common market, support investment programmes, promote research and development, and intervene in cases of market failure (Articles 5, 46, 55, 58 and 59). The ECSC also contained some corporatist elements, including a corporatistic advisory body, the Consultative Committee, and an emphasis on the necessity of integrating key economic actors (producers, workers and consumers) into the integration process (Article 48).

In social policy, two key aspects were built into the treaty: social harmonization and social improvement. Social harmonization was the idea that benefits and costs of market integration should be distributed equally among member states. A key aspect of this harmonization was the equalization of wage competition. In Article 68, the ECSC committed itself to minimizing wage undercutting (the forerunner of what the EU currently calls 'social dumping') within the common market. If firms used low wages to undercut other firms, the High Authority had the right to fine the firms for up to twice the amount of their savings from the low wages. In regard to social improvement, the Treaty of Paris clearly stated that employment creation, improving living standards and improving working conditions were all part of the goals of the ECSC (Articles 2 and 46). Article 56 committed the ECSC to various forms of unemployment aid, resettlement allowances and retraining policies for workers who lost their jobs due to technical innovation. Article 68 provided that, if competition between workers led to lower wages and living standards, the ECSC had the responsibility to lessen this competition in order to raise those wages and standards. Interpreted broadly, these social demands could have had a radical impact on the formation of the ECSC. However, as it turned out, social policies were of minimal importance compared with the social policies and rights that were developing at the national level and with the importance of economic policy in the ECSC.

Implementing the Treaty of Paris

Given the secondary importance of social policy, its ambiguous position within the treaty, and the weakness of the executive powers of the High Authority of the ECSC to implement them, how did the ECSC put its social policies into effect? As Doreen Collins, author of the most extensive study on early EU social policy, summarized:

> In practice, . . . social policy consisted primarily of methods of compensation for economic change affecting workers' jobs in which the impact of the introduction of the common market was originally the major factor. . . . the national welfare structures remained relatively untouched and were clearly intended to continue to carry the main responsibility for direct measures of social improvement. . . . Ideologically, however, it [social policy] was largely a defensive system quietening the fears of the timorous and enabling them to accept the new arrangements and to be willing to work within them. (Collins, 1975: 21)

As Collins indicated, ECSC social policy in the 1950s was predominantly reactive. Its limited powers and scope meant that it could do little that was innovative. However, it could be used to respond to specific problems in the larger economic integration process by helping 'buy off' and reassure economic losers. This reassurance strategy was demonstrated by a number of policies. In the late 1950s demand for coal was sharply declining due to competition from other energy sources. The ECSC quickly moved to regulate the market, stockpiling output, providing aid to help close uneconomic pits and imposing import restrictions. To help coal miners move out of the uneconomic areas and find new jobs, the ECSC provided unemployment aid, training and, perhaps most importantly, housing assistance. This support for mobility was directed predominantly towards intra-, not trans-, member-state movement. In the early 1950s, when the mines were booming, migrant workers were encouraged, particularly from Italy. However, as the mines began to experience difficulties, migration was greatly restricted. Throughout most of the 1950s, key ECSC members were afraid that low-wage migrants would flood their coal and steel sectors. At an intergovernmental conference in 1954, called to increase the rights of workers to work in different member states, only workers in fifty-six types of jobs (mostly highly skilled) were allowed to move freely. Moreover, very few individuals took advantage of this opportunity (Collins, 1975: 66–8).

When innovative policies did emerge, they were confronted with the limitations of the ECSC institutions and the divergent interests of the major interest group actors. For example, in order to promote tripartite consultations within the coal sector a Joint Committee on the coal mining industry was created in 1954, but due to disputes over the representation of member-state officials it did not meet until 1958. The High Authority hoped to make this a model of sector-based tripartite co-operation. The first issue it took up was the European coal miners' charter. In the mid-1950s, in an attempt to harmonize and raise the living and social conditions of miners, the High Authority submitted a series of draft proposals for better pensions, training, wages, regularity of employment and so on for the mining industry, incorporated into a European miners' charter. This charter would have been a precedential expansion of ECSC social policy, if approved and implemented. However, despite a series of meetings and strong trade union support, no agreements could be reached. Employers generally opposed the potential costs of the charter and some member-state governments disliked the expansion of ECSC social powers. By the early 1960s the miners' charter had failed and the Joint Committee had collapsed (Collins, 1975: 74–7).

The pattern of social policy established by the Treaty of Paris and implemented in the 1950s set the stage for future EU social policy. The treaty rested on a language of, and basic belief in, a neo-classical/free market economic interpretation of the advantages of expanding and integrating markets. In essence, the more the markets expanded and integrated and the less individual states and the European institutions interfered, the better off everyone would be. However, along with this central free market belief, the treaty recognized the need to 'harmonise and improve' social conditions of the workers and citizens taking part in this process. Interpreted broadly, the treaty gave the ECSC a mandate for extensive intervention and social policy development. However, lacking specific powers or financing for social policies the ECSC was dependent upon the co-operation of the major interest groups and member-state governments for social policy development.

The Treaty of Rome

Following the early success of the ECSC, plans were soon made to expand the integrated coal and steel market into a true common market. The 1956 Spaak Report, which laid the foundation for the EEC and EuroAtom treaties, focused on the potential of the common market to rationalize production, increase European economies of scale, and create a European market that would be capable of competing with the USA. Social policies were of minimal importance in the report and largely left to the national level. Interestingly, it was the French government, concerned about a flood of low wage competition from Germany(!) and desiring to defend its higher levels of social rights and provisions, that pushed for more social policies in the Treaty of Rome (Schmitt, 1962: chapter 12).

The 1957 Treaty of Rome, which established the European Economic Community (EEC), followed directly in the footsteps of the Treaty of Paris. The primary difference between the two was in scope, not content. Once again, the basic focus of the treaty was the creation of a common market. This market, once created, was to lead almost automatically to greater economic and social benefits. In creating this common market, the treaty emphasized free movement of goods, persons, services and capital within the common market. The EEC was empowered to force the signatories of the treaty to accept these free market rules. The EEC was also empowered to intervene in the free market structure of the common market during the twelve- to fifteen-year transition period. However, once this period ended it was expected that the institutions of the EEC would take a less interventionist position (Article 8).

On the social side, the Treaty of Rome extended the concern shown by the Treaty of Paris for social aspects in the creation of the common market by recognizing the importance of EEC state intervention. Although the treaty did not specify the types of state regulation, the EEC was clearly given the responsibility to ensure that appropriate member-state policy co-ordination was carried out (Article 43). Furthermore, in areas such as agriculture (Articles 38–47) and social policy (Articles 117–28) where the treaty emphasized the need for economic stability and fair living standards, the EEC was supposed to directly intervene in the functioning of the market, thus creating a regulated common market. Linked to the importance of regulation in the creation of the common market was the promotion of major interest groups in the policy-making process and the foundation of an early form of Euro-corporatism. The Treaty of Rome attempted to establish basic forms of co-operation and Euro-corporatism through the creation of the Economic and Social Committee. This advisory body, consisting of representatives of the primary economic groups (workers, employers and various interests), was a direct extension of the corporatist advisory committee in the ECSC and encouraged the integration of European interest groups into the EEC policy process, especially for social issues (Article 124) and in the agricultural sector.

The Treaty of Rome reflected, but did not radically extend, the basic pattern of social rights and responsibilities of the Treaty of Paris. Like Article 3 of the Treaty of Paris, Article 117 of the Treaty of Rome stated that 'Member States agree upon the need to promote improved working conditions and an improved standard of living for workers, so as to make possible their harmonisation while the improvement is being maintained.' Moreover, as Article 118 stated, the EEC was also responsible for promoting development in: 'employment; labour law and working conditions; basic and advanced vocational training; social security; prevention of occupational accidents and diseases; occupational hygiene; (and) the right of association, and collective bargaining between employers and workers'. Article 119 stated that 'men and women should receive equal pay for equal work', which was inserted primarily at the insistence of the French. Article 120 stated that 'Member States shall endeavour to maintain the existing equivalence between paid holiday schemes.' Articles 121–2 committed the EEC Commission to produce annual reports on social developments and gave the EEC Parliament the authority to request Commission reports on 'any particular problem concerning social conditions'. Finally, Articles 123–8 dealt with the creation and operation of the European Social Fund. This fund was an extension of the training and mobility enhancing policies of the ECSC, dedicated to reducing unemployment and opposition to the common market by making workers more skilled and mobile.

By the end of the 1950s, EU social policy was firmly established as a secondary element to the larger and more important policies of economic integration and the formation of the common market. As established by the treaties, EU social policy was predominantly a strategy for easing the transition to a common market. However, the breadth of EU social policy during this period was greatly constrained by its secondary role to the creation of the common market, opposition from member-state governments that were opposed either to social policies in general or to creating them at the European level, and resistance of employer groups who were afraid that EU social policies would increase costs and constrain their control over the economic process. In general, EU social policy focused exclusively on the working population and its rights and needs within the common market. Broad social policy issues such as education, health, poverty and old age were ignored. Despite the efforts of the Commission, Parliament and trade unions to expand the area of social policy and increase its importance relative to economic issues, EU social policy was slow to develop and limited to its foundation in the treaties. In the context of the three early theories of integration, this slow development would not be particularly surprising or disturbing. All expected or hoped to see economic issues dominate the early development of the EU. It was the benefits of co-ordinating on these issues that would provide the functionalist web that would capture, contain and eventually integrate the nation-state into a European federal system. Social policy would soon follow from the promotion federal structures, from the stimulation of functional integration and/or from the dynamics of spillover.

EU social policy in the 1960s

In the late 1950s and early 1960s the EEC appeared to be performing successfully. The treaties were in place and the key EEC institutions seemed to be functioning well together. Moreover, the economies of Western Europe were in the midst of the postwar economic golden age. Growth, unemployment and inflation rates for the six were among the best in Europe. From 1960 to 1967 growth averaged between 3 and 6 per cent a year, unemployment hovered between 0.8 per cent in Germany and 6 per cent in Italy, and inflation was contained to within 4–6 per cent per year (Armstrong et al., 1984; Marglin and Schor, 1991; Shonfield, 1980). Central to this economic revival was the growth of international trade, particularly intra-EEC trade. From negligible amounts in the immediate aftermath of the Second World War, intra-EEC trade jumped to 35 per cent of all international trade for the members of the EEC by 1960 and to 50 per cent by 1970. Intra-EEC trade not only helped to stimulate these economies, but also protected them from competition from low wage/social rights competitors, and developed in a manner that helped the member states to regulate their economies and minimize the social disruption caused by economic integration.[5] The result of this economic success and productive integration was the increasing attraction of the EEC to other European countries. In 1961 Britain, Ireland, Denmark and Norway applied for membership.

Despite this economic success and the growth of national welfare states and social policies during the first half of the 1960s, EU social policy continued its limited and distinctive pattern of development. As established under the ECSC, EU social policy was secondary to economic integration and strongly linked to promoting the common market by helping to assuage the costs and/or fears of the losers in the integration process. The few social policy developments which did occur in the early 1960s included the first regulation on the free movement of labour (1961), the operationalization of the European Social Fund (1962) and the creation of the Industrial Health and Safety Division within the Commission (1962). More important, in the field of social security, the EEC quickly built upon the nearly eighty bi-lateral agreements already in place between the EEC member states dealing with social security issues. Regulations 3 and 4 of 1958 established the fundamental principles of equal treatment for all workers while in another country, the aggregation of benefits for workers who worked in more than one EEC member state, and the exportability of benefits to other member states. These regulations were not comprehensive and only began the long-term process of integrating and co-ordinating the various social security systems in order to reduce barriers to worker mobility. Nevertheless, they clearly signalled an area of EEC concern and its willingness to decisively exercise its influence in that area. Overall, federalists, functionalists and neo-functionalists probably would like to have seen more progress, but would have argued that most of the major indicators of European integration were pointing in the right direction.

However, by the mid-1960s cracks begin to grow within the EEC framework. In January 1963 President De Gaulle claimed that the United Kingdom lacked the 'political will' to join the EEC, implied that it was dominated by American interests and unilaterally vetoed UK membership, whereupon the UK quickly suspended membership negotiations. Denmark, Ireland and Norway, all with substantial trade and political linkages to the UK, did the same. All turned their attention back to the competing European economic organization, the European Free Trade Association, whose members included Austria, Denmark, Finland, Norway, Portugal, Sweden, Switzerland and the UK.

In mid-1965 a much more severe crisis emerged. Wanting to stimulate integration and the EEC institutions, the Commission, with the influential Walter Hallstein as its President and strong backing of the German government, proposed a substantial expansion of EEC powers. It argued that in July 1967, when the EEC customs union was supposed to be created and common agricultural prices established, the EEC should create its own financial resources (previously derived from member-state payments) through a common external tariff and levies on imported foodstuffs, and that some budgetary powers should be given to the Parliament. It was hoped that this plan would revitalize economic integration and strengthen, democratize and legitimate the main EEC institutions. The French government, led by De Gaulle, was fiercely opposed to the plan. When a compromise did not emerge, De Gaulle demanded that all French officials boycott the EEC institutions. For the next seven months France operated an 'empty chair' policy which paralysed the unanimous decision-making procedures of the EEC. During this period, all EEC policy-making collapsed. A solution was finally reached in the 'Luxembourg compromise' of 1966 (Willis, 1968: chapter 11). This compromise paved the way for some strengthening of the Parliament and the Commission. However, it reaffirmed the right of a member state to veto any piece of EEC legislation when it believed its 'vital interests' were at stake. The result was that instead of moving towards more qualified majority voting within the Council, where the votes of one or possibly two member states could have been overridden and which would have given EEC legislation a substantial boost, unanimous voting procedures remained and EEC policy development came to a virtual standstill. The member states reasserted themselves at the cost of the European integration dynamic, and EEC social policy initiatives, always lagging behind other policy areas, had vanished by the late 1960s.

Theoretical evolution: the revenge of realism/ intergovernmentalism

The events of the mid- and late 1960s were crippling for the theories of federalism, functionalism and neo-functionalism. West European nation-states were refusing to fade away. The federal dream was waning. Functional integration seemed incapable of going beyond basic levels of economic integration. Neo-functional spillover seemed to lose its power. Likewise, as the nation-state appeared to reassert itself, classical theories of international relations, realism and intergovernmentalism re-established their intellectual dominance.

Realism traces its roots from Thucydides' writings of the fifth century BC on the Peloponnesian war between Athens and Sparta, to Machiavelli's early sixteenth-century advice to Italian princes in *The Prince*, and Thomas Hobbes's mid-sixteenth-century classic, *Leviathan*. During the Cold War it was probably the most influential theory in political science, particularly in the United States.[6] An article by Joseph Grieco provides one of the best and briefest summaries of realism. He pointed out that realism was based on five basic assumptions: 'First, states are the major actors in world affairs. Second . . . states are "sensitive to costs" and behave as unitary rational agents. Third, international anarchy is the principal force shaping the motives and actions of states. Fourth, states in anarchy are preoccupied with power and security. . . . Finally, international institutions affect the prospects for co-operation only marginally' (Grieco, 1988: 488). For realists, there was no overarching world or global order. States were the primary units of social organization, were rational, and pursued their interests until they were constrained by the interests of others. Realism was the major theory of Cold War confrontation between the US and USSR. The globe was the stage. All nations were caught up in this struggle and its parameters determined their fates. Co-operation between states under conditions of anarchy was limited.

The creation and success of the ECSC and EEC seemed to fly in the face of basic realist thinking. Nation-states were co-operating, integrating in a peaceful fashion, and an international organization seemed to be ordering the international environment. This was all the more difficult for realists to accept because just a few years earlier these states had been at each other's throats in one of the most vicious conflicts in human history. In the realist world view, this degree of co-operation and integration was an aberration.

In response to this, realism was slightly modified in the European context and labelled 'intergovernmentalism'. One of the most eloquent and best-known intergovernmentalists was Stanley Hoffmann. In his classic work, 'Obstinate or Obsolete? France, European Integration and the Fate of the Nation State',[7] originally published in 1960, he provided three main reasons why the ECSC and EEC had partially succeeded in a realist world and why it could not really achieve its dreams of true integration or federalist development. First, it was the development of the Cold War system that allowed for the creation of a co-operative West European sub-system. United by fear and opposition to the communist East, protected and encouraged to integrate by the US, early West European integration efforts existed in an international sub-system that allowed for and encouraged integration. In the early 1960s, when the US (with its growing nuclear arsenal) no longer needed Western Europe to unite into a defensive pact against the East, the international sub-system changed and the dynamic for integration changed as well. Second, the ECSC and EEC were successful because they concentrated on the area of low politics (economic and social issues) rather than high politics (foreign policy and military affairs). For Hoffmann, low politics were areas of little concern for nation-states. Bargains could be made and co-operation encouraged because it was only secondary interests that were involved. However, this situation was self-limiting. As integration continued and began to pressure key low politics areas or perhaps touch upon high politics, the integration process would grind to a halt as it ran into the divergent interests of nation-states. As Hoffmann noted regarding 'the limits of the functional method':

> its [functional integration's] relative success in the relatively painless area where it works relatively well lifts the participants of the EEC to a new level of issues where the method does not work well any more – like swimmers whose skill at moving quickly away from the shore brings them to a point where the waters are stormy and deep, at a time when fatigue is setting in, and none of the questions about ultimate goal, direction, or endurance has been answered. (Hoffmann, 1995: 87)

Third, opposed to what Jean Monnet and Ernst Haas saw as a logic of integration, Hoffmann argued that there is a much stronger 'logic of diversity' at work in the European context. To Hoffmann, nation-states were much more diverse and had more distinctive interests and goals than the functionalists envisioned. As such, nation-states were much more hesitant to commit to integration bargains out of fear of being the loser and much more tentative towards the integration process as a whole. The logic of diversity suggested that 'in areas of key importance to the national interest, nations prefer the self-controlled uncertainty of national self-reliance, to the uncontrolled certainty of the [integration] blending process. . . . losses on one vital issue are not compensated for by gains on other issues. . . . [and functional integration is] destructive past a certain threshold' (Hoffmann, 1995: 84). When De Gaulle pulled the empty chair trick, realist/intergovernmentalist theories were vindicated. The EC had reached its limit and the nation-state was reasserting its dominance. In the mid- to late 1960s the pessimism of intergovernmentalism easily replaced the hopeful optimism of functional/neo-functionalism.

What was the role of social policy for the intergovernmentalists? As deduced from their emphasis on the division between low and high politics, intergovernmentalists saw social policy as the realm of low politics and thus relatively unimportant. Ironically, its own unimportance gave it the chance to develop at the European level. Since it was of minimal consequence, co-operation would be relatively uncomplicated and could be carried out, so long as it did not interfere with higher political issues. Moreover, even within its realm of low politics, social policy would be strongly determined by the structures of the international system and the prevailing intergovernmental bargains that shaped the larger integration project. Like economic policy, social policy integration did not create a dynamic of integration. Integration was dependent upon the intergovernmental bargains of self-interested nation-states working within the Cold War international environment. Small-scale, low-level social policies could emerge where benefits were obvious and costs were low. However, these would not lead to spillover within social policy or to other policy areas. In fact, as social policy integration continued it would likely become more difficult and divisive and any achievements might easily be broken by demands from the arena of high politics. From the viewpoint of the mid- to late 1960s, it was hard to argue with this pessimistic position. The European integration project was stagnant, social policy was at a standstill, and no major intergovernmental bargain or structural transformation was on the horizon. What would it take to revive European integration and social policy?

During the 1950s and 1960s European integration and social policy evolved out of a complex set of international, European and national factors. Despite substantial developments at the national level, social policy at the European level remained weak for several reasons. First, it lacked the basic social and political support required for such a complicated policy task. No large-scale intergovernmental bargains were made over social policy. Second, social policy, as envisioned in the treaties, was subsidiary to economic integration, and primarily served to calm the fears of the threatened and buy off the losers in the integration process. In practice, social policy harmonization meant little more than encouraging member states to improve and increase their national level social policies. Third, the success of social policy development at the national level made European social policy creation redundant and robbed it of its political supporters. Fourth, economic integration in the 1950s and 1960s was relatively limited and did not have a major European-level social policy impact. Despite growing amounts of international trade and economic activity, the economies of the EC member states remained remarkably nationally oriented. National governments could be and were responsible for the performance of the national economy. Labour mobility between the member states was very limited. Hence, most social problems could be dealt with at the national level and did not have a direct linkage to European developments.

All of the early theories of European integration saw social policy as a secondary policy area. For pragmatic federalists, functionalists and neo-functionalists, social policy was secondary, but it had a radical potential. As economic and social issues were increasingly solved at the European level, the ECSC/EEC would increasingly ensnare the member states in a web of societal interests. As the benefits of European co-operation and integration expanded, more and more economic and social problems and policies would be transferred to the European level. National-level interest groups would increasingly demand more European policies. This radical potential is completely missing from the realist/intergovernmentalist interpretation of the development of EU social policy in the 1950s and 1960s. To them, European social policy developed because of its lack of importance, not because of its radical potential. Of the basic intergovernmental bargains that were made, none dealt with social policy. Social policy was a minor side issue, used to assuage doubts and buy quiescence. It had no radical potential and was completely dependent on the success of larger integration bargains. With the success of the ECSC and creation of the EEC, during the 1950s and early 1960s, it was the federalists and (neo-)functionalists who dominated the debate on European development and strategies. However, with the empty-chair crisis and the policy immobility of the mid- to late 1960s, the realist/intergovernmentalist vision made a strong comeback. The European Sisyphus had pushed the stone of integration further than it had ever been before. However, in the mid- to late 1960s, De Gaulle and the nation-state set it rolling back down again and European social policy along with it. Could it ever be pushed back up?

2

European Social Policy 1970–1999

The social dimension permeates all our discussions and everything we do. . . . Think what a boost it would be for democracy and social justice if we could demonstrate that we are capable of working together to create a better integrated society open to all.

Jacques Delors, 1989[1]

For an observer of European integration from the late 1960s to the late 1970s, comments like the above from the President of the Commission would have been unthinkable. At the time, the EU was a divided, fictionalized, and weak institution that had little impact on major economic and social problems. Moreover, social policy was completely stagnant and virtually non-existent. Intergovernmentalism reigned supreme. Federalist movements had vanished and neo-functionalist academics began to abandon the study of European integration and move into other fields of academic study. The main theoretical innovation, at the time, was the concept of confederalism. Nevertheless, by the late 1980s and early 1990s, European integration had made a remarkable recovery via the Single European Act (1987), the Maastricht Treaty (1991) and the 1992 Internal Market Project. Linked to this recovery was the extraordinary revitalization of social policy. In terms of total policy output, financial backing for the policy, and areas covered, social policy was still clearly secondary to national-level social policies. However, as the EU took on increasing powers and influence and was even perceived as a potential new superpower (Colchester and Buchan, 1990), the creation of an EU welfare state became conceivable and led to a Janusian controversy over the nature of the emerging EU social policies. As the 1990s progressed, the survival of national-level welfare states combined with the continued progress of EU social policy led social policy observers to ask new questions about the interaction of EU social policy with different types of national social policy regimes.

A brief revival, then collapse: from The Hague Summit of 1969 to the 'Eurosclerosis' of the early 1980s

As discussed in Chapter 1, although the mid- to late 1960s was a time of stagnation for the EC and its social policy, a number of events came together in 1968 and 1969 that laid the basis for a brief revival in the fortunes of the EC and its social policy. At the international level, European integration was strengthened by growing disagreement with the US over the Vietnam War and the increasingly disruptive influence of US economic and monetary policy on West European economies (Block, 1977; Gilpin, 1987). At the same time as US economic policy was becoming more disruptive, the control of international financial movements (a central element in postwar Keynesian economic policy) was becoming increasingly difficult (Giavazzi and Giovannini, 1989; Stewart, 1984). Hence, if West European governments were going to maintain their traditional economic controls and performance, a co-ordinated European strategy was seen to be necessary. Developing alongside these economic concerns were growing West European social developments, reflected in the demands of the students and workers during the 1968 uprisings in France and elsewhere in Western Europe. Responding to these demands, the Parliament became increasingly vocal in demanding stronger European social policies (Parliament, 1969). At the national level, key political changes were central to the recovery of European integration. In 1969, following his failure to win a national referendum, De Gaulle resigned as the President of France and was succeeded by Georges Pompidou, and Willy Brandt, the leader of the German Social Democratic Party, became Chancellor of West Germany. Almost simultaneously, the EC lost one of its most determined defenders of the prerogatives of the member states and gained two strong integrationists and supporters of social policy.

These changes led to The Hague Summit of December 1969. During this meeting the various heads of state attempted to revive the integration process. Major agreements were reached on the transformation of EC funding, the financing of the common agricultural policy, increased budgetary powers of the Parliament, the expansion of EC membership to include Britain, Denmark, Ireland and Norway, and, most importantly, the formation of some form of European Monetary

Union (EMU). The Hague Summit, and in particular Brandt (Shanks, 1977: 5), brought social policy back on to the EC agenda by arguing that it was a necessary complement to economic integration envisioned by the EMU. As the final communiqué of the 1972 Paris Summit stated: '[the member states] attached as much importance to vigorous action in the social field as to achievement of economic union . . . [and considered] it essential to ensure the increasing involvement of labour and management in the economic and social decisions of the Community' (Brewster and Teague, 1989: 66).

This led to the creation of the European Regional Development Fund and the reform of the Structural Funds. The idea behind these two developments was that EMU would cause substantial shifts in the economic map of the EC. Since workers were generally unwilling to move out of declining areas and into growing ones, it would be necessary to have a strong regional policy that would encourage development in declining areas, soften the economic blows of competition, and encourage movement to growth areas. Linked to this strategy was the 1974 Social Action Programme (Commission, 1974) which the Commission welcomed as 'the first attempt by the Community to draw up a coherent policy setting out in a purposeful way the initial practical steps on the road towards the ultimate goal of European Social Union' (Lodge, 1978: 123). The 1974 Social Action Programme (SAP) was the first major advance for EU social policy since the treaties of Paris and Rome and attempted to reach far beyond their basic social policy implications. Michael Shanks, Head of the Social Affairs Directorate of the Commission in the early 1970s, argued that this extension of EC social policy beyond the rigid boundaries of the treaties 'reflected a political judgement of what was thought to be both desirable and possible, rather than a judicial judgement of what were thought to be the social policy implications of the Treaty of Rome' (Shanks, 1977: 13). The SAP laid down three broad areas for policy action (the 'attainment of full and better employment', 'improvement of living and working conditions so as to make possible their harmonisation while the improvement is being maintained', and 'increased involvement of management and labour in the economic and social decisions of the Community, and of workers in the life of undertakings') and thirty-five specific proposals for action. Each of these actions had to be debated and approved individually by the Council.

As it happened, just as this radical plan for the expansion of social policy was created, the EC lapsed into another period of stagnation and uncertainty. Following the massive currency fluctuations of the early 1970s, the attempt to create EMU was abandoned. The best that the West European nations could manage was a modified 'snake' system established in April 1972 which merely tried to limit exchange rate fluctuations between various West European currencies by encouraging member states to peg the value of their currencies to the value of the most stable currency, the German Mark (Giavazzi and Giovannini, 1989; Tsoukalis, 1997). Further, the OPEC oil shocks of 1973–4 quadrupled the price of oil, on which Western Europe was highly dependent, and double-digit inflation ensued. Instead of pursuing a co-ordinated response to the oil crisis, inflation and growing recession, each of the member states increasingly pursued their own nationalist strategies. Finally, during the 1970s and early 1980s there were several changes of membership and quarrels that crippled further EC developments. After joining in 1973 and the positive result of the 1975 EC referendum, Britain remained an 'awkward partner' (George, 1990), demanding special consideration and challenging entrenched EC policies. Meanwhile, with the addition of Greece in 1981 and Spain and Portugal in 1985, the EC became a much more economically diverse organization, making integration more complex.

This stagnation and division were reflected in EC social policy and the implementation of the SAP. All three of the main areas of the programme produced mixed results. In the area of full and better employment, the EC did create a new European Centre for the Development of Vocational Training (CEDEFOP) and increase and reform the European Social Fund. However, no major legislation in this area was passed. In the area of the improvement and harmonization of living and working conditions, only a few directives were passed in the fields of labour law, equal treatment for men and women, and health and safety. Finally, in the area of democratization of economic life a number of attempts were made to increase the degree of participation at the European level and within European firms. However, despite these efforts and the promotion of the 'social dialogue' between the ETUC (European Trade Union Confederation) and UNICE (Union of Industrial and Employers' Confederations of Europe), co-operative decisions and policy developments were extremely limited. This area of policy development was particularly weak due to the impact of the general economic crisis which tended to make most economic actors more nationalist, the difficulty of co-ordinating and implementing policy in nations with very different industrial relations and social policy traditions, and the relative weakness of the European-level interest organizations of labour and capital.

In all three areas of the SAP, developments were limited not only by the international situation, but by the internal structure and dynamics of the EC itself. First, social policy during this period was based on the idea of 'harmonization'. Harmonization, as established under Articles

117 and 118 of the Treaty of Rome, meant that for the common market to function properly the complex and interdependent web of member-state social policies, old and new, would have to be continually and increasingly harmonized by the EC, a daunting task. The two enlargements of the EC in the early 1970s (Britain, Ireland and Denmark) and 1980s (Spain and Portugal and Greece) increased this difficulty. The second enlargement alone added 70 million people to the EC whose per capita income was half that of West Germany's and whose social policies were very distinct from the Northern European model. Second, the institutional weakness of the European Parliament (not even directly elected until 1979) and the Economic and Social Committee meant that social actors, such as the ETUC and European socialists, were less capable of promoting social policies within the EC. Third, the power of the Council and the demands of unanimous voting on all major social policy questions clearly limited the development of those policies. Finally, with the rise of Margaret Thatcher in Britain in 1979, all European social policy initiatives had to pass the barrier of militant free-market ideology. With veto power within the Council, the British government blocked a number of social policy directives: proposals to give more rights to part-time workers in 1981, to temporary workers in 1982, for parental leave in 1983, and to discourage sex discrimination in 1986. In conclusion, the period of the 1974 SAP saw a large increase in the demands for EC social policies, but the limitations of the international environment and internal institutional dynamics prevented their translation into European social policies.

Theoretical developments: confederalism

The mid- to late 1960s were the time of the intergovernmentalists. Reflecting the revival of the West European nation-states and the stagnation of the EC, federalist movements evaporated and neofunctionalists began to drift towards other areas of academic study. Intergovernmentalists were vindicated. The nation-state, once again, demonstrated its power and resilience in the face of attempts at European organization. The brief revival of the EC following The Hague Summit (1969) and the proposals for EMU gave some pause to intergovernmentalist interpretations, but with the nationalist responses of the member states to the currency and energy crises of the early 1970s and the stagflation of the mid- to late 1970s, intergovernmentalist theory seemed ascendant. The only new major challenger was confederalism.

Confederalism was a theoretical balancing act between the nationalism of intergovernmentalism and the supranationalism of federalism. The key author behind confederalism was Paul Taylor (Taylor, 1975, 1983, 1984). For Taylor and others, confederalism offered a bridge between the contending theories of European integration. Taylor's view of confederalism had four main elements. First, similar to regime theorists (Keohane and Nye, 1977; Krasner, 1983), Taylor saw nation-states as both the primary actors in the international arena and constrained within an interdependent web of economic, social and political arrangements. They could chose to break this web, but there would be costs. Second, the international order was not stable. In the realist/intergovernmentalist vision, the international order was, and always had been, anarchical. Nation-states competed against one another for position and advantage. For the neo-functionalist, this anarchical order could and would be transformed by the processes of integration, creating a new co-operative West European system. The assumption was that once this new order was created, it would be stable as well. For confederalists, the international system could shift from a more anarchical to an ordered one, and back again. International circumstances, regional dynamics, and national-level situations would all contribute to the creation of periods of order or disorder. Third, nation-states might chose to integrate into stable forms of co-operation. Given that nation-states existed within a web of interdependent economic, political and social relationships, under acceptable circumstances they might choose long-term co-operative and integrative strategies to help them deal with this web of complexity and interdependence. This did not imply that the nation-state was 'withering away', or that integrative strategies were a permanent condition. However, it did indicate that nation-states could choose to pursue long-term co-operative strategies as opposed to short-term self-interested ones. Fourth, for confederalists, international institutions mattered. Appropriate institutional activities and policies could bolster national-level co-operation and integration. Nation-state participation in the EC did affect the perceptions and actions of member states. However, these impacts were not the predominant ones. International factors and national developments could easily override the emerging co-operative relationships.

From these four assumptions, Taylor argued that the EC had gone through varying phases of development that displayed different integration dynamics. Taylor was not particularly consistent with his categorization of the time periods of particular integration dynamics. In 1975 he wrote that the EC had gone through three phases of development: the federal (1950–54), the neo-functional (1955–69), and confederal phase (1970–75). In 1984, he spoke of an ideal integration phase in the early and late 1950s and early 1960s, a period of rational-utilitarian integration in the 1960s and 1970s, and an emerging phase of 'constrained actor' integration in the mid-1980s. The key point was not over the appropriate definition of the various phases or periods, but that different phases/periods could develop and exist. Taylor had moved away from the more grandiose theorizing on integration and recognized a degree of complexity, variation and uncertainty that marks all subsequent EU theory. As he pointed out, European integration was limited by a 'combination of circumstances and antagonistic pressures which are the product of chance – and different – developments in the various periods of integration' (Taylor, 1984: 587).

Confederalism did not have any special interest in social policy. Overall, social policy was expected to follow the general developments of EU integration. For example, despite the high hopes of the 1974 SAP, when the EC began to stagnate in the mid- to late 1970s, so did the programme. The interesting points that confederalist thinking raised for EC social policy were fourfold: there could be waves and troughs of social policy development, changes in the international system could influence the success or failure of social policy, and appropriate EC institutional structures and policies would affect social policy outcomes. Finally, and perhaps most important, the recognition of uncertainty and complexity of EU social policy development was a substantial shift from earlier thinking.

The SEA and the White Paper on the internal market project

As mentioned above, the late 1970s and early 1980s represented a period of 'Euro-pessimism'. The stagflationary recession of the 1970s encouraged the member states to pursue autonomous economic strategies. The vision of EMU was crushed and the Exchange Rate Mechanism (ERM) struggled to operate on a tumultuous economic sea. Some EC social policies did develop in the wake of the SAP, but only in relatively limited areas. Attempts at creating more substantial EC social rights, particularly in the areas of labour rights and participation, were blocked, diluted or abandoned.

However, by the early 1980s several interrelated changes were taking place which would allow for both the revival of the European integration and, subsequently, the revival of European social policy. These changes included: the abandoning of nationalistic economic policies and the growing acceptance of an increased marketization of society, the continued disruptive nature of US economic and foreign policy, the demands of European business elites, and the activities of the successful EC Commission headed in 1985 by Jacques Delors. By 1983–4 all of the major EC member states had abandoned nationalist economic strategies and were embracing more liberal and open economic policies. Thatcher in Britain, Kohl in Germany and even Mitterrand in France realized that traditional national economic controls had failed to deal with the economic difficulties of the 1970s and early 1980s. Linked to this abandonment of nationalist strategies was the revival of neo-classical economic thinking. Brought about by the inability of Keynesian policies to deal with the economic difficulties of the 1970s, neo-classical economic thought experienced a major academic and political revival. Claiming that the state had become too big, society too demanding and the market too constrained, free-market thinkers called for the expansion of market forces in all areas of economics and society (Hall, 1989). These demands were articulated most clearly in the Reagan and Thatcher 'revolutions' in the US and UK. By 1983–4, not only were the main EC member states turning away from nationalist strategies, but they were also beginning to adopt similar basic policies for economic recovery.

Other major factors were also laying the foundation for the revival of the EC. The US continued to act as a disruptive economic hegemon in the 1970s and 1980s. As opposed to the 1950s and 1960s, when the US maintained a stable exchange rate policy (linking the dollar to gold at $35 an ounce), the US was seen in the late 1960s and early 1970s as exporting inflation due to its lax monetary and fiscal policies and as contributing to international economic dislocation due to its floating exchange rate policy. In the early 1980s the US implemented a very tight monetary policy combined with increased government deficit spending which resulted in raising international interest rates and pulling international capital away from Western Europe. The US had moved from being an inflationary stimulant in the mid-1970s to a deflationary drag in the early 1980s (Andersen, 1984; Ploeg, 1990). For many West Europeans, the US had become an active destabilizer and was 'unsafe at any speed' (Kenen, 1984: 18). Therefore, if Europeans were ever going to step out of the shadow of the disruptive American economic giant, then they needed to work together to create an economic area of European co-operation and stability.

At the European level, two key groups were evolving and demanding EC developments. Although European business interests had been co-ordinated by UNICE since 1958, no strong European business organization had emerged. With the creation of the European Business Roundtable in the 1980s, European business found a strong co-ordinated voice that supported EC integration based on the creation of a true common market, the reduction of internal economic 'rigidities', and a free-market framework. Linked to the emerging free-market consensus, this business–state alliance was a potent political force. Finally, supporting all of these other factors was the creation in 1985 of the EC Commission headed by Delors, which promoted and sustained the movement towards European integration and eventually social policy.

The combination of these social and economic forces led to a revival of European integration based upon two main documents, the 1985 White Paper on the completion of the internal market and the 1986 Single European Act.[2] The 1985 White Paper listed nearly 300 specific proposals for identifying and eliminating the physical, technical and fiscal barriers to the free movement of goods, individuals, capital and services. This laundry list of proposals, many of which had been circulating within the EC institutional system for some time, would have been relatively meaningless without an accompanying transformation of the EC institutional structure to speed the policy-making process.[3]

Initially, EU decision-making power had been concentrated in the hands of the Council of Ministers. The Commission had the right to initiate policy, but legislative power remained firmly in the hands of the Council. Furthermore, within the Council, decisions were made through unanimous voting procedures. The dominance of the Council and unanimous voting procedures were reaffirmed by the 1965 Luxembourg compromise. Decision-making and voting procedures remained unchanged until the mid-1980s.

In the mid-1980s decision-making and voting procedure reform became linked to the creation of the 1992 Internal Market Project. At the 1984 Council meeting at Fontainebleau, the Dooge Commission was created to suggest institutional and decision-making reforms. The report from this commission recommended that the EC should be relaunched by limiting the Luxembourg compromise, especially over decision-making involving the creation of the internal market. The 1986 SEA, which integrated these proposals, established qualified majority voting (QMV) within the Council for most issues directly involved with the creation of the internal market, especially those outlined in the White Paper. QMV was not extended to the more contentious areas of social and economic policy and various loopholes were created to allow states to veto legislation that they strongly opposed. Despite this weakness, Council decision-making was significantly streamlined.

A second major transformation ratified by the SEA was the acceptance of a new integration strategy, 'mutual recognition' and 'subsidiarity'. As discussed in chapter 1, before the 1980s, integration of technical, industrial, working, product and social standards was supposed to be based on a strategy of harmonization. Through negotiation, EC-wide standards would be set and national actors would be forced to progressively accept those standards. The harmonization approach had a number of weaknesses which were aggravated by the integration of new member states in the 1970s and 1980s.[4] The first major challenge to this strategy came from a 1979 judgement of the European Court of Justice (ECJ).[5] German alcohol regulations prohibited the importation of the French liqueur 'Cassis de Dijon' because its alcohol content was too high for wine and too low for spirits. These regulations were challenged and the case was taken to the ECJ. It ruled that since the liqueur was produced to acceptable French standards, the Germans must accept those standards. Using the concept of 'mutual recognition', the ECJ argued that every member state had to accept the standards of other member states, so long as those standards did not demonstrate a clear threat to health, safety, the environment or other aspects of the public interest. This strategy of mutual recognition shifted the burden of policy formation from the EC to the member states. Standards would no longer be set harmoniously ahead of time by the EC, but would create themselves through a decentralized competition of standards. An interest group or member state would bear the burden of demonstrating that the standards were harmful, rather than the EC. As the White Paper implied:

> if a product is lawfully manufactured and marketed in one Member State, there is no reason why it should not be sold freely throughout the Community. Indeed, the objectives of national legislation, such as the protection of human health and life and of the environment, are more often than not identical. ... What is true for goods, is also true for services and people. If a Community citizen or a company meets the requirements for its activity in one Member State, there should be no valid reason why those citizens or companies should not exercise their economic activities also in other parts of the Community. (Sydow, 1988: 93).

For social policy, the transition from harmonization to mutual recognition had substantial implications. Whereas harmonization implied a levelling of policies between the various member states, mutual recognition implied a market-like competition between social policy and standards that threatened a 'race to the bottom' as member states were forced to accept each others' policies and standards. These fears were accentuated by the growing mobility of capital in the 1980s. If investors and firms were able to easily move from one member state to another, then they might be able to 'shop' for the least regulated environment and weakest social policy regime. Member states with advanced social policies feared for their social policies and their competitiveness. These fears were encapsulated in the term 'social dumping' and would later be a driving force behind the creation of the Social Dimension and Social Charter.

Similarly, the concept of subsidiarity had substantial potential for influencing the future of EC social policy. Subsidiarity emerged through the debates of the 1980s, but was not enshrined in the basic treaties of the EU until the 1991 Maastricht Treaty (Article 3b). Subsidiarity was basically the idea that any decision and/or policy that could be made/carried out by levels below the EU should be done so, stressing that policies should be made at the EU level only if they could not be made at the national or sub-national levels. Obviously, this was a strategy for calming the fears of member states who were afraid of giving away too much power to the EC and reflected the decentralizing implication of mutual recognition. Regarding EU social policy, subsidiarity added an extra hurdle for its development to overcome. Not only would social policy have to go through the normal policy channels, but now it would have to demonstrate that the problems it was addressing could only, or best, be dealt with at the European level. The combination of mutual recognition and subsidiarity significantly strengthened the boundaries around EU social policy development. For those hoping to see the creation of some form of EU welfare state these were major setbacks.

Overall, the role of social policy in the White Paper and SEA was minimal. The only policies mentioned were those for encouraging the elimination of barriers to the freedom of movement of workers and creating a true common labour market. The SEA did alter the basic EC treaty in three social policy areas. Article 118a established QMV in the Council 'to encourage improvements, especially in the working environment, as regards the health and safety of workers'. This seemingly clear extension of social policy was substantially constrained by Section 2 of Article 118a which stressed that: 'Such directives shall avoid imposing administrative, financial and legal constraints in a way which would hold back the creation and development of small and medium-sized undertakings'. This paragraph greatly limited the opportunities to create social policy and clearly subordinated it to demands from economic actors who would be most opposed to its creation. The second and third social policy elements of the SEA were the encouraging of a social dialogue between European capital and labour in Article 118b and the reorganization of the EC social funds in Article 130a–e.

Why were social policies so secondary to the revival of the EC in the mid-1980s? The dominant economic philosophy at the time was free-market economics. The assumption was that as the protected economies of Europe integrated and barriers to trade were reduced, Europe would develop a more flexible and dynamic economy. As the famous Cecchini Report (Cecchini, 1988) concluded, the costs of not completing the internal market would be a 7 per cent decrease in GDP, 6 per cent increase in prices and 5 million lost jobs. This philosophy and its conclusions were supported by powerful international and European business organizations and key member-state governments. Social policy had no role to play in this economic revival. Moreover, in order to keep the larger integration process moving, social policy was intentionally downplayed or ignored. Insistence by some member states on more extensive social policies could easily have wrecked the delicate negotiations over the internal market project. Exclusion of social policy concerns was particularly important in keeping Thatcher and the Conservative British government committed to the internal market. Hence, social policies were sacrificed for the larger goal of economic integration and recovery. Finally, pro-EC social policy forces were particularly weak at this time. The European left was still divided over the degree to which social policy should be moved to the European level and European-level social policy NGOs were still in their infancy. Even the Delors Commission was hesitant to push for EC social policy too quickly. Using a logic that was remarkably similar to early neo-functionalist thinking, Delors chose to restrain social policy proposals in order to let the basic agreements on the internal market occur. Once these agreements were set and the market was developing, then political demands for social policy would develop on their own and EC social policies could be promoted without threatening the entire internal market project (Ross, 1995).

The creation of the social dimension

Interestingly, the Delors strategy on social policy appeared to work. Following the creation of the White Paper and the SEA, European economic activity and integration greatly accelerated, the internal market project appeared to be on track, and discussions were proceeding for the revival of monetary integration. Accompanying this activity was the revival of social policy under the general concept of the Social Dimension. Its key elements were first seen in the proposals of the Belgian Employment Minister Alan Hansenne. In 1987 Hansenne, responding to the British government's free-market-oriented

'Action Programme for Employment Growth', proposed that the EC adopt a list of basic social rights (which he based on the Council of Europe's European Social Charter). This specific proposal was defeated in 1987. However, neither it nor the attempts at other social policies were expunged from the European agenda. In fact, the Social Charter, plus proposals in other social policy areas including free movement of workers, a reform of the structural funds (European Social Fund, Agricultural Fund and European Regional Development Fund), working conditions and employee participation, re-emerged in the 1988 Commission working paper, entitled *The Social Dimension of the Internal Market* (Commission, 1988).

The Social Dimension working paper performed a delicate balancing act between general support for the internal market project and specific proposals for curbing the excesses of the common market. The basic argument was that EC social policy was an essential element in the creation of the internal market. It was not designed to stop the development of the market, but to facilitate its creation. Promoting the free movement of workers and reforming the structural funds to make them more effective were obvious elements of the market-supporting strategy, and neither was strongly resisted by conservative governments in the Council. Demands for improved working conditions, predominantly in the areas of health and safety, were also seen as a clear complement to the market process. Health and safety issues had been a part of the founding treaties and the SEA gave them QMV status. The two remaining aspects, worker participation and the Social Charter, were much more divisive.

The Social Charter was composed of three sections: an introduction; a listing of twelve areas of fundamental social rights for workers;[6] and a final section on the implementation of the charter. With strong support from the European Parliament, the Economic and Social Committee, the activist Delors Commission and the ETUC, the Social Charter was put before the Council for its Strasbourg Summit meeting (8–9 December 1989) and passed by eleven votes to one, but only in the non-binding form of a 'solemn declaration' (which required only a qualified majority). Even in this non-binding form, the Conservative British government still voted against it. With the passage of the Social Charter in a non-binding form, the battle over the creation of EU social policy shifted to the implementation of the charter through the 1989 Social Action Programme (Commission, 1989). This was divided into thirteen sections, twelve corresponding to the sections in the Social Charter and one on the use of the European structural funds. The SAP thus presented a multitude of directives, recommendations, decisions, regulations and other instruments for implementing the Social Charter. On 12

January 1990 the Commission adopted the SAP and argued that many
of the individual directives would be presented to the Council in the
form of qualified majority voting directives under the SEA's Article 118a,
which requires qualified majority voting in order to encourage 'improvement, especially in the working environment, as regards the health and
safety of workers'. This interpretation of the qualified majority voting
procedures for social policies was strongly supported by the European
Parliament, which threatened to bring 'the motion of censure out of the
cupboard' (*Agence: Europe*, 12 January 1990), and by the European
Trade Union Confederation (ETUC), but was firmly opposed by the
UNICE and the British Conservative government.

Due to a variety of delays and divisive debates, social policy proposals did not begin to reach the Council until 1991 and progress remained slow for several international and European reasons. In
December 1989 the Berlin Wall fell, the iron curtain around Eastern
Europe soon collapsed and along with it the USSR. Questions of foreign policy, new members and security issues pushed social policy issues off the European agenda. Similarly, the Maastricht Treaty
negotiations consumed a tremendous amount of policy-making time
and effort. Social policy was part of the treaty, but the issues of EMU
and completing the internal market dominated most discussions. When
a British national election was called for April 1992, the EU did not
want to raise delicate social policy concerns before the election and so
put most social policy on hold until the second half of 1992.

This lull in social policy activity appeared somewhat reminiscent of
the years immediately following the 1974 SAP, when, following a brief
flurry of activity, social policy became bogged down in endless debates and was continually delayed due to larger issues. However, even
before the Maastricht Treaty took effect in 1992 there were a number
of reasons why social policy in the early 1990s was better positioned
than in the mid-1970s. To begin with, the EU and the internal market
project were much stronger in the latter period. Because it could no
longer be ignored, national- and European-level actors were increasingly turning to the EU as an arena for pursuing policy development.
Internal institutional changes also helped social policy developments.
The direct election and increasing power (through the co-operation
procedure introduced by the SEA) of the generally supportive Parliament gave social policy a needed lift. A friendly and activist Commission made a continued push for social policy possible. The expansion
of QMV, even if granted only to limited areas, gave social policy activists a new lever within the Council. New social policy NGOs were
developing, expanding their influence, and beginning to take an active
role in promoting European social policy. Finally, the majority of trade

unions and leftist parties had become committed to the EU and were playing a growing role in its development (Featherstone, 1988; Geyer, 1997a; Haahr, 1993).

The importance of this last factor should not be underestimated. One of the major weaknesses of European social policy in the 1970s was that its natural supporters, trade unions and leftist parties, still embraced strongly nationalist economic and social strategies. EC opportunities were ignored and substantial resources were never allocated to the European level. (The ETUC was not created until 1974!) By the late 1980s virtually every major leftist party had abandoned rigidly nationalist economic strategies. This is not to say that they had abandoned their national orientations and had all become 'good Europeans'. Instead, they had adopted a more pragmatic strategy towards the EC which allowed them to focus on EC costs and opportunities.

Further theoretical developments: combining Sisyphus and Janus

In the late 1980s a noticeable transformation occurred in the academic importance of the EC. Previously, European integration studies had been a relatively esoteric and isolated branch of international relations or international political economy. The revival of the EC in the late 1980s was accompanied by an explosion of new work. Courses proliferated, students multiplied and huge numbers of EC-based books and articles appeared. The EC was being extolled as the new superpower. In terms of academic interest, it certainly was.

Ironically, all of this interest generated only a limited amount of theoretical innovation. On the one hand, 'new wave' intergovernmentalists were arguing that the revival was based on a new core agreement between the main member states (Lange, 1993; Moravcsik, 1991, 1993). New wave neo-functionalists argued that the neo-functionalist dynamic had returned (Mutimer, 1989; Tranholm-Mikkelsen, 1991; Caporaso and Keeler, 1995). Other authors, following in the footsteps of Taylor, maintained that the revival and continuing success of the EC were due to a combination of an evolving international context, intergovernmental bargains, neo-functional spillover and institutional activities (Keohane and Hoffmann, 1991; Peterson, 1995). Neo-institutionalists stressed the importance of the Commission, the European Court of Justice, and transformation of the Council for reinvigorating the integration process (Sbragia, 1992). Moreover, as the importance of the EC grew, academics began to interpret both the EC and member-state policy-making processes as an increasingly two-dimensional (Putnam,

1988) and/or multi-dimensional game (Smith and Ray, 1993) where not only would EC-level actors have to take account of national dynamics, but national-level actors would now have to pay attention to EC costs and benefits. Subsequently, this evolved into a concept of multilevel governance (Marks, 1993; Marks et al., 1996, 1996a; Scharpf, 1994). In short, the recognition of the complexity and contingency of the EC and its policy-making process was perhaps the major theoretical achievement of this period.

Similarly, as social policy evolved in the late 1980s and early 1990s a more complicated debate emerged regarding its status and future development. EC social policy development came to be a debate not just over whether or not it would develop, but over whether its development was good or bad. While earlier academics and activists had strong views on the type of social policy that should emerge, these views and debates had been largely ignored because of the earlier weakness of the EC and its social policy. With their revival in the late 1980s, these issues were brought together in a fascinating mix of theoretical debate and political struggle.

With some obvious oversimplification, such as ignoring institutional (Parliament and Commission vs. Council) and national (wealthy Northern member states vs. poor Southern member states)[7] divisions, this mix can be summarized as follows:

EU Social Policy is:

	Positive	Negative
EU social policy cannot develop	1 Traditionalist and nationalist left, national corporatists	3 Free-market-oriented conservatives ('EU sceptics')
EU social policy can develop	2 Modernizing left EU-oriented socialists and social democrats	4 Free-market-oriented conservatives ('EU believers')

The first category under 'Positive' contained a mix of the traditional and nationalist left and supporters of corporatist strategies. In the context of increasing economic globalization and a growing number of new member-state applications, this group was highly sceptical of the potential of significant EC social policy development. The EU level was too institutionally weak, non-democratic, dominated by conservative and/or business forces, too pluralistic and so on to create a viable social policy that could enhance or take over from the existing national social policies and welfare states and protect European citizens against the forces of globalization. Moreover, since EU social policy was so weak and its economic integration dynamic so strong, then on balance it must have a deregulatory tendency. National political forces would be better off defending their national social policies, corporatist structures and welfare states, rather than turning towards the EU in a useless attempt at creating a Euro-welfare state. As W. Streeck and P. Schmitter eloquently summarized in 1991:

> For some time to come, whatever will occupy the place of the supranational Single European State governing the Single European Market, will likely resemble a *pre-New Deal liberal state*, with, in Marshall's terms: A high level of *civil rights*, . . . A low level of *political rights*, . . . An even lower level of *social rights*, . . . [and the] almost complete absence of a European system *of industrial citizenship*. (Streeck and Schmitter, 1991: 152; emphasis in original)

The second 'Positive' group was dominated by the moderate pro-EU social democratic left at both the national and European level. For them, the creation of some advanced form of EU social policy/welfare state was not only feasible, but essential. Social democracy was born out of a struggle to organize society peacefully on the national level (Schwarzmantel, 1991). Through political and economic organization, social democrats would progressively reform their national societies and economies. As global economic forces intensified, the European economies became increasingly integrated, and the ability of the various member-state governments to control and direct their economies was steadily undercut, the obvious place to turn to maintain Europe's social standards and social democratic developments was the EC. Social democratic ideology had always demanded a substantial degree of social/political control over economic activities. If those economic activities were moving to a European level, the obvious response was to move politics and society to that level. As Enrique Crespo, Vice-President of the Parliament, argued:

> The left must install itself in this new framework . . . to give positive impetus to European construction, consolidating the most progressive aspects of a borderless Europe as a common economic and social area and bring a new dimension to the Welfare State. . . . Faced with this opportunity offered to it to actively build the future, the left must find again one of its original distinguishing features: internationalism. (Crespo, 1989: 44)

Under 'Negative', the first group is difficult to clarify since those who were in it had little reason to express their views openly or to take part in a public debate. One could call them conservative or business-oriented Euro-sceptics. In general, they were opposed to an extension of EC social policy for a number of reasons: opposition to government interference in the free market, fear of government oppression, libertarian concerns, concern for the return of governmental overload, and so on. However, due to their scepticism of the success of the integration project and/or the difficulties of EC social policy development they remained relatively unconcerned with its prospects. Hence, the difficulty with tracking this group. On the other hand, one could argue that the reason why some business groups and conservative parties/governments were willing to make certain concessions towards EC social policy development was exactly because they did not expect much to come out of it. They could maintain a co-operative and pragmatic position largely because they did not expect EC social policy to develop into a substantial threat.

The final group consists of the readily identifiable market-oriented conservative EC social policy opponents. The most vocal of them were found within the British political and academic contexts. For this group, EC social policy was a considerable threat. As with the Euro-sceptics, EC social policy threatened the benefits of growing economic globalization, workings of the free market, positive deregulatory impact of economic integration, the marketization of society, and ability of Europe to compete internationally. It was a disruptive and destructive potential, but the threat was real and needed to be countered at all possible levels within the EC. For them, European business must refuse to take part in the social dialogue, member-state governments must block all social legislation in the Council, and the ECJ must refuse to recognize the broad interpretation of social rights in the treaties. As Thatcher argued in her famous speech at Bruges:

> The aim of a Europe open for enterprise is the moving force behind the creation of the Single European Market by 1992. . . . It means action to free markets, to widen choice and to produce greater economic convergence through reduced government intervention . . . And before I leave the subject of the Single Market, may I say that we emphatically do not need new regulations which raise the cost of employment and make Europe's labour market less flexible and less competitive. (Salmon and Nicoll, 1997: 212–13)

The Maastricht Treaty and the recovery of EU social policy?

Despite grand plans and substantial effort, the late 1980s produced rather limited results in EU social policy. During the late 1980s and early 1990s most of the legislative elements of the social dimension had been rejected, put on hold or watered down. There were several obvious constraints on the development of EU social policy. Structurally, these included: the prevailing free-market ideology which viewed social policy with scepticism and scorn, the inherent difficulty of creating an EU-level social policy that integrated the diverse social policy regimes of the EU member states, the focus on mutual recognition rather than harmonization and the EU's limited budgetary capacities (controlling only 1.5 per cent of EU GDP) to create and fund large-scale social policies. Politically, the British Conservative government remained adamantly opposed to all social policy developments that came to the Council. Moreover, the power balance between pro- and anti-social policy interest groups, particularly the ETUC vs. UNICE, though improving, remained tilted against social policy development. Institutionally there were a variety of problems as well. The weakness of the Parliament, the Economic and Social Committee and the Commission (all strong social policy supporters) and strength of the Council (with the British veto) meant that proposing social policy was quite easy, passing it quite difficult. Further, the unanimous voting procedures in the Council for most social policy legislation magnified the influence of the British veto.

However, in the late 1980s integration had been so successful that talks began on the creation of a new treaty to promote the integration project and drive towards full economic and increasing political and social integration. This effort culminated in the December 1991 Maastricht Treaty on European Union, the cornerstone of which was the revival of European Monetary Union (EMU). As mentioned above, European monetary integration had been a dismal failure in the 1970s and early 1980s. However, between 1983 and 1988 currencies within the European Monetary System increasingly stabilized. Following the success of the SEA and internal market strategy, an EU committee (headed by Delors) presented its plan in 1989 for a European monetary union (Delors Report, 1989). This plan envisioned a three-stage process towards full EMU by 1999. Step by step, national controls over monetary policies would be transferred to the European System of Central Banks at the same time as national currencies were increasing replaced by the Euro. The plan was debated throughout 1990 and 1991 and finally agreed upon at the Maastricht meeting of the European Council. The Maastricht Treaty committed all member states of the EU (except the British who had negotiated an opt-out clause) to a rapid and irreversible march towards monetary union. The main points of the treaty closely reflected the basic strategy of the Delors plan. First, as Article 105 of the Maastricht Treaty stipulated, 'the primary objective of the European System of Central Banks (ESCB) shall be to maintain price stability'. Second, the ESCB would, following a German model, be independent of national and European political and institutional structures. Third, national monetary policies and currencies would progressively shift towards the ESCB and the Euro. Fourth, increasingly strict criteria would be applied to member states wanting to participate fully in the EMU. Inflation rates could be no more than 1.5 per cent higher than the average of the three member states with the lowest inflation. Interest rates could be no more than two percentage points higher than the average of the three countries with the lowest rates. Central government budget deficits could not exceed three per cent of GDP. Public debt could not exceed 60 per cent of GDP. And, the national currency was required to remain within the narrow bands of the ERM (2.25 per cent) and not be devalued against any other currency in the EU.

For Delors, and many others, it was obvious that this degree of monetary and fiscal restraint could be quite difficult for the member states to maintain, might cause substantial disruption in certain regions and be politically unpopular. To deal with this, he proposed a substantial expansion of EU regional and social policies (Ross, 1995). In essence, to move integration forward, several policy areas had to move forward together. Neo-functionalism had returned in a strategy of instantaneous spillover. After months of lengthy bargaining Delors got most of his policies. Regional policy was greatly enhanced through an expansion of the structural funds (170 billion ECUs for 1994–9) and the creation of other regional support agencies. In social policy, the Protocol on Social Policy annexed to the Maastricht Treaty created a number of institutional changes which generated the potential for a substantial intensification of social policy development. The changes included: an expansion of the consultative powers (the 'co-decision procedure') of the Parliament (Corbett et al., 1995), the creation of qualified majority voting in the Council in new areas of social policy (health and safety, working conditions, information and consultation of workers, equal opportunities and treatment for men and women, and integration of people excluded from the labour market), promoted the 'social dialogue' between capital and labour, and created a new form of social policy initiative by agreement between European capital and labour. This seemingly clear advance for EU social policy was complicated by the unique procedural device of the British 'opt-out' clause. Using this device, Britain was allowed to 'opt out' of future qualified majority-approved social policies. At first glance, this appeared to remove a major source (British opposition) of Council resistance to many social policies. However, since new policies were not supposed to affect Britain, legally or financially,[8] the 'opt-out' greatly complicated both the legal foundation and implementation of EU social policies.

During the ratification difficulties of the Maastricht Treaty, social policy development came to a near standstill. This was accentuated by a number of developments. First, in order not to antagonize British (especially Conservative) voters, EU social policy was put on hold until after the British general election of April 1992. Following the victory of the Conservatives in that election, it was Britain's turn to be President of the Council (July–December 1992). Consequently, the newly re-elected Conservative government was able to stifle EU social policy development with relative ease since most attention was directed towards overcoming the Danish rejection of the Maastricht Treaty in June 1992.[9] At the beginning of 1993 the Danes took over the Presidency of the Council and were determined to bring social policy back to the forefront. However, ratifying the Maastricht Treaty in the second Danish referendum (May 1993) became the focus of most Danish actions (Geyer and Ayres, 1995). No major directives were passed during this period.

The successful second Danish referendum on the Maastricht Treaty in May 1993 removed the last obstacle to its implementation. In the second half of 1993, under the Belgian Presidency of the Council and with the new institutional changes in place, social policy began to move forward again. By the end of 1993 the Commission had initiated all of the Social Charter's Action Programme. By 1995, of the forty-seven initiatives in the programme, sixteen had been approved. However, twenty-nine of the initiatives required Council approval, and of those only four had been passed (Commission, 1995b).

More important, in 1994–6 two main Maastricht Treaty innovations were implemented, the British 'opt-out' and the creation of social policy based on a social dialogue between the ETUC and UNICE. As will be explored more thoroughly in chapter 4, in 1994 the European Works Council Directive was passed by a vote of 10–0 (Portugal abstained) in the Council. This was the first piece of EU social policy legislation to be passed against the British veto, using the Maastricht Treaty's 'opt-out' clause. Meanwhile, in 1995, after a lengthy process, an agreement was reached between the social partners, primarily the ETUC and UNICE, for legislation on the Parental Leave Directive. This was passed by the Council in 1996 and became the first successful use of the social dialogue to create EU legislation through the Social Protocol of the Maastricht Treaty.

Besides these institutional innovations, a number of other factors developed in the 1990s which improved the situation of EU social policy development. Throughout the 1990s European social policy

NGOs were rapidly emerging and establishing themselves, often with direct and extensive support from the Commission (Greenwood, 1997: chapters 7 and 8; Greenwood and Aspinwall, 1998: chapters 3 and 7). In 1994 three new member states chose to join the EU: Austria, Finland and Sweden (Norway voted to stay out, again!). All three countries were well above the EU economic average, had strong social democratic traditions, advanced social policies, substantial welfare states, and were strong proponents of EU social policy. Moreover, in May 1997 the arch opponent of EU social policy, the British Conservative Party, was decisively defeated by the British Labour Party. Labour immediately promised to end the British social policy opt-out, but was cautious towards new social policy developments. Hence, despite a number of basic constraints, it would appear that EU social policy may be set for a period of expansion.

Reflecting these developments, the EU Social Affairs Commissioner Padraig Flynn developed a much more co-operative and consolidating strategy on social policy. In 1993 Flynn and the Commission presented a Green Paper on EU social policy (Commission, 1993). The purpose of the paper was threefold: to develop a debate on social policy and direct it into certain key areas, to gauge the opinions and reactions to various proposals from key member states and organizations, and to use the debate and opinions as a basis for outlining a set of feasible Commission proposals. The areas covered by the Green Paper included employment improvement, convergence of social policies, strategies for fighting poverty and social exclusion, policies on the young and elderly, free movement policy, sex equality policy, promotion of the social dialogue, and the role of the European Social Fund. Overall, it was a very general document, focused on finding areas of agreement. The response to it was generally positive except, unsurprisingly, from the British Conservative government (Commission, 1995).

This co-operative and consensual process led to the creation of the 1994 White Paper (Commission, 1994b), which summarized the responses to the Green Paper, and the 1995–7 Medium-Term Social Action Programme (Commission, 1995a), which set the framework for the subsequent period. In general, it was primarily a repetition of the White Paper, calling for a number of existing proposals to be finally enacted, promoting the creation of a number of new discussions, debates and conferences, but demanding few new pieces of legislation except in relatively consensual areas of health and safety and freedom of movement.

During the debates preceding the 1997 Amsterdam Treaty revisions, social policy was completely overshadowed by concerns with EMU, integrating new East European members, and the new sections in the treaty dealing with employment policy. With the defeat of the British Conservative government in May 1997, the British social policy opt-out was ended and the Social Protocol was quickly integrated into the basic text of the Amsterdam Treaty. The treaty gave a clear commitment to address a variety of forms of discrimination in Article 13 (consolidated texts). However, the treaty refrained from making substantial spending commitments to new social policy areas and dropped measures for improving the position of the elderly and disabled from Article 137 (consolidated texts) (Duff, 1997: 73).

The most recent major publication of the Commission on social policy, *Social Action Programme 1998–2000* (Commission, 1998e), again reflected this consolidating approach. Focusing on just three main areas – *jobs, skills and mobility*; *the changing world of work*; and *an inclusive society* – it contained the usual array of social policy proposals, but framed many of them in the new light of employment policy. With the integration of the employment section into the Amsterdam Treaty and the subsequent creation of the employment policy guidelines, the Commission clearly saw an opportunity for justifying and expanding social policies through their linkage to employment creation. The success and constraints of this linkage are explored in chapter 9.

The current state of EU theory

Despite the efforts of a growing number of Euro-academics, there has been no substantial macro-level theoretical development in EU social policy since the late 1980s. I would argue that there are two main reasons for this. First, as mentioned above, macro-level integration theory reached an impasse in regard to the EU in the 1970s and 1980s. Since that time, most works on the dynamics of integration have used a combination of earlier theories, culminating in the concept of multi-level governance. Second, as more detailed work on the EU proliferated in the 1980s and 1990s, different theories from comparative politics, political economy, state theory and other areas were all brought to bear on the question of integration dynamics and policy development. A multitude of meso- and micro-approaches have emerged, but none which claims to capture larger-level integration dynamics.

As the 1990s progressed, three key developments altered the nature of these debates. First, despite the growth of Europeanization and globalization, West European national welfare states proved to be remarkably resilient. Overall spending on welfare remained noticeably stable. Political support was strong. Different welfare states maintained their distinctive structures (Geyer, 1998; Geyer et al., 2000; Hirst and Thompson, 1996; Swank, 1992, 1998). In essence, national social policy regimes were being pressured and altered, but not radically. Second, despite hopes and fears, it became obvious that the EU was not capable of creating a substantial social policy regime which would replace national-level regimes. Third, despite this limitation, EU social policy was continuing to make slow progress and becoming increasingly important to the member-state social policy regimes. The growth of the European Social Fund, the expansion of social policy in the Amsterdam Treaty (1997), the growth of European social policy interest groups, and the integration of social policy groups and concerns into the Employment Guidelines (1998) were all indications of slow but continuous development (Sykes and Alcock, 1998).The combination of these factors changed the central question of EU social policy research from 'Could the EC protect/replace national level social policies?' to 'How does EU social policy interact with distinctive national level social policy regimes?'

This overview demonstrates the uneven and irregular development of EU social policy. Following The Hague Summit (1969), there was a brief expansion of social policy in the early 1970s. However, this was soon followed by a lengthy period of 'Eurosclerosis' and social policy stagnation. The revival of European integration under the SEA sparked the recovery of European social policy under the auspices of the Social Dimension. This forward momentum was stalled during the tortuous debates over and ratification of the Maastricht Treaty in the early 1990s. Nevertheless, when the treaty was finally passed and its institutional innovations put into place, EU social policy again began to move forward. Currently, EU social policy is in a phase of consolidation. The institutional changes in the Maastricht and Amsterdam treaties seem to encourage continued progress.

The three major theoretical developments in EU social policy which occurred during the 1970s, 1980s and 1990s were the growing recognition of the complexity and contingency in EU social policy, the growth of the left–right debate over the Janusian nature of EU social policy, and the shift towards studying the micro- and meso-level aspects of EU social policy and its impact on national-level social policy regimes. The key question for current theorists is not whether the EU can save the European welfare state, but how it interacts with national-level regime types.

3

Labour Policy: Core Areas

Freedom of movement for workers shall be secured within the Community by the end of the transitional period at the latest.

Article 48, Treaty of Rome, 1958

The institutions of the Community shall . . . in the common interest . . . promote improved working conditions and an improved standard of living for the workers in each of the industries for which it is responsible.

Article 3, Treaty of Paris, 1951

EU labour policy has been a contentious and divisive area of EU social policy.[1] The creation of a common market always implied the development of some form of common labour market and policy. However, such a policy lies at the heart of the division between socialist and capitalist philosophical traditions in Western European thought. At the European level, socialist/labour parties and trade unions concentrated on regulating and limiting the impacts of marketization on the national labour markets, while market-oriented parties and capitalist organizations of the right promoted the creation of a true European labour market in order to maximize Europe's economic potential and deregulate its economic structures. As demonstrated by the above quotations from the founding treaties, the EU has generally performed a balancing act between these two traditions which has been greatly complicated by the diversity of national-level industrial relations systems and multi-layered EU polity. The result of this balancing act was the division of EU labour policy into acceptable 'core' and disputed 'extended' areas. Core areas, where both sides could agree to some basic parameters, included free movement of labour, health and safety issues, and training. Extended areas, such as working conditions and employment rights, grew out of the development of the core areas and the success of European integration, and remain very divisive.

This chapter focuses on the development of two core areas, freedom of movement and health and safety. Training policy will be integrated into the review of the structural funds and youth policy. Despite obvious differences, their development presents a number of commonalities. Both were clearly mentioned in the founding treaties and appeared regularly in all major subsequent social policy documents; they were integrated into the functioning of the European Social Fund and gained early QMV status in the Council under the Single European Act. Subsequently, this QMV status led the Commission to use these core areas as 'Trojan horses' for other areas of social policy, including gender, social dialogue and labour rights. Most recently, as more areas of social policy have gained QMV status and the British Conservative Party veto of social policy was surmounted and eliminated, the Trojan horse strategy has been used less frequently. At the time of writing, central aspects of these policies have been firmly established and represent core issues on which both sides of the capitalist/socialist divide can agree. Nevertheless, the fringes of these policy areas and their extensions (including such questions as whether third country nationals have free movement and whether health and safety issues should encompass limiting working hours) remain divisive.

Free movement

The free movement of labour in the ECSC/EEC: liberal vision, nationalist constraints

The free movement of labour would appear to be one of the fundamental elements of EU policy, along with the freedom of movement of goods, services and capital. It is obviously essential to the creation of a true internal market. However, the early history of EU free movement policy is much more one of constraints upon that freedom, rather than its promotion.[2] In 1950 the economies of the six member states of the ECSC were still focused on postwar revival. International labour mobility had vanished during the Second World War and most of the members of the ECSC were desperately afraid of large-scale labour movement, particularly of the low skilled into their national economies. Reflecting this, the Treaty of Paris was noticeably silent on any broad right of workers to move freely between the member states. The treaty did encourage the mobility of skilled workers to areas that lacked expertise or were experiencing a shortage of skilled workers and the possibility of reabsorbing existing coal and steel workers within other areas of the ECSC (Collins, 1975: 65). However, it also built in safeguards against influxes of cheap labour by forbidding the cutting of wages as a competitive strategy (Article 68) and by refusing to allow pay discrimination between nationals and non-nationals (Article 69). In general, the treaty was built on the idea of the eventual creation of a common market where market forces would lead to the eventual 'equalization of conditions of life and work'. However, in reality, international labour mobility was greatly feared and tightly controlled. Even highly skilled workers were given little incentive to confront the difficulties of international mobility. A first small step towards mobility promotion, following the recommendations of a 1952 working group and a 1954 intergovernmental conference, was the creation of a 'European labour card'. This card was available to only fifty-six highly skilled job categories in the coal and steel industries and would give the holder limited rights to work in other member states (Collins, 1975: 67).

The Treaty of Rome had a much larger and encompassing vision than the Treaty of Paris. For the ECSC, freedom of mobility was only a distant goal. Promoting 'acceptable' (among the highly skilled) and protecting against 'unacceptable' (among the low skilled) forms of mobility was its primary mission. For the EEC, 'the abolition as between Member States of obstacles for free movement of persons' (Article 3c) was seen as an essential element of the creation of the common market. Further, for many of the EEC actors at the time (Levi-Sandri, 1968), freedom of mobility was a key element in the promotion of a social and political European identity. This was essential not only to federalists who wanted to see to creation of European civil and social rights, but to functionalist and neo-functionalists who saw this as an integral part in the formation of the spillover dynamic. Articles 48–51 are the primary ones to establish the right of freedom of mobility for workers.[3] Article 48, reiterating the principle of non-discrimination set out in Article 7, demands the prohibition of all national discrimination in the areas of 'employment, remuneration and other conditions of work and employment'. It confirmed the rights of workers to accept an offer of work in any member state, to remain in the country after the term of employment expired, and to take up employment under the same conditions as nationals. An important exception to this freedom of employment and mobility was in the area of public sector employment where no rights were granted. The article also specified that movement could be limited on the grounds of public policy, public security or public health.[4]

Why were the six founding member states of the EEC willing to accept this substantial expansion in the freedom of movement for workers? Had the European ideal captured the heart of the working class? This was unlikely. What was actually occurring was the 'golden age' of West European capitalism. As economies boomed, workers became more and more difficult to find. It was increasingly obvious that one of the major constraints on production was labour force limitations. Labour migration was no longer feared, but actively promoted by the member states. The key area of internal EEC migration was from southern Italy to the other member states. Over half a million Italians moved and stayed in the other member states during the 1950s and 1960s. In 1958 around 50 per cent of the EEC's first work permits were issued to Italians (Collins, 1975a, chapter 4). Moreover, during this period, intra-EEC migration was overwhelmed by migration into the EEC by non-member-state nationals. Key examples of this trend were the immigration of North Africans (former colonial areas, particularly Algeria) to France and Turks to Germany. By 1968 only 27 per cent of internal EEC work permits went to Italians while 69 per cent went to third country nationals (Collins, 1975a: 114). In general, under the boom-time conditions of the golden age, these migrants were seen as helping to expand production within the member states, particularly since they often took jobs that were no longer desired by the national workforce.

In the early years after the creation of the EEC, there was very little legislative development in terms of freedom of movement policy. In many ways, it was a study period for the EEC. One of the first things the EEC did was to create a Technical Committee to examine the legal and administrative constraints to labour mobility that needed to be identified, eased and eventually eliminated. These included aspects of passport and visa regulations, labour and residence permits, and family rights as well. It was not until 1961 that the first major piece of mobility legislation was developed. Regulation 15/61/EEC (plus a linked directive) established the dominance of the Community over issues regarding the treatment of EEC nationals, emphasized the 'equality of treatment' between nationals and other EEC nationals, and created a general obligation on member states to allow their nationals to work in other member states. In 1964 Regulation 38/64/EEC and Directives 64/240/EEC and 64/221/EEC expanded mobility rights to frontier and seasonal workers, standardized administrative procedures for work permits, abolished work and residence permits for stays under three months, and limited the ability of member states to restrict workers on the grounds of public order, safety and health. Clearly, not only was the EEC committed to, but the member states appeared willing to accept, a growing right to worker mobility. The problem was, as Doreen

Collins summarized, 'that these legal requirements . . . , although important as a first step, could not deal with the manifold problems of socio-economic reality' (Collins, 1975a: 105). As the 1960s progressed, it became increasingly apparent that legal constraints were not the only ones that were limiting worker mobility. The EEC quickly realized that if it were to promote the freedom of movement, as the Treaty of Rome directed it to do, it would soon be forced into such policy areas as those regarding family or training, which were not specified under the treaty and were new to the EEC. As discussed in chapter 2, this was exactly what the neo-functionalists had hoped would happen.

There was, however, one important exception to the early period of 'study' activity in the EEC, the right of mobile workers to social security. In the Treaty of Rome, it was clearly recognized that an important limitation of worker mobility was uncertainty over the rights of workers to, or the loss of, social security rights while working in another EEC member state. Article 51 empowered the Council with the ability to adopt 'such measures in the field of social security as are necessary to provide freedom of movement for workers; to this end it shall make arrangements to secure for migrant workers and their dependants'. Immediately after the ratification of the treaty, Regulations 3/58/EEC and 4/58/EEC were passed, setting out some of the basic rights to social security in the EEC. These regulations did not attempt to create a harmonized EEC social security system, but encouraged the member states to co-ordinate their social security systems so that migrant workers and their families would be covered whenever they moved within the EEC. Social security rights proved to be a particularly complicated and technical field. At the time, various bilateral agreements existed between Western European countries to promote labour mobility (particularly of the highly skilled) and the ECSC did recognize it as a problem area and attempted to encourage greater co-ordination between the systems for coal and steel workers. The EEC's basic strategy was to create a co-ordinated system that was non-discriminatory between EEC nationals, in which social security benefits would be exportable and would be cumulative if a worker moved between the systems.

Early consequences of the right to free movement

As the golden age of West European capitalism continued in the 1960s, pressure mounted for greater worker mobility. Following agreements at the Council meetings in May 1966 to promote the completion of the EEC customs union and the right to freedom of movement within the EEC, a key Regulation (1612/68/EEC) and linked Directive (68/360/EEC) were passed. This legislation attempted to '[take] into account, firstly, the importance for the worker, from a human point of view, of having his entire family with him and, secondly, the importance, from all points of view, of the integration of the worker and his family into the host Member State without any difference in treatment in relation to nationals of that State' (Barnard, 1996: 116–17). The regulation, intended to abolish all forms of discrimination based on nationality, accepted the fundamental right of workers and their families to work anywhere within the EEC, and to have the same opportunity to work as nationals of any given member state. It also recognized the need to go beyond the simple legal recognition of this right and to affirmatively promote equality of treatment at work, access to housing (a major problem for families at the time) and the integration of the worker and the family into the host nation. It also encouraged the member states to develop co-ordinated training, vocational and employment policies and created the SEDOC (European system for the international clearing of vacancies and applications for employment) system to promote greater information and transparency in the EEC labour market. Moreover, in 1970 Regulation 1251/70/EEC broadened the right of workers and their families to remain in host member states.

During the early 1970s there was a substantial expansion in the rights of freedom of movement and social security for the self-employed. For example, Directive 73/148/EEC, similar to Directive 68/360/EEC, confirmed the legal right of the self-employed to freedom of movement and their ability to provide and receive services in another member state. Directive 75/34/EEC, similar to Regulation 1251/70/EEC, broadened the right of the self-employed and their families to remain in host member states. Regulations 1408/71/EEC and 574/72/EEC expanded and clarified the social security rights of EEC migrants. As earlier, the EEC had no intention of creating a harmonized EEC social security system, but merely a co-ordinated system that promoted mobility. Regulation 1408/71 laid out the four main principles of that co-ordination and designated the major areas of policy co-ordination: there was to be non-discrimination between EEC nationals; workers were to be governed by the state social security system where they worked; the principle of 'aggregation' was to ensure that the host member state would take into account periods of insurance completed in other member states; and the principle of 'exportability' was to preserve social security rights previously acquired by workers. It also designated the major forms of social security covered by the regulation, for example those relating to sickness and maternity, invalidity, old age, occupational sickness and accident, death, unemployment and the family.

Concurrently freedom of mobility was institutionalized within the EEC, though substantial constraints remained. The public sector remained closed to the mobility rights of EEC nationals and the three derogations of the right to mobility based on public policy, public security and public health were still legislatively unchallenged. However, the actions of the European Court of Justice (ECJ) in a variety of cases were gradually restricting the definition of the public sector and the justifications for limiting mobility based on the three derogations. This judicial action created a delicate balance of promoting the freedom of mobility, while maintaining the rights of member states to limit that mobility. This balancing act is evident in the summary of the Van Duyn Case (41/74) of 1974:

> All derogations from a fundamental freedom of the Union must be interpreted strictly so that their scope cannot be determined unilaterally by each Member State without being subject to control by the Union institutions. Member States do, however, have a certain amount of discretion, within the limits of the Treaty, to determine what constitutes public policy in light of their national needs. (Barnard, 1996: 157)

The central point to recognize from these developments was that by the early 1970s, not only was the legal right to mobility by EEC nationals firmly established, but the EEC realized that the legal creation of this right was not enough. Effective promotion of freedom of mobility to develop a common market and encourage European 'citizenship' would require active policies of training, job information, social security and family support. This realization culminated in the proposed 1974–6 Social Action Programme, which encouraged the creation of common vocational training, employment and social protection policies and established an action programme for migrant workers and their families for EEC and non-EEC nationals. The Action Programme for Migrant Workers dealt with both EEC nationals and non-nationals. For member-state nationals, it encouraged the continued fight against non-legal barriers to mobility, including rights to social benefits, to trade union recognition, the mutual recognition of qualifications, and residence. It also encouraged more social security reform (to cover areas previously excluded and to eliminate any final areas of discrepancy between nationals and migrants), increased vocational and language training, improved social services for migrants and their families, education for the children of migrants, and housing and health benefits.

The early 1970s: constraining the freedom of movement

Ironically, at the same time as the recognition of the need for policy 'spillover' was occurring and developing political momentum, the West European golden age was coming to an end. As the recession deepened, unemployment rates began to climb steadily. Economies that had previously been desperate for more labour (the German and French in particular) were now struggling to find employment for their own nationals. By the mid-1970s, like many other areas of EC legislation, the freedom of movement policy came to a standstill. Member states had little desire to promote labour mobility, once again fearing large influxes of low-skilled labour. They were now trying to repatriate third country nationals to their home countries or limit their ability (or their families) to stay in the EEC. A key EC legislative example of this change in policy can be seen in the 1976 Council Resolution (OJ C 34, 14.2.1976) for implementing the 1974 Action Programme for Migrant Workers and their Families. This (non-binding) resolution stressed that the EC's 'prime objective' was to 'enable workers who are nationals of Member States to find employment in their own region'. However, if these individuals did not find employment in their own region, they had the right to find it anywhere within the EC. Moreover, the EC should continue to promote 'genuine equality of treatment', co-operation between national employment services, 'appropriate assistance' to migrant workers and their families to help them integrate into the host country, and (importantly) 'appropriate assistance' to those migrants who want to return to their home country. For non-EC nationals, the resolution was much more negative. The resolution argued that legal third country nationals should receive full equality with EC nationals. However, it also encouraged the EC to 'undertake appropriate consultation on migration policies *vis à vis* third countries' and to 'strengthen co-operation between Member States in the campaign against illegal immigration'. Thus, as the economies of the major EC member states began to falter, the burden of these problems was quickly shifted on to third country nationals. The right of freedom of movement within the EC was not sacrificed, but the promotion of that right and the previous position of third country nationals were quickly and efficiently ignored.

From the mid-1970s to the mid-1980s there were few new developments in the area of freedom of movement. Some directives were developed for promoting the mutual recognition of diplomas for certain professions (doctors, nurses, veterinarians, dentists and midwives); the European Social Fund was revised and restructured to deal directly with the growing employment crisis; the SEDOC system, established by Regulation 1612/68, began operating in 1973 and achieved some modest successes; the Commission attempted to promote more employment policy co-operation; and new initiatives were created to promote youth employment and training. The European Centre for the Development of Vocational Training (CEDEFOP) was established in 1975 (Regulation 337/75/EEC) and in 1976 the right of migrants to undertake trade union activity in the host country was reaffirmed (Regulation 312/76/EEC). Most of these issues were relatively minor, technical/administrative in nature, and non-controversial. They reflected the limited abilities and vision of the EC of this period.

The 1980s: liberal revival, external constraints and Trojan horses

As with many other policy areas, it was not until the creation of the 1985 White Paper on *Completing the Single Market*, the Single European Act (SEA) and Delors' Social Dimension initiative that freedom of movement policy began to take its current shape. The mid-1980s revival of the EC was based strongly on liberal economic ideas. As argued in the White Paper, the creation of a true single market would require the freedom of movement of goods, services, capital and labour. In theory, labour mobility was a crucial ingredient in the single market. The first major piece of EC legislation adopted was a new Action Programme for Migrants, which was based on the premise that the legal right to EC mobility was already in place. Nevertheless, 'the purpose of this legislation is to promote genuine equality of treatment with national workers in living and working conditions and in social security provision' (Commission, 1985: 7). The document specified six main aims: to improve existing EC legislation; to encourage the application of EC mobility rights at the member-state level; to make EC texts more readily available and comprehensible; to adapt and strengthen social security provisions; to promote the exercise of full political and civil rights of migrants in host countries; and to provide greater protection for certain categories of persons (such as frontier and seasonal workers) not covered, or inadequately covered, by existing instruments. For third country migrants, the programme offered a contradictory dualistic approach. On the one hand, the document encouraged the protection of the rights of those who were legally working in the EC and the promotion of their integration into EC society. On the other, it also stressed that relations between the EC and third countries should concentrate on 'keeping migration of foreign workforce under control', encouraging the voluntary return of foreign workers, and campaigning against illegal migration and clandestine employment. In essence, the cost of opening up migration within the EC was the limiting of migration from outside it. As Geddes pointed out, this contradictory approach was generated by 'single market integration: namely, that free movement of EU nationals within the single market seems to require tighter control of external frontiers. . . . So, at the same time as internal barriers are reduced, external ones are tightened within a co-ordinated policy framework at EU level' (Geddes, 1995: 205).[5]

More specifically, in the White Paper the freedom of mobility, for member-state nationals, was seen as one of the central elements of the creation of the single market. Similar to the 1985 Action Programme, it recognized that legally there were few restrictions to mobility, but other barriers remained. These included cumbersome administrative procedures for migrants and the difficulties of comparability of occupational and vocational standards. The SEA did support the freedom of mobility for member-state nationals by altering Article 49 of the Treaty of Rome to give the Council the ability to pass mobility legislation with a qualified majority. The SEA complicated this support by requiring the Council to use a qualified majority in 'co-operation' with the Parliament, and after 'consulting' the ESC, and did not give social security issues QMV status. Nevertheless, in the EC's social policy documents, promoting mobility became a primary concern. For example, as *The Social Dimension of the Internal Market* stated: 'Social policy must, above all, contribute to the setting up of a "single labour market" by doing away with the barriers which still restrict the effective exercise of two basic freedoms: the freedom of movement of persons and the freedom of establishment' (Commission, 1988: 2–3). Linked to the Social Dimension was the Social Charter, in which freedom of movement was the first social right to be mentioned and which encouraged the harmonization of conditions of residence, the mutual recognition of diplomas and occupational qualifications, and the improvement of living and working conditions of frontier workers. The Action Programme for the Charter outlined a number of proposals, including new regulations for extending social security rights, a directive for protecting the rights of workers posted in other member states ('posted workers'), and a number of lesser proposals. In 1989 Directive 89/48/EEC (later extended by Directive 92/51/EEC) provided for the recognition of higher education diplomas. At the same time as these legislative proposals were emerging, the Commission took steps to limit the exemption of the public sector employment (Article 48) from freedom of mobility legislation by strictly defining the parameters of the public sector (OJ C 72, 18.03.1988) and opening up areas such as public administration of commercial services, public health care services, and teaching and non-military research sectors. Meanwhile, as discussed below, the Commission was also creating, via funding from the European Social Fund, an impressive variety of training and vocational programmes linked to the promotion of mobility.

Where did all of this freedom of mobility activity come from? During the mid- to late 1980s there was an EC revival based on the abandoning of national policy autonomy and a growing market-oriented consensus. Under such conditions, freedom of mobility was a prime candidate for legislative activity. It was also an important area for bringing in new social policy areas; freedom of movement legislation is a prime area of social policy spillover. The legal right to mobility was relatively easy to establish, but creating the conditions for actual mobility required the EU to take a much larger role in related social policy areas such as the rights of families, social security rights and training. Moreover, when freedom of mobility for member-state nationals (excluding issues of social security) gained QMV status under the SEA, it offered social policy proponents a new strategy for expanding social policy. Not only was this a way to get around the militant British veto, but it also legitimized the policy as necessary for the promotion of the single market.

The result was the creation of the Trojan horse strategy for broadening social policy through freedom of mobility. A key example was the directive for 'posted workers'. In 1991, the Commission argued that in order to promote a true single market a basic framework of rules for these workers would have to be created in order to avoid market 'cheating'. For example, firms could not be allowed to post a worker in another member state solely for the reason of reducing his/her basic economic rights (including minimum rates of pay, maximum hours, public holidays, etc.). This was similar to the broader social dumping arguments and despite obvious linkages to labour rights policy was submitted by the Commission under freedom of movement policy. Predictably, this proposal generated a substantial amount of debate and opposition from key member states (particularly the UK) and the European employers organization, UNICE. It was only after five years of intensive legislative struggle and a substantial weakening of the provisions in the legislation that the directive was finally passed in 1996 (96/71/EC). This strategy was used in a variety of areas and led to a very antagonistic relationship between DGV and the British Conservative government throughout the late 1980s and early 1990s.

The 1990s: the contradictions of internal openness and external control

In the 1990s, with the freedom of movement legislation well established, the EU turned to specific strategies for promoting the realization of that freedom. The Maastricht Treaty had relatively little impact on freedom of mobility legislation. A new section was added on European citizenship (Articles 8a–8e). However, no new areas were given qualified majority status. One institutional change was in Article 49, where the QMV procedure in the Council for mobility legislation would have to be taken in regard to the 'co-decision' procedure with the Parliament, rather than the 'co-operation' procedure (Corbett et al., 1995: chapter 11). Other legislative and non-legislative developments relating to freedom of movement did occur. In 1992 the new European Employment Services (EURES) were set up to replace the ageing and inefficient SEDOC system and 'inform, advise and place jobseekers throughout Europe and as a forum for examining . . . any question concerning employment in Europe' (Commission, 1996e: 14). In other areas, a virtual alphabet soup of organizations and programmes was being created (Rees, 1998). These included the 1989 PETRA programme for vocational training for the young, the 1990 LINGUA programme to support language acquisition, the COMETT programme to link businesses with universities, and many others. In July 1992 and June 1993 Regulations 2434/92/EEC and 1945/93/EEC were adopted; these modified and extended the mobility rights and application of social security schemes to employed and self-employed persons and their families. In January 1994 the European Economic Area agreement came into effect, creating a zone of freedom of labour mobility between the EU and the remains of the nations of the European Free Trade Association. Theoretically, this created a right to freedom of mobility for 375 million people.

In the more recent social policy developments of the mid-1990s, freedom of movement policy has played a relatively secondary role. It was only mentioned in passing in the Delors White Paper, *Growth, Competitiveness, Employment* (Commission, 1994). In the 1993 Green Paper on European Social Policy, *Options for the Union* (Commission, 1993), the Commission put forward a number of proposals for completing and enhancing freedom of mobility. These included lifting the final legal barriers to free movement, promotion of the EURES network, equal treatment in regard to social and tax advantages (particularly students and pensioners), better protection of mobile worker occupational pension rights, deepening and extending social security co-ordination, and providing more information to legal actors who deal with the implementation of EU freedom of movement legislation. In the subsequent discussion of the Green Paper, most of the Commission's proposals were supported. All were seen as relatively small-scale demands, administratively oriented, inexpensive and not politically divisive. On the other hand, proposals for the increasing of rights of third country nationals met with a more mixed response. Most NGOs and special interest groups that were contacted in the Green Paper consultation process strongly supported an extension of these rights in order to promote the social and economic inclusion of the beneficiaries into the European integration processes. However, some member states, particularly Luxembourg and Germany, called for caution in any extension of these rights to third country nationals (Commission, 1995: 13). In the 1994 White Paper *European Social Policy: A Way Forward for the Union*, the Commission summarized its conclusions from the Green Paper consultation process. Reflecting the general perception of the previous ten or more years, the Commission argued that, for member-state nationals and legal residents: 'The challenge to the Union now is . . . to create a real European mobility area, in which freedom of movement becomes not only a legal entitlement but also a daily reality for people across Europe' (Commission, 1994b: 26). The document made no mention of strategies for integrating illegal residents and immigrants.

The Commission clarified these proposals in its 'Medium-Term Social Action Programme 1995–7' (Commission, 1995a), promoting new legislation on pension rights, rights of residence, social security and taxation, launching a series of debates on free movement issues (education, social security and rights of third country nationals),[6] and promoting the EURES system for transnational employment promotion and the TESS (modernization of the exchange of information between national social security institutions) system for social security co-ordination. These demands manifested themselves in the 1997 *Modernizing and Improving Social Protection in the European Union* (COM (97) 102 final), the Action Plan for Free Movement of Workers (COM (97) 589 final), the Commission proposal for safeguarding the supplementary pension rights of employed and self-employed persons (COM (97) 486 final) and the Green Paper on Supplementary Pensions (COM (97) 283 final).

The Amsterdam Treaty confirmed the importance of freedom of movement and pushed its internal implications. Article 62 (consolidated texts) demanded that within five years the Council should adopt 'measures with a view to ensuring . . . the absence of any controls on persons, be they citizens of the Union or nationals of third countries, when crossing internal borders'. Furthermore, the Schengen Agreement on open borders between certain member states was attached to the treaty. Also, a small article (Article 286, consolidated texts) was inserted to encourage 'the protection of individuals with regard to the processing of personal data and the free movement of such data'. This bold goal of internal openness was substantially complicated by British, Irish and Danish 'opt-outs' and the complexity of the Schengen Agreement (Duff, 1997: 46–54). This demonstrated that certain core member states (France, Germany, the Benelux countries) were determined to substantially increase free movement rights and mobility, while others (Britain, Ireland and Denmark, particularly following its rejection of the Maastricht Treaty) remained reluctant. With the requirement of unaminous voting (UV) in the Council, the only option was a compromise letting France, Germany and the others push ahead, while protecting Britain's, Ireland's and Denmark's right not to take part. Similarly, linked to the deepening of free movement rights were the development of more co-ordinated asylum, immigration and policing policies (Articles 61–9, consolidated texts). As established in the early 1990s, EU member states were unwilling to see the growth of internal borders without greater co-operation and strengthening of external borders and internal policing powers.

At the time of writing, EU freedom of movement policy is in a strangely contradictory position. On the one hand, the basic legal elements of freedom of movement have been in place for ten to twenty years. Any new legislation in this area is generally dealing with new circumstances (changes in social security provision, social structures, etc.) or extending the legislation to cover the last cracks in the legal edifice. In these areas, freedom of movement policy is primarily administrative, technical, and less political. On the other, creating true freedom of movement has forced the EU into a number of highly contentious and possibly expensive areas where it has neither the political will nor economic muscle to go. The policy regarding training and education (see chapter 8 below) is one area in which it has been politically and economically acceptable to see an expansion of EU competencies. However, when EU proposals move beyond its core areas it immediately runs into a hornet's nest of difficulties, such as deeper citizenship rights, social security issues, and the rights of third country nationals and illegal immigrants/residents. Finally, despite the creation of a legal framework of mobility rights, the substantial EU legislative output, and the multiple attempts by the EU to promote mobility, intra-member-state mobility remains extremely low. During the 1990s only 4 per cent of the EU population was working in other member states.

Health and safety

Like policy on freedom of movement, that on health and safety was one of the early core areas of EU social policy: it was mentioned in the early treaties, became established in the 1970s and gained QMV status under the SEA. Further, in the late 1980s and early 1990s, it was used as a Trojan horse for related areas of social policy.[7] It now combines relatively non-political technical and administrative policies, such as determining acceptable levels of asbestos and lead in the workplace, with extremely contentious ones, such as protections for atypical workers and the regulation of working time.

The 1950s and 1960s: early treaty bases and slow developments

EU health and safety policy originally evolved as a response to particular conditions of the coal and steel industries. Especially in coal mining, health and safety issues were extremely important. The numerous industrial accidents and the discovery of mining and industrial diseases made prevailing conditions less and less tolerable, and governments and trade unions became increasingly concerned. In this sense, the inclusion of health and safety areas in the Treaty of Paris was a way to promote acceptance of the treaty by socialist parties, trade unions and workers (Haas, 1958). As the ECSC itself argued: 'Quite apart from the importance of caring for the worker's physical well-being . . . it is essential that efforts should be made to reduce the relatively heavy direct and indirect charges on operating budgets (of firms) resulting from industrial accidents and occupational diseases. The recruitment of workers is incidentally facilitated if the work is made less arduous and less dangerous' (Collins, 1975: 82). Arguably, even European business had an interest in promoting health and safety.

Article 3 of the Treaty of Paris empowered the ECSC to promote the improvement of working conditions 'so as to make possible their harmonisation while the improvement is being maintained'. Article 55 directed the High Authority to encourage research into safety through organizing contacts between research institutes, encouraging joint projects and distributing research results. The ECSC acted as a research centre, distributing information and encouraging member states to improve their laws and regulations. Although it had no direct right to legislate in this area, the ECSC took its research and promotional activities seriously, in 1954–7 spending the equivalent of $1.2 million supporting sixty-six different research projects (Collins, 1975: 85). The year after a serious mining disaster in Marcinelle, Belgium, in August 1956, the ECSC created the Permanent Mines Safety Commission[8] to monitor mine safety and encourage national authorities to deal with safety problems.

Following in the footsteps of the Treaty of Paris in regard to health and safety, Article 117 of the Treaty of Rome stated: 'Member States agree upon the need to promote improved working conditions and an improved standard of living for workers'. Article 118 gave the Commission the task of promoting close co-operation between the member states in the 'prevention of occupational accidents and disease . . . [and] occupational hygiene'. Despite this clear foundation in the treaties, there was little activity in health and safety policy during the late 1950s and early 1960s. It was not until 1962 that the EEC began to set up the Industrial Health and Safety Division within the EEC's Commission.[9] In the early to mid-1960s, following the primarily educational and advisory role of the ECSC, the EEC passed a number of recommendations designed to promote minimum European standards in protection for young people and women, industrial medicine, compensation for victims of industrial disease, and the defining and listing of occupational diseases. The first proposals for health and safety directives did not emerge until 1964. Of the three that were proposed, only one directive concerning the classification, labelling and packaging of certain dangerous substances was passed in 1967 (OJ 196, 16.8.1967) and its implementation was delayed until 1972.[10]

Why was the EEC so reluctant to develop health and safety policy in this period? A few reasons come quickly to mind. The EEC was following the pattern of the ECSC in being at a learning stage (Neal, 1995: 83). The best way to chart and promote health and safety issues was to study the nature of the problems, create lists of diseases, compare safety standards and to promote information exchange and policy on 'best practice'. Meanwhile, the health and safety regimes of the member states were drastically different from each other and undergoing remarkable change and expansion in the 1950s and 1960s. In this period of change, there was apparently little political will or interest to develop European-level policies. Also, since the Health and Safety Division of DGV was not even set up until 1962 there was no European-level actor to promote health and safety policy.

The 1970s and 1980s: slow development and institutional embeddedness

Like social policy in general, a rush of health and safety legislative expansion occurred in the wake of the 1974 Social Action Programme,

which called for the 'humanisation of their [workers'] living and working conditions . . . with particular reference to . . . improvement in
safety and health conditions at work'. This programme precipitated
the creation of the Advisory Committee for Safety, Hygiene and Health
Protection at Work in 1975; the next year the European Foundation
for the Improvement of Living and Working Conditions was established. These two institutions represented the new dualistic approach
to the creation of health and safety policy. The tripartite Advisory
Committee, bringing together governmental, employer and employee
representatives, would provide the co-operative and consultative institution for policy formation; meanwhile the European Foundation
would provide the research and technical knowledge behind future
proposals.[11] Following this programme, two health and safety directives were approved in 1977 and 1978, the first (77/567/EEC) relating to the provision of safety signs at places of work and the second
(78/610/EEC) protecting workers from vinyl chloride monomer. The
second was particularly important in being the EEC's first attempt to
control worker exposure to a chemical carcinogen.

The 1974 programme also led to what Alan Neal called the
'programmatization' of health and safety. The first Action Programme
for health and safety at work was approved by a Council Resolution
(78/C 165/1) in June 1978, covering the period to the end of 1982. It
proposed a range of developments under four main topics: prevention
of work-related accidents and diseases; protection against dangerous
substances; prevention of the dangerous and harmful effects of ma-
chines; and improvement of attitudes towards workplace health and
safety. The main result was the creation of one 'framework' directive
and the subsequent creation of four 'daughter' directives. The former
(Directive 80/1107/EEC), approved in November 1980, agreed to the
harmonization of measures for the protection of workers with respect
to chemical, physical and biological agents at work. It aimed to limit
worker exposure to dangerous agents in the workplace and protect
workers who were likely to be exposed to them. The procedure thus
established had four aspects: to attempt to limit the use of the dangerous substance; to limit workers' length of exposure to the substance;
to measure procedures for evaluating results; and to encourage individual and collective protection measures. In the 1980s the four 'daughter' directives aimed to cover such areas as protecting workers from
exposure to lead (82/605/EEC), asbestos (83/477/EEC), noise pollu-
tion (86/188/EEC) and from other dangerous substances or activities
(88/364/EEC).

The Second Action Programme of 1984, covering developments until
1988, included twenty-one statements of intent covering seven general

areas: protection against dangerous substances; protection against accidents and dangerous situations; promotion of health and safety training and information; statistics; research; organizational management; and promotion of health and safety co-operation between the member states, the EEC and other international bodies. It led to a number of new proposals by the Commission, but little policy output. Due to the growing institutional capabilities of the Commission, health and safety issues began to appear on the EC agenda in the 1970s and 1980s. However, they were clearly limited by the requirement of unanimous voting in the Council and the technical difficulty of deciding what constituted 'safe' or 'unsafe' levels of exposure to dangerous chemicals or activities in the workplace. The result was that when legislation was passed, it was generally weakened to such a degree that it was equal to or below the standards of the least regulated member state (James, 1993: 142).

The revival of health and safety and the Single European Act

What transformed this rather uninspiring area of EU social policy development was the creation of qualified majority voting status for health and safety issues under the 1986 Single European Act and the subsequent Social Charter and Social Action Programme. Under Article 118a of the SEA: 'Member States shall pay particular attention to encouraging the improvements, especially in the working environment, as regards the health and safety of workers, and shall set as their objective the harmonisation of conditions in this area, while maintaining the improvements made.' Furthermore, in order to achieve this objective, the SEA gave health and safety proposals qualified majority voting status in the Council. The only limitation to this transformation that was specified within the SEA was that the Commission must avoid proposing directives that would impose 'administrative, financial and legal constraints . . . which would hold back the creation and development of small and medium sized undertakings'. As with much of the EU social policy process, it was a case of moving forwards and back at the same time. QMV was established for health and safety issues.[12] However, new health and safety proposals could not be allowed to impose onerous costs on small and medium-sized enterprises. Obviously, the key battles would occur over the broad or narrow interpretation of health and safety issues and the acceptable level of 'constraints' that could be imposed.

The Commission was quick to promote a broad interpretation of health and safety and paid little attention to the costs that would be incurred by small firms. In 1987 it adopted the ambitious and wide-ranging Third Action Programme on Safety, Hygiene and Health at Work (COM (87) 520 final), also proposing sixteen new health and safety directives, a number of new recommendations and various non-legislative actions. Five of the proposed directives would amend existing ones, while others were concerned with safety in relation to organization, factory plants and machinery, construction, personal protective equipment, warning signs, medical assistance on ships, and the use of pesticides, carcinogenic and biological agents and cadmium compounds. In December 1988 the Commission announced that it would expand these recommendations to include proposals covering temporary and mobile work sites, health and safety for fishing vessels, agriculture, modes of transport, extractive industries and nuclear plants.[13] The 1988 Social Charter and 1989 Social Action Programme built upon the Commission's expansive strategy. Paragraph 19 (1) of the Social Charter argues that: 'Every worker must enjoy satisfactory health and safety conditions in his working environment. Appropriate measures must be taken in order to achieve further harmonisation of conditions in this area while maintaining the improvements made.' The 1989 SAP restated some of the existing health and safety proposals and called for the protection of workers exposed to physical hazards; it also offered proposals for pregnant women and young people at work and announced its intention to revise and update the European schedule of industrial diseases, to create a new EC agency for monitoring health and safety in the workplace, and to promote health and safety issues in the social dialogue between European business and labour.

With QMV for health and safety issues established in the Council and a substantial number of proposals being presented by the Commission, substantial legislative developments soon followed. A key example was the 1989 framework Directive (89/391/EEC) for improving health and safety at work. Its main importance was that it established a new method of creating health and safety policy and spawned a variety of 'daughter' directives. Instead of concentrating on detailed technical arguments and requirements, it focused on creating broad general principles that could be flexibly interpreted and dealt with through a 'technical adaptation procedure' (Barnard, 1996: 269). This made the legislation more acceptable to the member states and less susceptible to never-ending delays based on technical arguments. While the directive did lay down minimum standards, it also encouraged member states to improve on existing standards. Most important of all, the directive attempted to encourage the creation of broad general duties for employers and workers and the promotion of the social dialogue between employers and workers over health and safety issues. The duties of employers included: awareness and evaluation of health and safety risks; planning and taking action to deal with these risks; training and educating the workforce to these risks; informing the workforce and workforce representatives of risks; encouraging participation from the workforce in dealing with these risks; and reporting illnesses and accidents to member-state authorities. Employees were responsible for: correctly using all machinery and safety devices; immediately informing the employer or worker representatives of dangers to health and safety in the workplace; and co-operating with the employer to ensure that health and safety measures are correctly implemented and that working conditions are safe. Despite this apparent balancing act between employers and employees, 'the overarching principle is that the employer must take full responsibility and the employer must bear the financial burden of any health and safety measure' (Barnard, 1996: 300–1).

The creation of employer/employee duties, based on the fundamental responsibility of the member states 'to encourage improvements in the safety and health of workers on their territory' (preamble to the directive), was seen as a significant step forward for health and safety legislation and led to the formation of a substantial number of daughter directives. By the end of 1992, marking the end of the 1992 Project and the European Year for Safety, Hygiene and Health in the Workplace, twelve major health and safety directives had been passed in two main categories: directives relating to work equipment (e.g. video display units, personal protective equipment and safe machinery) and to the working environment (e.g. on construction sites, in the mining industries and on fishing vessels).

Similar to freedom of movement policy, following the attainment of QMV status for health and safety policy the Commission attempted to use it as a Trojan horse for other social policy areas. Using a very broad interpretation of health and safety policy, the Commission developed a number of proposals including directives for protecting young people at work, protecting pregnant women, protecting atypical workers and regulating working time. All of these proposals were met with stiff opposition from the British Conservative government, which argued that they were only tenuously linked to health and safety issues and that the Commission was unfairly shifting these issues into the health and safety arena in order to avoid the British veto. Despite British resistance, all four policy extensions were eventually passed by the Council: the 1991 Atypical Worker Directive (91/383/EEC), the 1992 Pregnancy Directive (92/85/EEC), the 1993 Working Time Directive (93/104/EEC) and the 1994 Young People at Work Directive (94/33/

EEC). However, these were delayed and revised, weakening or watering down the original proposals. Moreover, the Working Time Directive was directly challenged by the British government before the ECJ (C–84/94), which rejected the challenge in November 1996. What the Commission ultimately achieved was the expansion of the definition of health and safety to include general issues of working conditions, further legitimized by the Social Protocol of the 1991 Maastricht Treaty, which concluded that proposals regarding 'working conditions' could now be decided by qualified majority voting. Even though any immediate practical consequences were minimized by the British social policy opt-out, the Commission had, using a broad interpretation of health and safety criteria, set the stage for the expansion of EU social policy into a new area of working conditions. This legislation and its expansion is explored more thoroughly in chapter 4.

Developments in the 1990s: slow expansion and the end of the Trojan horse strategy

In the traditional areas of health and safety, legislative and non-legislative developments continued throughout the 1990s. The 1993 Green Paper on social policy argued that the costs of workplace accidents and illness (8000 work-related deaths and 10 million cases of work-related illnesses in 1990) remained stubbornly high and called for the rigorous application of existing EU health and safety legislation by the member states. The response of the member states and the major interest groups to the Green Paper was mixed. All agreed that substantial progress had been made and that a period of consolidation and concentration on the implementation of the new legislation was necessary. However, some (Spain and the ETUC in particular) claimed that new legislation was also needed. The 1994 White Paper on social policy reaffirmed this more limited and consolidating approach to health and safety policy development. It called for no new legislation, a 'consolidation of existing provisions', promotion of 'information, education and training activities' and 'risk assessment', a study of the 'problems' encountered by small and medium-sized firms, and the development of non-legislative measures (including the creation of the Safety Action for Europe – SAFE – programme for the promotion of health and safety in small and medium-sized enterprises and the European Agency for Health and Safety at Work) (Commission, 1994b: 24–5). This approach was confirmed by the 1995–7 Medium-Term Social Action Programme and the Fourth Action Programme (COM (95) 282 final) covering health and safety legislation for the years 1996–2000. The

Fourth Action Programme was divided into three main parts: the preparation and promotion of non-legislative measures (such as SAFE); the promotion of member-state implementation of EU policy, progress on EU health and safety proposals, a review of existing legislation and new proposals for certain high-risk work activities; and the improvement of Commission performance, links to third countries, and improved co-operation within the EU. This clearly implies that new legislation is of secondary importance. Updating existing legislation and passing existing proposals are the primary legislative activities. Co-ordinating existing health and safety programmes and promoting implementation have taken on new importance.

This emphasis on the effective implementation and application of existing legislation was demonstrated in the 1997 Amsterdam Treaty and in the 1998–2000 Social Action Programme. The Amsterdam Treaty did little to expand the area of health and safety policy. Health and safety issues were already granted QMV status. The treaty merely confirmed their importance by including them in the list of key social policy areas to which the member states should pay attention (Articles 136, 137 and 140, Consolidated Texts). The 1998–2000 SAP stated that: 'Over the past decade a legislative framework for minimum European health and safety standards has been put in place. . . . Attention now needs to be focused, first, on the effective implementation of this framework and, secondly, on adapting these standards to new risks and changing work practices brought on by technological developments and scientific advances' (Commission, 1998e: 9). The document went on to promote the effective implementation of existing programmes, the updating and completion of existing legislative instruments, and aid for the dissemination of information through the European Agency for Health and Safety at Work.

A key question for the 1990s is: Why did the EU adopt this more cautious approach towards health and safety policy in the post-Maastricht period? There were a number of interwoven reasons. First, the successful attainment of QMV status for other areas of social policy under the Maastricht and Amsterdam treaties and the end of the British social policy opt-out eliminated the need for health and safety policy to act as a Trojan horse for other areas of social policy. Second, it became increasingly obvious that the transposition and implementation of the new health and safety legislation at the member-state level was much more complicated and difficult than anticipated by the Commission. By the end of 1994 only one member state (France) was able to transpose all of the main health and safety directives of 1989–93. Implementation of more recent legislation was also poor. Third, as the responses to the 1993 Green Paper demonstrated, most member states were not interested in developing new health and safety policies. Therefore, despite QMV status, there was little political will to develop more.

Overall, the area of health and safety has been a particularly successful one for EU social policy. The policy was established at the founding of the EU, but not until it was given QMV status did it began to develop substantially. As Phil James summarized:

> The availability of qualified majority voting in respect of health and safety Directives has clearly been a crucial factor influencing the speed of recent developments. . . . Directly it has made the process of securing agreement over draft Directives much easier and quicker. Indirectly it has prompted both the Commission and the Council to accord the area of health and safety at work a far greater priority in their programmes of work. (James, 1993: 144)

The result of the creation of QMV status was the successful development of earlier legislative proposals made under the Social Dimension, and the expansion of health and safety issues into new areas, working conditions and public health. With the election of the new British Labour government in May 1997 and the subsequent elimination of the British social policy opt-out, conditions remain propitious for further legislative developments. However, health and safety has become a victim of its success. Following the significant development of health and safety legislation, a period of consolidation seems inevitable.

EU labour policy has always walked a fine line between the creation of a liberal and regulated common labour market. A key example of this balance can be seen in the development of the two main core areas of labour policy. Both freedom of movement and health and safety policy were recognized by the original treaties, struggled to develop between the 1960s and the early 1980s, experienced substantial expansion following their achievement of QMV status, and were used as a Trojan horse for other policy areas. In general, both of these policy areas have seen their core domains largely established and institutionalized with a resulting shift to concerns over consolidation and implementation. In many ways, these two areas have become the 'motherhood and apple pie' issues of EU labour policy. However, the 'extensions' of EU labour policy, employment rights and working conditions, worker participation and the social dialogue, have remained limited and politically divisive.

4

Labour Policy:
Extensions

In conclusion, UNICE fully understands the political pressure on
Governments to be 'seen to be doing something' about the unacceptable levels of unemployment. Yet it urges them to resist the tempta-
tion to take the easy way out, by seeking popularity for the EU through
incorporation of rights and freedoms. . . . EU social policy henceforth
must concentrate far more on improving the employability of those
out of work, than on improving still further the acquired rights of
those in work.

Z. Tyszkiewicz, UNICE conference speech, 1996

The Community and the Member States . . . shall have as their objectives the promotion of employment, improved living and working
conditions . . . proper social protection, dialogue between management and labour, the development of human resources with a view to
lasting high employment and the combating of exclusion.

Article 136, Amsterdam Treaty, 1997

Throughout the 1950s and 1960s, EU labour policy remained constrained within its core areas. Despite brief references to broader working and employment rights, worker participation and capital–labour
dialogue, little activity emerged beyond a few vague proposals and a
number of non-binding recommendations and decisions. It was not
until the 1970s, when growing economic difficulties, the rise of the
ETUC and the development of the 1974 Social Action Programme
triggered an expansion. During the 1980s and early 1990s, under the
Social Charter, Social Dimension and the Maastricht Treaty, labour
policy began to make significant headway into new arenas. Driven by
trade unions frightened by the erosion of national labour rights, Commission activists determined to promote the 'human face' of Europe,
and the socialist majority in the Parliament, the EU significantly ex-

panded its influence in the areas of employment rights and working conditions, worker participation and the social dialogue.

Although each of these areas developed its own particular trajectory, some general characteristics did emerge. First, the evolution of these policy areas seemed to occur in fits and starts, blocs of legislative proposals and activity occurring at uneven intervals linked to major social policy developments. Second, all of these areas developed from broad interpretations of core treaty articles. Third, as evidenced from the above quotation from Z. Tyszkiewicz, Secretary General of UNICE, labour policy extensions generated significant opposition from employer groups and political parties with free-market philosophies (particularly the British Conservatives). Finally, despite this late start and strong opposition, all of these areas have become embedded within the labour policy process, firm bases within the treaties (as demonstrated in the above quotation from Article 136) and a growing body of legislation and case law.

Employment rights and working conditions

In the original treaties, employment rights and working conditions were mentioned only indirectly or through broad interpretations of key social policy articles.[1] Article 3 of the Treaty of Paris demanded that the ECSC should 'promote improved working conditions and an improved standard of living for the workers in each of the industries'. Likewise, Article 117 of the Treaty of Rome spoke of the need to improve 'working conditions' and the 'standard of living' while promoting 'harmonization' and Article 118 stated that the EEC was responsible for encouraging development in 'labour law and working conditions'. However, beyond these limited references, the treaties did not provide a substantial base for the expansion of EU labour policy into the areas of employment rights and working conditions. Furthermore, with the member states experiencing high growth and full employment within economies that were primarily nationally oriented, there was little political or social interest in creating new European-level labour policy. Consequently, there were no legislative developments in the 1950s and 1960s.

Employment rights

This disinterest was diminished by the economic difficulties and growing economic internationalization of the late 1960s and early 1970s.

The early midwife of EU labour policy expansion was the 1974 Social Action Programme (SAP). Among its various proposals, the 1974 SAP demanded that the EC promote 'a reform of the organization of work giving workers wider opportunities . . . [and] protect workers' interests, in particular with regard to the retention of rights and advantages in the case of mergers, concentrations or rationalization operations' (Commission, 1974: 9). From these demands, particularly the second one, came the first proposals for the three main legislative achievements in EC employment rights in the 1970s: the 1975 Collective Redundancies Directive (75/129/EEC), the 1977 Acquired Rights Directive (77/187/EEC) and the 1980 Insolvency Directive (80/987/EEC).

The 1975 Collective Redundancies Directive grew out of three contradictory developments: a growing need for industrial restructuring in Western Europe; increasing levels of industrial unrest and resistance to restructuring; and the spreading fears of the ability of transnational firms to subvert national-level labour market rules and regulations. Consequently, the directive had to walk a delicate balance between promoting the needs of restructuring and the demands for increased labour protection. It avoided directly limiting the freedom of employers to carry out collective redundancies, and did not try to harmonize national practices. Instead, it merely laid down minimum requirements for consultation between employers and workers' representatives and 'competent public authorities' before redundancies were to be carried out.[2] The idea behind this directive was to integrate workers and the public authorities into the process of economic restructuring in order to protect the rights of workers and to promote a smoother restructuring process. It was a small first step of EU policy into employment rights. Case law developing from this directive and its subsequent modification (92/56/EEC) came to have a substantial impact on the development of employment rights in some member states (Barnard, 1996: 385).

The basic strategy of the second main directive, the 1977 Acquired Rights Directive (also known as the 'Transfer of Undertakings Directive'), was very similar to the first. During the growing economic turmoil of the 1970s, business takeovers and mergers at the national and international level became increasingly common. While perhaps necessary for the industrial restructuring of Western Europe, there were legitimate concerns that workers' rights would be compromised in the process. This directive avoided direct limitations on business transfers, but protected workers' rights during a transfer in three ways. First, it provided for the automatic transfer of the employment relationship from the old to the new employer. Second, it protected workers from dismissal by the new employer due solely to the process of the transfer. Although workers could be dismissed on general economic or performance grounds, they could not be dismissed solely due to the transfer process itself. Third, it required employers to inform and consult the workers' representatives in the firm about the forthcoming transfer. The directive established the minimum standards for these rights, size of firms and workforces affected, defined what constituted a transfer, encouraged member states to develop and adopt higher standards, and gave member states the right and responsibility to sanction firms not in compliance with the directive.

The directive met with little opposition from the Continental legal systems. For example, in the French legal system new employers had been traditionally required to take on all rights and responsibilities towards the existing workforce. However, in the British legal system, the directive created a number of difficulties. Under the British system, the employment relationship was seen as a personal contract. Therefore, when a business was transferred, all contractual relations with the workforce ended and new ones would have to be created; in theory, this meant automatic dismissal of the entire workforce. The directive directly challenged this approach. In response to these difficulties, the UK forced the modification of the directive and later delayed and did not fully implement it. In 1993 the UK was taken to the ECJ, found guilty in 1994 (Case C–382/92), and has since fully implemented it. Also in 1994, the Commission recognized that the directive needed to be updated and clarified in the light of economic developments; the replacement directive was adopted in June 1998.

The Insolvency Directive was the weakest and least influential of the three. This is not particularly surprising given that it was passed in 1980, during a period of EU policy stagnation. The directive was not aimed at easing the process of restructuring, but on the rights of workers in insolvent firms. It provided two main forms of protection for workers against insolvent employers. The employer had to pay outstanding claims (particularly wages) to the employees, and member states had to guarantee that insolvent employers' non-payment of state social security contributions would not adversely affect the employees' benefit entitlement or old-age benefits. Most member states had already adopted national provisions that mirrored these new EU requirements. Consequently, few difficulties have emerged over the legal definition or implementation of the directive (Burrows and Mair, 1996: 236).

These three directives indicate a curious and distinctive element of EU employment rights. They were the first major EU legislative developments to emerge outside the core areas of labour mobility and health and safety. Their development was caused by changing economic circumstances and the demands of the 1974 SAP. Despite the high hopes of some,[3] no further developments for employees' rights in restructuring firms have occurred. This was attributable to the basic shift in economic thinking in the 1980s towards the promotion of market-oriented strategies and the relative weakness of the left and labour unions at the EU level. In deference to strong opposition to further legislation in this area, Article 2 of the Social Protocol of the Maastricht Treaty, later integrated into the Amsterdam Treaty, stated that unanimous voting in the Council would be required on issues for the 'protection of workers where their employment contract is terminated'. Hence, one would certainly not expect to see further developments in this area. Nevertheless, two of the three directives were updated and revised in the 1990s and, despite their limited impact, they did foreshadow the later struggle over working conditions and lay the foundation for the expansion of worker consultation and participation.

Working conditions

As with employment rights, the first glimpse of EU policy on working conditions was seen in the 1974 SAP. Under the section for 'improvement of living and working conditions', the 1974 SAP called on the EC 'to establish an action programme for workers aimed at the humanization of their living and working conditions, with particular reference to . . . [among other things] the gradual elimination of physical and psychological stress which exists in the place of work'. The EC failed to produce the action programme, but did create the European Foundation for the Improvement of Living and Working Conditions in 1976. The focus of the foundation was to monitor progress of living and working conditions in the member states, undertake research and analysis of the major developments in conditions, and promote the dissemination of knowledge and research on these conditions and strategies for improving them.

There was no substantial legislation on working conditions until the early 1980s due to the requirement of UV in the Council, a sense of Euro-stagnation and the Commission's focus on the creation of employment rights. In 1981 the Commission presented a proposal for a directive which would have extended the rights of full-time employees to part-time employees (COM (82) 830 final). The proposal was strongly opposed by the British government and soon rejected by the Council. British opposition was particularly fierce due to the strong free-market ideology of the Thatcher government and the voluntaristic and unregulated nature of British industrial relations. After several attempts to find a compromise, it became obvious to the Commission that legislative activity would be futile in the area of working conditions as long as unanimous voting was required in the Council. A similar fate awaited the 1984 Commission proposal for the reduction and reorganization of working time.

As in several other areas of social policy, the legislative door to creating a policy on working conditions began to open under the SEA. As discussed above, the key changes in the SEA were Articles 100a and 118a. Article 110a created QMV in the Council for the 'approximation' of laws relating to the creation of the internal market. Article 118a created QMV for areas relating to the 'working environment, as regards the health and safety of workers' and promoted the improvement of working conditions. Given this new treaty base and a broad interpretation of the 'working environment' and 'working conditions', the Commission quickly moved to expand legislation in these areas.

This expansion occurred through the Social Charter and the 1989 SAP. In the section on Improvement of Living and Working Conditions, the Social Charter reiterated the importance of improving living and working conditions, particularly 'the duration and organization of working time and forms of employment other than open-ended contracts, such as fixed-term contracts, part-time working, temporary work and seasonal work'. The ensuing Social Action Programme raised a number of new initiatives, later strengthened by the Maastricht and Amsterdam treaties, to promote the 'improvement in particular of the working environment to protect workers' health and safety'. The legislation that resulted from these changes included the Proof of Employment Directive (91/533/EEC), the Pregnant Workers Directive (92/85/EEC), the Working Time Directive (93/104/EC), the Young Workers Directive (94/33/EC), the Posted Workers Directive (96/71/EC) and the Atypical Workers Directive (97/81/EC).

The first to pass and possibly least controversial was the Proof of Employment Directive, which required all employees to be given a written statement setting out basic employment and job information. This information included the identity of the parties, place of work, title/grade of work, type of work, date and length of employment, holiday arrangements, termination notice requirements, initial pay and working hours. The directive was aimed at providing a minimum degree of information and legal documentation for the growing sector of atypical work (part-time, seasonal, short-term). Most member states already had similar legal requirements in place. Even the UK did not oppose the directive since it required only a slight modification of its own legal system.

The second major piece of legislation to pass was the Pregnant Workers Directive in 1992. Part of the Health and Safety Framework Directive (89/391/EEC), it was the tenth offspring of that 'parent'. As such, it fell under Article 118a and thus could be voted on by QMV in the Council. It was based on that framework directive and required employers to assess the health and safety risks of the workplace to pregnant workers, taking steps to avoid such risks and informing the worker of both the risks and the steps taken. So far, it was a straight-forward health and safety directive. However, it went beyond this by providing that pregnant workers were not obliged to work at night, would be allowed time off for ante-natal examinations and be entitled to fourteen weeks' maternity leave, during which they would be pro-tected from dismissal. This was a clear example of the Commission's Trojan horse strategy. The UK opposed the directive, but did not choose to challenge the legality of placing it under health and safety criteria. Its passage in 1992 made it one of the earliest successful Trojan horse directives.

The 1993 Working Time Directive, which arose directly out of the Social Charter and SAP, attempted to use a similar strategy. It argued that flexible working time and situations were essential for economic growth and competitiveness, but held that the needs of flexibility should not have negative repercussions on the health and safety of workers. Therefore, it was essential for the EU to regulate certain elements of working time in order to avoid these negative consequences. As the preamble to the directive stated: 'research has shown that the human body is more sensitive at night to environmental disturbances and also to certain burdensome forms of work organisation, and that long pe-riods of night work can be detrimental to the health or workers and can endanger safety in the workplace' (Barnard, 1996: 308). Using this logic, the Commission argued that the directive should be placed under Article 118a on health and safety and thus subject to QMV in the Council. The directive concentrated on laying down minimum re-quirements that were likely to 'improve the working conditions of workers in the Community'. The key features of the directive included: a minimum daily rest period of eleven consecutive hours; a rest break in a working day of more than six hours; minimum rest period of twenty-four hours a week; forty-eight hours a week maximum work; and four weeks paid annual leave. It also recommended that night work should not exceed eight hours in a twenty-four-hour period, and that night workers should receive free and confidential health assess-ments, being transferred to day work if their health was being affected.

On the surface, this was an extensive expansion of EU policy influence and could impact a broad array of economic activities. In order to avoid unreasonable burdens on certain economic activities and increase the directive's chances of passage, the Commission integrated a number of derogations. These included allowing derogations if a collective agreement was reached by capital and labour and exempting three main categories[4] of workers from some elements of the directive.

Despite this flexibility, the British government not only firmly opposed the directive, but also opposed its legal base in the treaty as a health and safety issue. Again, British industrial relations had never developed a substantial body of legal regulations for working time and the regulations which it did have were eliminated by the Conservatives during the 1980s (Pelling, 1992; Sheldrake, 1991). This was exactly what Thatcher meant when she complained about seeing the 'frontiers of the state' being reimposed from Brussels. After the directive was passed in 1993, the UK immediately initiated ECJ proceedings, arguing that the directive should not have been based on Article 118a (and therefore subject to UV procedures in the Council), went beyond the setting of minimum standards, was a misuse of power by the EU, and was an overly broad interpretation of the definition of 'working environment' in Article 118a. In March 1996 the ECJ rejected all the British complaints (Case C–84/94), holding that the directive did fit under Article 118a, that the minimum standards were not set too high and that the interpretation of the working environment was not too broad. It was one of the major victories of EU social policy over British Conservative government opposition.

Similar to both the Pregnancy and Working Time Directives, the 1994 Young Workers Directive was a combination, or hybrid, of traditional health and safety issues with broader employment rights. Related to the 'parent' health and safety framework directive (89/391/EEC), but not a direct 'daughter', the Young Workers Directive was based on setting minimum standards in the working environment for young workers to protect their health and safety. It was concerned with two types of young worker: children (less than fifteen years old and required to attend school) and adolescents (fifteen- to eighteen-year-olds). The basic premise of the directive was that work by children should be prohibited, while work by adolescents should be regulated by the conditions of the directive. Similar to the Working Time Directive, these conditions included constraints on daily and weekly working hours and night work, and requirements for increased protection from health and safety hazards and limitations on night work. Employers were made responsible for assessing the health and safety of the workplace for young workers and informing the young worker of the risks and the steps taken to address them. Despite the seemingly firm position in regard to the rights of young workers, a number of derogations (again similar to those of the Working Time Directive) were integrated into the directive in order to ensure flexibility for training schemes and for a number of economic sectors (shipping, armed forces and police, hospitals, agriculture, etc.).

Regardless of the concessions and a four-year extension on the implementation period, the British opposed the directive. However, unlike the Working Time Directive, they did not challenge its legality in the ECJ, probably because their existing challenge to the Working Time Directive served as an adequate test case. Moreover, since the UK had a substantial body of national legislation regulating child labour, it was less concerned with the impact of the Young Workers Directive.

The 1996 Posted Worker Directive emerged out of a combination of legal concerns and social demands regarding the rights of posted workers within the EU. With the creation of the SEA and the drive to create a true internal market, a number of difficult issues arose over the role and rights of workers from one member state posted for a limited period of time in another member state. This was particularly true in the area of services, especially construction, and led in the late 1980s and early 1990s to a number of legal controversies. For example, in the case of *Rush Portuguesa* (Case C–113/89), a Portuguese company was subcontracted to do work on a French railway line. The company transported and used its own workforce, including non-Community nationals with work permits in Portugal. The French claimed that the company could not do the work because it had not obtained French work permits for its non-Community nationals. The ECJ ruled that according to Articles 59 and 60 (regarding freedom of services), member states could not prohibit persons and their staff from moving freely within the EU. This ruling strengthened trade union fears over unfair competition and 'social dumping' between the member states. The Commission, in the 1989 SAP, integrated this trade union concern with an argument that it would also distort competition: 'Due to the fact that these working conditions are different, there is a risk that, in addition to disadvantages for workers, this will give rise to distortions of competitions between undertakings' (Commission, 1989: 23). It chose this strategy as a way of highlighting the importance of the issue and linking it to an area of QMV within the Council.

The proposed directive applied to three main employment relationships: workers posted by a firm to the host member state; workers posted by an agency; and workers placed by a firm in another branch of the firm in another member state. In all three cases, the host member state must ensure that 'the guest service provider does not deprive the worker of the terms and conditions of employment which apply for the work of the same character in the host state' (Barnard, 1996:

330). These terms and conditions included areas such as maximum hours and rest periods, public and paid holidays, minimum rates of pay, health and safety conditions, protection of special categories of workers (pregnant, young) and equal treatment of men and women. In short, the EU was proposing to create minimum standards for posted service sector workers that would avoid undercutting social standards in the host country and coincide with the creation of minimum standards in other EU labour policy areas, while allowing a number of exceptions for particular sectors to reflect the diversity of labour relations in the EU. For example, the directive applied only to those workers with a posting of longer than one month and gave member states, in consultation with employers and labour, the right to grant exemptions in the provisions relating to pay and holidays.

Despite its QMV status and the derogations, the directive generated strong political opposition from a number of member states within the Council – in particular Britain, Portugal, Ireland and Italy. Consequently, the draft directive was shelved by the Council in 1994. However, the Commission was determined to keep up the pressure for its adoption and included it as one of its main demands for legislative action in its Medium-Term Social Action Programme 1995–7. In June 1996 the Council reached a common position on the directive, based on modifications made by the Italians, and it was finally adopted by the Parliament and Council in December 1996. The Posted Worker Directive demonstrates the difficulties of passing labour policy even when a clear QMV basis exists. Differences in national labour relations systems, struggles between low-wage/low-regulation and high-wage/high-regulation member states, and disagreements between Euro-labour and Euro-business all contribute to the difficulties in the this area.

The next legislative achievement in the area of working conditions was the 1997 Atypical Workers Directive. Concerns for the rights of 'atypical workers' (part-time, short-term, seasonal) had been a growing concern of the Commission since the 1970s. The 1974 SAP mentioned the need to 'protect workers hired through temporary employment agencies' and 'gradually to extend social protection . . . to categories of persons not covered or inadequately provided for under existing schemes'. In the early 1980s several directives regarding the rights of atypical workers were proposed by the Commission, but strongly rejected by the Council. Following the economic difficulties of the 1980s and the substantial growth of atypical employment, these demands were revived and articulated by the Social Charter and the 1989 SAP. The Social Charter encouraged the improvement of living and working conditions for those in 'fixed term contracts, part-time working, temporary work and seasonal work'. The SAP revived the two earlier proposals on atypical workers and argued that: 'Unless safeguards are introduced, there is a danger of seeing the development of terms of employment such as to cause problems of social dumping, or even distortions of competition, at Community level' (Commission, 1989: 16).

As a result, the Commission produced three related directives, all based on different parts of the treaty (Benson, 1993: 79). The first of these three proposals was based on Article 100, requiring unanimous voting in the Council, and proposed that atypical workers should have the same access and rights to vocational training and social services as permanent workers, be included in bodies of worker representatives, be informed of permanent positions, and be given the grounds for the firm's choice of atypical employment. The second proposal was based on Article 100a, requiring only QMV to combat distortion of competition. It required atypical workers to be granted the same rights as permanent workers in regard to social security schemes, dismissal, paid leave and bonuses. It also set a three-year limit on the continuation of fixed-term contracts. The third proposal was based on the health and safety provisions of Article 118a, thus requiring only QMV in the Council. This proposal was linked to the framework Health and Safety Directive 89/391/EEC and argued that atypical workers had the same rights to health and safety protection as permanent employees.

Originally, the Commission maintained that these three directives should be considered as a group, so that either all or none of the proposals had to be accepted. However, when it became clear that the first two directives would run into serious opposition within the Council, while the third would be passed with relative ease, the proposals were separated. The third proposal, being related to health and safety and largely duplicating the well-established health and safety rights of permanent employees, was passed with little opposition in December 1990 and became Directive 91/383/EEC.

On the other hand, the first two proposals ran into several difficulties. The proposal based on Article 100, requiring unanimous voting in the Council, was strongly opposed by the British government and had no hope of passing through the Council. Ironically, it was the Parliament that scuttled it, arguing that it should have been considered under Article 100a and thereby passed using QMV (Benson, 1993). Since the proposal based on Article 100a had generated a substantial amount of opposition as well and was uncertain to be passed, even with QMV, the 1994 German Presidency combined both proposals and based the new proposal on Article 100, requiring unanimous voting. This unified proposal was basically a watered-down version of the former proposal under Article 100, promoting equal treatment for atypical workers; despite these changes, it remained blocked in the Council. Thus, in 1994 the Commission announced it would use Article 3 of the Social Protocol and consult the social partners over the creation of an acceptable proposal. The consultations began in September 1995 and resulted in an agreed proposal in June 1997. The provisions of the new proposal included: the rights of full-time workers in shifting to part-time work; the provision of information on part- and full-time positions; access to part-time work; the right to training; and the promotion of further negotiation of the rights of atypical workers at the national level. This agreement was approved by the Commission in July 1997 (COM (97) 392 final), but ran into difficulties in the Parliament, which was concerned about the weaknesses of the proposal, and in the ECJ.[5] It was finally passed in December 1997.

Most recently, issues of working conditions and the promotion of workers' rights have become less important in the Commission's legislative strategies. As the Medium-Term Social Action Programme 1995–7 clearly demonstrated, there are no major new proposals in the area of working conditions. Instead, the programme concentrated on consolidating and updating existing proposals and legislation (including an eventually successful expansion of the Working Time Directive in November 1998) and launching new debates on flexibility and work organization, illegal work, telework and workers' privacy. The Amsterdam Treaty did give working conditions issues QMV status in Article 137 (consolidated treaties). However, the Commission has yet to use this as a springboard for announcing a plethora of new proposals. Instead, it seems to be taking a much more co-operative and consolidating strategy towards the development of new policies on working conditions, co-ordinated with the 1998 Employment Guidelines. Primarily, the guidelines seem to shift the creation of working rights and organization to the social partners and the member states. The social partners are encouraged to 'negotiate, at the appropriate levels, in particular at sectoral and enterprise levels, agreements to modernise the organisation of work'. Meanwhile, each member state should 'examine the possibility of incorporating in its law more adaptable types of contract' (Commission, 1998). The 1998–2000 SAP mirrored these proposals.

In general, the Commission has moved from an active to a passive position on the promotion of employment rights and working conditions. During the 1970s, 1980s and early 1990s, the Commission developed and initiated a variety of legislative proposals in these areas with mixed results. In the second half of the 1990s, particularly in the area of employment rights, the Commission appears to be unwilling to push for further EU-level legislation. Instead, it has attempted to push the issue back down to the member states or on to the shoulders of the social partners. This strategy reflects the transformation of economic ideology and global economic forces in Western Europe in the 1980s and 1990s and the Commission's recognition of the difficulty of passing legislation in these areas.

Worker participation

Worker participation in decision-making within European firms was promoted in the early integration strategies, reflecting the corporatistic orientation of the founding members of the EU.[6] Article 46 of the ECSC Treaty emphasized the importance of informing and co-operating with primary market actors. Article 48 went even further, stating that:

> the High Authority shall normally call upon producers' associations (for obtaining information or carrying out its activities) on condition either that they provide for accredited representatives of workers and consumers to sit on their governing bodies or on advisory committees attached to them, or that they make satisfactory provision in some other way in their organization for the interests of workers and consumers to be voiced.

The EEC Treaty did not have such a clear emphasis on worker participation at the level of any given firm. However, with the creation of the Economic and Social Committee (ESC), composed of representatives of workers, employers and various other economic groups, the EEC was clearly trying to promote more co-operative and participatory forms of European industrial relations.

Despite these bases in the treaties, worker participation issues failed to materialize in the 1950s and 1960s. Some attempts were made by the ECSC to promote tripartite consultation in the coal industry, but these efforts were dashed by resistance from the employers and the emerging coal crisis (Collins, 1975: 75). The earliest attempts at creating EC firm-level worker participation (also referred to as industrial democracy) were linked to the efforts to create an EC company law. In the late 1960s and early 1970s European elites became increasingly concerned about the comparative advantages of US firms in the European common market (Shanks, 1977: 48). US multinationals, based in the massive US market, had economies of scale which no European firm could match. In order to counter this, EC industries would need to combine. To encourage this merger process, the EC decided to create a European company law (*Societas Europaea*), under which new pan-European companies could form.

Worker participation became intertwined with the formation of EC company law through the demands of the West Germans. At the time, West German law required that all large firms had to have two governing bodies (an executive and a supervisory board) and that the supervisory board should be composed of between 33 and 50 per cent worker representatives. Furthermore, it specified that all large firms must have independent works councils (elected by the entire workforce within a firm). Through law, precedent and collective agreements, these councils gained the right to full information and consultation with management over issues directly affecting personnel (working conditions, rates, performance, etc.). Hence, to avoid an exodus of German firms from their national system, any new European company law had to be set equal to or above the German standard.

Subsequently, proposals for worker participation were integrated in the 1972 Fifth Directive, which obliged all firms with at least 500 workers to establish a system of two governing bodies (similar to the German). In the supervisory body, workers' representatives should compose 33 to 50 per cent of the members. The directive recognized that each member state would have to implement the directive in its own manner. However, over the long term, systems were expected to converge.

This proposal met with a huge barrage of opposition when it reached the Council. Employer groups were strongly opposed, trade unions were divided, and member states such as Italy and France, which had very different systems of industrial relations, firmly objected (Daubler, 1977). The proposal was quickly shelved and a new study created. This led to the 1975 Green Paper, which increased the flexibility of the proposal. However, even with these concessions it was unable to pass the Council, let alone be implemented by reluctant European firms.

Throughout the 1970s various less direct attempts were made to get some form of EC worker participation rights established. The 1975 European Company Statute included provisions similar to those of the Fifth Directive and proposals for EC-wide works councils and collective bargaining. It differed from the Fifth Directive in that it was voluntary (a Resolution). Firms wishing to become EC-wide and adopt an EC legal character could choose to come under the statute. However, once again, primarily due to the opposition of employer groups, the proposal was shelved. More limited proposals that required worker information, consultation or participation in respect to certain specific issues were passed by the Council including the 1975 Collective Redundancies Directive and the 1977 Acquired Rights Directive.

The next direct attempt to create firm-level worker participation was the 1980 Vredeling Directive (Blanpain et al., 1983). In this case, the issue was not supervisory boards or work councils, but information and consultation. Large firms, especially multinationals, were increasingly making decisions without informing their dispersed workforce. The proposal attempted to rectify this by requiring firms with more than 100 employees to provide workforce-relevant information (the firm's financial and economic situation, production and investment strategies and related information) on their activities at least once every six months. Further, if a subsidiary refused to give out information on these issues, the employees had the right to directly request the information from the head office.

Opposition to this proposal from European and international employer groups was fierce. Moreover, by this time the Thatcher government had come to power and Britain strongly opposed the proposal. A second attempt was made to pass the proposal in 1983. The number of firms affected was decreased (only subsidiaries with over 1000 workers would be involved), information was to be passed on annually, not bi-annually, and employees were not given an automatic right to consult the parent corporation. Nevertheless, these amendments were insufficient for the Conservative British government, which vetoed the proposal in 1983. The proposal was again revised and revived in 1986 and 1989. Both attempts were blocked and the proposal was seen as perceived to be indefinitely shelved.

It was not until the presentation of the Social Charter and the 1989 SAP that issues of worker participation returned to the EC agenda. Articles 17 and 18 of the Social Charter encouraged the creation of information and consultation between the two sides of industry, while the section on employee participation attempted to revive it through a revised European Company Statute. For greater flexibility, potential European firms were given a choice of establishing one of three types of worker participation: a German type based on worker representation through supervisory boards; a French/Italian type based on worker representation through separate worker bodies; and a Swedish type based on worker participation through collective agreements (COM (89) 268/1 final). However, to make sure that firms did not use the statute to avoid national legislation, all companies would have to observe existing national laws on workers' rights. Despite these revisions, both the British government and UNICE remained opposed. As Martin Rhodes pointed out, despite the benefits of a European Company Statute, multinational employers remained strongly opposed: 'for even if it [the worker participation proposal] amounts simply to a statutory regulation of the *status quo* – as seems likely given its flexible framework – large companies are wary of any legislation which might legitimise demands for transnational collective bargaining' (Rhodes, 1991: 260).

The Maastricht Treaty had mixed consequences for the development of European worker participation policy. On the one hand, the treaty strengthened the consultative powers of the European Parliament (generally a strong supporter of worker participation), encouraged labour–capital 'consultation' and gave the Council the 'opt-out' clause with which it could bypass the British veto. On the other, tensions raised during the prolonged ratification struggle brought EU labour policy development to a near standstill. It was not until early 1993, when the pro-social policy Danes took over the Presidency of the Council, that the events at the Hoover factory in France[7] combined with this to bring worker participation issues back on to the EU agenda. In response, the Danes revived the modified Vredeling proposals from 1989, but a threatened British veto shelved them again in June 1993.

However, with the final ratification of the Maastricht Treaty in November 1993, Padraig Flynn, EU Commissioner of Social Affairs, decided to push the proposal forward in early 1994 through the use of the Social Protocol, the first use of the protocol to overcome the British veto. Accordingly, several steps were necessary to surmount the British veto. First, the social partners must be consulted. If an agreement between the partners was reached, then the Commission must approve it. If no agreement was reached, then the Commission must rework the proposal and return it to the social partners for a second consultation. If no agreement was reached again, then the Commission had the right to put the proposal before the Council for a vote by the eleven (later fourteen) member states.

In January 1994 Flynn put the proposal before the two social partners. Due primarily to employer resistance, no agreement was reached. The Commission then revised the proposal in February, eliminating the requirement of a specific form of works councils, extending the time for implementing the councils from one to two years, and strengthening the employers' right to protect 'vital' information. This weakened proposal was returned to the social partners in mid-February for the second consultation. However, once again, no agreement was reached. On 13 April Flynn announced that the consultations were over and that a legislative solution was the only way that works councils could be implemented. At the meeting of the Social Council on 23 June 1994 the Works Council Directive was passed by 10–0 votes (Portugal abstained) and became Directive 94/45/EC following its second reading in the Council on 22 September 1994. After more than twenty years of legislative struggle, the EU finally had a substantial law for the promotion of European worker participation.

By 1998 the directive applied to seventeen countries (the fifteen EU countries plus the two EEA countries, Iceland and Norway) and required that 'community-scale' firms (with over 1000 workers with at least 150 in two or more of the involved European countries) must form a European Union Works Council or a 'procedure for informing and consulting employees' in these firms. Of the 1200 companies in Europe which the European Trade Union Institute estimated would come under the directive, eighty had already formed European works councils by the end of 1995; by early 1998 over 400 had been formed (*European Works Councils Bulletin*, 1996, 1998).

Finally, since the success of the Works Councils Directive, the focus has been on establishing and consolidating the councils, rather than on expanding EU legislation in this area. The 1995 Medium-Term Social Action Programme mentioned that the Commission was currently examining the case for expanding the system of worker involvement through the European Company Statute (and three other related statutes) and, prompted by the Parliament, would 'initiate consultations with the social partners on the advisability and possible direction of Community action in the field of information and consultation of employees in national undertakings'. Concurrent with these consultations the Commission published two Green Papers: 'Partnership for a New Organization of Work' (Commission, 1997g) and *Partnership for a New Organization of Work: Case Studies* (Commission, 1997h). These documents laid out broader arguments for a rethinking of EU work organization including the role of national-level information and consultation. However, despite the efforts of the Commission, the consultation process did not produce an agreement on this. Key opponents to an agreement were the German, British, Greek and Portuguese employers' organizations.

Most recently, worker participation policy has been consolidated, but not extended. The Amsterdam Treaty, which integrated the social protocol into the basic treaties, confirmed the QMV status of 'the informating and consultation of workers'. With the end of the British social policy 'opt-out', the Works Council Directive was extended to cover British firms. Further, attempts were made in early 1998 to revive the European Company Statute and to encourage the social partners to develop legislation on national information and consultation procedures (COM (98) 612 final). However, despite these developments, the Commission has been cautious towards promoting further legislation. The extension of worker participation legislation was not mentioned in either the 1998–2000 SAP or the 1998 Employment Guidelines.

The social dialogue

The concept of a social dialogue between peak organizations of capital and labour is a distinctly continental European one.[8] The Anglo-American industrial relations systems never developed similar institutionalized forms of labour–capital dialogue and co-operation. Thus, it is not surprising that the ECSC and the EEC developed a European-level social dialogue, mirroring national-level capital–labour consultations, or that the British were generally opposed to it.

Although mentioned in Article 48 of the Treaty of Paris, the first significant institutional embodiment of the social dialogue was the EEC's Economic and Social Committee (ESC). The ESC was composed of three main groups: employers, trade unions and others (farming, professions, crafts, etc.). It was given no direct role in EEC decision-making, but it could present its opinion and was expected to be consulted on all matters concerning social policy. By virtually all accounts, the ESC failed to become an influential EU institution (Lodge and Herman, 1980).[9]

The weakness of the ESC was compounded by the weakness of European-wide peak associations of capital and labour. Although the major capital organization (UNICE) was founded in 1958, sector-based organizations retained much more power and influence in relation to the EC. Furthermore, trade unions lacked a central European-wide organization until 1973, when the ETUC was finally established. Some attempts were made by the Commission in the 1960s to develop a social dialogue at the sector level through the creation of Joint Committees of Workers and Employers. However, these Joint Committees did not develop substantial influence or powers and atrophied during the economic difficulties of the 1970s. Hence, in the early years of the EU, the creation of a genuine and broad-ranging European social dialogue between peak associations of capital and labour was little more than an idea.

However, in the early 1970s, a number of surprising developments occurred. Linked to the push for greater social policy development in the early 1970s, the EC held a number of 'tripartite conferences' between European and national peak associations of labour and capital and member-state elites and the Commission. Six of these meetings were held between 1972 and 1978. A number of issues, including full employment, inflation, wage restraint and fiscal policy, were discussed.

A standing committee on employment was created and plans were laid for the creation of tripartite sectoral councils. However, this progress ended in 1978 when the ETUC withdrew from the proceedings, blaming the failure of the EC to take any concrete steps towards establishing positive social legislation, and in particular, the failure of the worker participation proposals. In addition, ETUC members were very divided over the usefulness of the EC. As the EC member states turned inward in the late 1970s and early 1980s and Eurosclerosis was at its height, the social dialogue vanished from sight.

The next attempt to revive the social dialogue between capital and labour occurred under the leadership of the new Commission President, Jacques Delors. This attempt was a part of Delors' 1985 'l'espace sociale' initiative (Vandamme, 1985) to create a new dynamism in EC social policy. According to Paul Teague and John Grahl, Delors' strategy:

> appeared to base EC legislation on agreements emerging from the social dialogue between management and labour rather than relying on the Commission for ideas or proposals. In other words, the trade unions and employers would become the initiators of policy in the social field. It was such thinking that lay behind Delors' statement to UNICE and the ETUC in 1985 that if they entered into a social dialogue the Commission would refrain from developing any new social policy initiatives. (Teague and Grahl, 1989: 66)

Delors chose this strategy in order to circumvent the institutional bottlenecks, particularly the British veto in the Council, obstructing social policy development.

The UNICE and ETUC responded to Delors' strategy by setting up two working groups: one relating to economic policy and employment, the other to technology and work. Unfortunately for Delors' strategy, the meetings, nicknamed the 'Val Duchesse talks', produced no substantial results. UNICE saw the talks as purely advisory. The two papers that were produced were vaguely written documents of general principles (more growth, less inflation, more employment, etc.) and had no impact on EC legislation. At the time, Delors was forced to abandon his strategy of using the social dialogue as a cornerstone for the creation of social policy and returned to a legislative strategy via the Commission and the creation of the Social Charter. Nevertheless, the social dialogue did not die. In fact, Val Duchesse accomplished two important things: it brought the main European social partners back together (they had ended regular contacts in 1978); and it established a continuing dialogue between them. Also, in the wake of the talks, Article 118b of the SEA codified the importance of the social dialogue and recognized that they had the right, if they chose to exercise it, to make European-wide collective agreements: 'The Commission shall endeavour to develop the dialogue between management and labour at a European level which could, if the two sides consider it desirable, lead to relations based on agreement'.

Immediately after the SEA, UNICE remained uncommitted to the social dialogue and refused to agree to any significant 'joint opinions'.[10] Nevertheless, as progress on the Social Charter (which recognized the social dialogue and promoted the legitimacy of collective agreements) continued, UNICE began to reconsider its intransigent position. In 1990 Belgian, Dutch and Italian employer representatives began to break ranks within UNICE, arguing that it was better to shape EC social policy through bargaining than through EC statutes. In Autumn 1991 UNICE shifted its policy and agreed with the ETUC to involve the social partners in the formation of social policy (Rhodes, 1992: 39). This recognition of the social dialogue and the ability of capital and labour to make collective agreements and influence EU social policy was integrated into the Social Protocol of the Maastricht Treaty. Article 2 of the Protocol gave member states the right to 'entrust management and labour, at their joint request, with the implementation of directives [relating to social policy]'. Article 3 stated that:

> The Commission shall have the task of promoting the consultation of management and labour at Community level and shall take any relevant measure to facilitate their dialogue by ensuring balanced support for the parties. To this end, before submitting proposals in the social policy field, the Commission shall consult management and labour on the possible direction of Community action.

Article 4 gave labour and management the right to have the social dialogue 'lead to contractual relations, including agreements' that could be approved by the Council using QMV procedures.[11] Obviously, this greatly enhanced the position and potential of the social dialogue, whose actors could now be requested to implement EU legislation, would be directly informed of and consulted regarding new social policy developments and could adopt legally binding agreements, if they so chose.

During the early 1990s the social dialogue was neglected as all efforts were focused on passing the Maastricht Treaty. It was not until June 1993 that the social partners finally met under the auspices of the Standing Committee on Employment. The focus of talks was to find a common position on preliminary proposals for Delors' new White Paper, *Growth, Competitiveness, Employment,* and on the EU Works Councils Directive. However, on both issues no common positions were developed. During 1994 no major talks occurred between the ETUC and UNICE despite the attempts by the Germans (who controlled the Council Presidency in the second half of 1994) to bring them together. Moreover, as mentioned above, the social partners were unable to come to a common position on EU works councils in 1994, despite several required ETUC–UNICE meetings over the directive. Both the ETUC and UNICE were determined to be inflexible during the discussions, since the Commission was committed to bringing forward legislation if an appropriate agreement was not reached. Given this position, the ETUC had no reason to agree to anything below the Commission's demands and UNICE did not see the point of making a separate agreement if there was nothing to bargain over.

The social dialogue seemed to revive in 1995 due to a new willingness of UNICE to co-operate and a continued desire in the Commission to promote the social dialogue process. In the 1995 Medium-Term Social Action Programme, the Commission proposed three substantial pieces of legislation to the social dialogue actors: the Parental Leave, Atypical Work and Burden of Proof of Employment Directives. In December the social partners reached an agreement on parental leave. This was passed by the Council in March 1996 and became the first successful use of the social dialogue to create EU legislation through the Social Protocol. As Padraig Flynn stated during the signing of the agreement: 'Today is an historic date. It is the first time that the social partners at European level have agreed according to the procedures of the Social Protocol. The agreement signed today paves the way for the development of European social policy' (*Agence: Europe*, 16 December 1995). In June 1997 an agreement was reached on the regulation of atypical work and adopted by the Council in December that year. In addition, under the auspices of the Confidence Pact on Employment, the Commission brought the social partners together for several high-level meetings to examine what could be done to solve Europe's employment problem. Unfortunately, neither the legislative nor Confidence Pact consultations led to any substantial outcomes. At the sectoral level, a number of agreements did develop, but only in areas with a high degree of dependence on or linkage to the public sector. These included agreements in the postal services, telecommunications, railways, aviation, shipping, road transport and agriculture (Commission, 1996b).

Since 1997, the social dialogue has continued to function, but rather quietly. The Amsterdam Treaty modifications incorporated the Social Protocol into the main treaty text and reaffirmed the QMV status of social dialogue agreements, so long as they did not involve areas that required UV procedures (Article 139, consolidated treaties). The Commission document, *Agenda 2000*, recognized the continued importance of the social dialogue. Moreover, in 1997 the Commission initiated a new Green Paper, entitled *Partnership for a New Organization of Work: Case Studies* (Commission, 1997h), which expected the social dialogue to play a substantial role in developing legislative proposals for the transformation of work organization, preparations for EMU, and strategies to counteract unemployment.

In 1996 the Commission initiated a consultation process on the future of the social dialogue (COM (96) 448), which involved the Parliament, ESC and member states and major European labour and capital organizations. The result of this process was the 1998 Commission Communication 'Adapting and Promoting the Social Dialogue at Community Level' (COM (98) 322), which proposed the strengthening of existing cross-industry advisory committees, the promotion of the sectoral dialogue through the creation of new Sectoral Dialogue Committees, and the reform of the Standing Committee on Employment. These proposals encouraged necessary changes in the social dialogue and reflect the general broadening strategy of the Commission for social policy.

Overall, the social dialogue grew substantially in the 1980s and 1990s and was occasionally seen as the forefront of the creation of a nascent form of Euro-corporatism (Falkner, 1998). The impact of economic globalization, the growing importance of the main EU-level actors (ETUC and UNICE), the institutionalization of the dialogue in the Maastricht and Amsterdam Treaty revisions, and the continued promotion of the dialogue by the Commission as another avenue for developing EU social policy all point to the growing importance of the social dialogue. At the same time, the current state of the dialogue also demonstrates its weaknesses, including the continued ineffectiveness of the European peak organizations of labour and capital, legal challenges to the exclusive nature of membership in the social dialogue, the inherent difficulties of developing Euro-corporatism at the EU level, the dependence of the social dialogue on the Commission, and the poor performance of the dialogue at producing legislative outcomes and large-scale framework agreements. Despite these weaknesses, as a strategy for surmounting legislative opposition, generating debate and support for EU labour and social policy proposals, and integrating EU actors and interest groups into the policy process, it has shown promise and achieved some successes.

The three main extensions of EU labour policy developed in very different ways. Employment rights development in the 1970s derived from fears of the growing power of multinational firms and the desire to show that the struggling EU could do something concrete about them. Policies on working conditions grew directly out of the historical concern for health and safety standards in the workplace. Given a broad interpretation of the meaning of health and safety and what constituted working conditions, these policies found a base in the treaties and, following the Single European Act, even gained QMV status in the Council. Issues of worker participation could be also found in the early treaties, but it took over twenty-five years of political and legislative struggle before a substantial policy, the Works Council Directive, emerged. Finally, the social dialogue was built into the early treaties, but due to the weakness of the social actors and divisions over the role of the dialogue, it did not gain substantial legislative influence until the 1990s. Despite these differences, these policy areas exhibited a number of similarities. All were a response to the changing economic climate of the 1970s, 1980s and 1990s; they were strongly influenced by the creation of the Social Action Programmes and the Commission's 'Trojan horse' strategy, and had to contend with weak justifications in the early treaties. Overall, recent treaty modifications have done much to open up these areas to further expansion. However, basic institutional constraints, the diversity of member-state industrial relations systems, economic globalization and other factors will continue to limit their expansion.

5

Gender Policy: From Article 119 to 'Mainstreaming'

Each Member State shall during the first stage ensure and subsequently maintain the application of the principle that men and women should receive equal pay for equal work.

Article 119, Treaty of Rome, 1958

The re-enforcement of equality provisions in the Treaty on the European Union is only the first step in achieving defacto equality between women and men. It is generally accepted that we also need a shift in attitude and a re-examination of the stereotyped gender roles which have been perpetuated up until now . . . It is time for women to cast off the shackles of inequality and prove they represent more to society than the archetypal mother and home-maker, whose prime responsibility is to bear and nurture the next generation of EU citizens.

European Women's Lobby, 1997

In the field of social policy, one area of tremendous development has been gender policy. Founded on one article (quoted above) in the Treaty of Rome by a government (France) more concerned with being economically undercut by EU competitors than with women's rights, gender policy had a less than propitious beginning and subsequently languished for over two decades. However, since the 1970s a number of factors have come together to energize its development, including: the growing political and social power of 'second wave' feminism in Western Europe; the increasingly effective organization of women's groups' lobbying efforts at the EU level; the general economic transition from the traditional family occupation structure of full-time employed husband and home-maker wife to a multitude of family structures (divorce, single parents, etc.); and occupational arrangements (movement of women into full- and part-time employment); the ability and willingness of the Commission and Parliament to promote and develop gender policy; and the opportunity which Article 119 presented to legal actors and the ECJ for the expansion of EU law in this area.[1]

As shown below, these changes and others combined to enable the EU to create a number of legislative and non-legislative instruments for combating gender inequality. However, as is made plain by the second quotation above, despite the successes of gender policy in creating *de jure* equality (particularly in aspects relating to the labour market), for many women's groups and political actors these developments only begin to deal with the topmost layer of the multi-level problem of *de facto* gender inequality. The difficulty with expanding policy activities beyond their current labour market orientation is that it would take the EU into both new and potentially controversial areas in which its capabilities are greatly restricted. As Ilona Ostner and Jane Lewis argued in 1995: 'The existing body of directives and rulings is sufficient to generate a continuing stream of important policy adaptations, but . . . the employment nexus and the constraints of member-state cultural and political diversity . . . greatly narrow the space for EU policymaking' (Ostner and Lewis, 1995: 193). This chapter focuses on how gender equalization policy attained its success and the current limits of that success.

Beginnings: Article 119

Unlike many other areas of EU social policy, gender equalization policy did not begin with the ECSC. In fact, the ECSC was remarkably silent on gender issues, probably attributable to the predominantly male character of the coal and steel workforce. Moreover, the primary occupational model was a traditional one: full-time employed male and unemployed female home-maker. ECSC social policy considered women and their needs only in the context of promoting the mobility and social needs of their husbands and families. For example, the ECSC developed a substantial housing policy to improve worker and family mobility and living standards. The first major step in EU gender policy was not taken until Article 119 of the EEC's Treaty of Rome.

Demands for 'equal pay for equal work' were becoming increasingly common by the late 1950s and early 1960s. At the international level, the United Nations (in the Universal Declaration of Human

Rights), the Council of Europe (in the European Social Charter) and
the International Labour Organization (in Convention 100) all committed their members to work towards this goal. Moreover, several
EU member states (France, West Germany and Italy) already had ver-
sions of it contained in their constitutions. At the time, it was common
for wage rates to be set along gender lines, with higher male and lower
female rates. All of these various declarations, conventions and demands were aimed at eliminating this practice.

The primary actor behind Article 119 was France. Why was France
so interested in gender equalization policy? In the immediate aftermath of the Second World War, French women gained a number of
political and economic victories. These included the right to vote in
1944, equal rights 'in all domains' under the Constitution of 1946,
and, perhaps most important, a unisex national minimum wage in
1950. Although this latter legislation was fairly limited – it was justified
as giving women more status as 'mothers' (Hoskyns, 1996: 55) and
covered only a small number of employed women – it was enough to
raise competitiveness concerns of both French employers and government. In economic sectors with large numbers of female employees
(particularly textiles), the greater legal rights for French women and
inability to maintain a lower female wage could lead to a substantial
competitive disadvantage in the forthcoming common market. Forcing other countries to adopt similar social standards was an obvious
strategy for dealing with this threat. According to the documentary
work done by Catherine Hoskyns (1996), there was relatively weak
opposition to Article 119 from the other member states except for the
Dutch, who did not have the constitutional provisions against unequal
pay and had several economic sectors that relied heavily on low-paid
female labour. Although they failed to block the article, they were
probably instrumental in limiting its scope.[2]

In retrospect, the clarity and strength of Article 119 was remarkable. Whereas other social policy articles spoke of 'promoting' or 'improving' social policies and standards, Article 119 directly obliged
member states, within a specified period, to 'maintain the application
of the principle'. Why was it so clear and direct? According to Hoskyns
(1996: 57), the article was originally intended for a treaty section on
distortions of competition, where the language would have been considered appropriate. When that section was restructured, and growing
demands were heard from trade unions and some member states for
more social policy in the treaty, a natural response was to move the
article to the social policy section. Later, as the European women's
movement developed, the clarity and strength of Article 119 would be
put to substantial use.

The 1960s and 1970s

From stagnation to development

After the ratification of the Treaty of Rome, no immediate steps were taken to implement the gender policy reflected in Article 119. While other common market policy areas were rapidly developing, social policies, in particular gender policy, were at a standstill. With this neglect and with the approaching end of the 'first phase' of the common market in December 1961 in mind, the Council (probably under French pressure) published a declaration which encouraged the development and implementation of EU social policies (Collins, 1975a: 85). The Commission then sent a draft recommendation to the Council in July 1960 which, among other things, re-emphasized the member-state obligations towards Article 119 and asked the member-state governments to notify the Commission of action taken by the governments to address the obligations by June 1961. By June 1961 not a single member state could point to any 'practical initiative' which had been taken in response to the recommendation (Collins, 1975a: 86). The Commission then created the Article 119 Group, composed of governmental and Commission representatives and aided by legal and statistical experts, to document and develop policy proposals for implementing Article 119. As the December 1961 deadline approached, under French pressure, an intergovernmental resolution was passed which set out clear objectives for the creation of equal pay, emphasized the responsibility of the member states, and created a deadline for the implementation of the policies and the elimination of pay differentials by June 1964 (Hoskyns, 1996: 62).

Following this flurry of activity, equal pay policy slowly slipped from the EC agenda. In 1964, when the second deadline was reached, the Commission noted that there had been substantial progress, but that Belgium and the Netherlands had not established the required overall provisions or suitable means of judicial remedy (Hoskyns, 1996: 63). By 1965–6, when the EC was embroiled in the 'empty chair' controversy, equal pay and gender issues vanished. There were a number of reasons for this lapse. First, during this early policy period women were completely excluded from both the political and bureaucratic EC hierarchies. Hence, other than the occasional male reformer, the actors involved had little direct interest in the issue. Second, by the early to mid-1960s, the French government, the former champion of equal pay, was becoming increasingly uninterested in the issue. The French economy was performing extremely well, and fears of cut-rate competition from industries with low-cost female labour were fading. Third, by the mid-1960s, implementation of Article 119 encountered the twin problems that beset other social policy areas: lack of information and a general decline in EU policy dynamism. Despite the creation of the Article 119 Group, many of the member states lacked a basic knowledge of the socio-economic position of women and the legal parameters of equal pay issues. Developing this knowledge and expertise would take time. Likewise, when the EU experienced its internal difficulties in the mid-1960s, equal pay policy was ignored along with all the other social policy areas.

The rise of gender policy

Several interrelated developments led to a resurgence of EU gender policy in the 1970s. These included 'second wave' feminism, legal developments and the creation of the 1974 Social Action Programme (SAP). The rise of second wave feminism[3] in the 1970s was linked to major economic, social and political changes, including the growth of female employment, a decline in large families and a consequent reduction in the years of child-rearing linked to the growth of life expectancy, and the growing rate of divorce. These changes constantly forced women into contradictory positions within their societies. While attempting to break out of traditional family roles, they were being constantly confronted with discrimination and segregation based on those previous roles. Inequality in pay, unequal rights on the job, lower opportunities, work that was 'female', all confronted women in the marketplace that they were increasingly entering. Thus, while for some women the labour market was an escape, it also reaffirmed their traditional subservient and secondary status. Politically, the 1970s were years of growing feminist activism and gradual female entry into political elite groupings. Gender attained the status of a major public policy issue during this period. Several Western European states enacted substantial gender equality legislation and women began to reach the upper levels of political parties in some countries.

EC gender policy development reflected the growing economic, political and social importance of gender issues in the 1970s. Distinctive initial features were landmark legal events, the Defrenne case[4] and the special status of gender issues in the 1974 SAP.

In 1968 Gabrielle Defrenne, an air hostess since 1951 for the Belgian airline Sabena, was forced to resign at the age of forty. Although pay discrimination between male and female air hostesses had been eliminated in 1966, it was standard practice for the airline to force the resignation of female air hostesses at forty, while male air stewards were allowed to continue to work until fifty-five. Ignoring the obvious impacts on the personal feelings of the women and difficulties of obtaining another job at that stage in life, the forced resignations for women had drastic impacts on their economic standing, preventing them from benefiting from seniority, higher wages and male pension levels. Sabena's justification for this policy was linked to the popular, but increasingly challenged, gender roles of the times. Air hostesses were supposed to be attractive and, therefore, young, if they were to properly serve the predominantly male air traveller.[5] At the request of two female Belgian lawyers, Elaine Vogel-Polsky and Marie-Therese Cuvelliez, Defrenne allowed her name and situation to be used to form a basis for a case against Sabena, citing Article 119.[6]

The litigation of the Defrenne case(s) was complex and lengthy. Two major cases and one minor one grew out of Defrenne's complaint against Sabena. The first began in March 1968 before a Brussels labour court where Defrenne claimed that she had suffered a loss of earnings in three respects: due to discriminatory pay scales before 1966; reduced severance pay caused by her early retirement; and reduced pension entitlements also caused by her early retirement. In December 1970 the tribunal decided to dismiss all of the charges. The case was then sent to the labour appeal court where it was stalled for another four years. While waiting for the first tribunal decision, Vogel-Polsky and Cuvelliez decided to launch a second case. This time it was against the Belgian state for a 1969 decision by Sabena to create special pensions for all air crew, except air hostesses, arguing that this was contrary to Article 119. The Belgium administrative court referred the matter to the ECJ in 1970. Despite being initiated later, this aspect of the Defrenne case was the first to be heard at the European level. The position of Defrenne and the Belgian air hostesses apparently elicited a sympathetic response from the ECJ judges, but the case hinged on the definition of whether state pensions were seen as 'pay' or not. A reluctant ECJ, which clearly considered Article 119 to be directly applicable and to have 'direct effect'[7] and wished to see it applied to the maximum, found that pensions could be considered pay only if they were 'directly or indirectly' paid by the employer and that the Sabena pension scheme, being a statutory social security scheme, fell outside this definition. The judges were aware that the Sabena provisions were out of date and even that the provisions had competitive implications against other member-state airlines (the French in particular) who were not allowed to discriminate against their female employees in such a blatant fashion.

Given this sense of 'unfinished business', the ECJ was in a very re-

ceptive mood when the original Defrenne case reached the European
level in 1976. Moreover, second wave feminism was emerging and the
EC, in the aftermath of the 1974 SAP, was beginning to substantially
expand its gender policy. The original case, brought before the Belgian labour courts in 1968, dealt with the loss of earnings which
Defrenne had suffered by being forced to retire at forty and through
unequal pay scales up until 1966. After four years, the court rejected
all of Defrenne's claims except her claim for 12,716 Belgian francs
(about £240) for pay lost due to unequal pay scales between 1963 and
1966. The Belgian court then passed the case up to the ECJ, raising
two key questions: 'first, is Article 119 directly enforceable in the national courts and if so, from what date?; and secondly, has Article 119
become applicable in national law by virtue of European Community
measures or does the national legislature alone have competence in
the matter?' (Burrows and Mair, 1996: 17).

Interestingly, the case was argued on the one hand by Defrenne's
lawyers, Vogel-Polsky and Cuvelliez, and on the other by representatives from two of the new member states, Britain and Ireland, the other
member states choosing not to make submissions. This new European-
level case hinged around whether Article 119 was 'clear and simple'
and directly applicable. The British and Irish governments argued that
the article was insufficiently clear and concise to satisfy the conditions
of direct effect. Moreover, the Irish emphasized that other articles given
direct effect status had been ones dealing with the 'fundamental
freedoms' of the treaty, whereas Article 119 was merely 'pursuing a
social objective which is limited to a specific class of persons' (Burrows and Mair, 1996: 18). Finally, Britain and Ireland complained
about the economic consequences of extending direct effect to Article
119 retroactively. This time, in very different circumstances, the ECJ
strongly supported the position of the Defrenne lawyers and ruled that
Article 119 pursued a dual objective of eliminating distortions to competition and 'forms part of the social objectives of the Community'
(Barnard, 1996: 173). As such, Article 119 was directly applicable not
only to public authorities, but to collective labour agreements as well.
On retroactivity, the opinion of Advocate General Trabucchi confirmed
that the article took effect from 1962 for the original member states
and 1973 for the new member states. Nevertheless, in response to the
economic concerns of the UK and Ireland and for reasons of legal
clarity, individuals were granted the direct effect of the article only
from the date of the judgement in 1976.

After the resolution of the second case, a final Defrenne case was
launched in which (Case C-149/77) the ECJ declared that 'respect for
fundamental personal human rights is one of the general principles of

Community law. . . . there can be no doubt that the elimination of discrimination based on sex forms part of those fundamental rights' (cited in Barnard, 1996: 171). With this position, the ECJ reaffirmed the direct applicability of Article 119, elevated its status and that of gender equalization policy in general, and later used this status to make a number of progressive legal decisions and open the gates to further legal developments and challenges by women in the 1980s and 1990s. Before returning to these legal developments later in this chapter, it is necessary to explore the role of gender policy in the 1974 SAP and the three main directives that emerged from that programme.

As seen earlier, the 1974 SAP was a watershed development in early EU social policy. Under the section entitled 'Attainment of full and better employment in the Community', the SAP encouraged the EU and member states to 'undertake action for the purpose of achieving equality between men and women as regards access to employment and vocational training and advancement and as regards working conditions, including pay . . . [and] to ensure that the family responsibilities of all concerned may be reconciled with their job aspirations' (Commission, 1974: 8). This statement was a reflection of the limits and potential of EU gender policy at the time. While the boundaries of gender policy depended upon access to and activities within the labour market, a clear area of EC concern and expertise, concerns for reconciling job aspirations and family obligations clearly implied a realization that factors beyond labour market dynamics would be influential in gender policy.

In response to the SAP and to show that the EC was responsive to the UN's 1975 International Women's Year, the Commission developed three main legislative proposals: the 1975 Equal Pay Directive (75/117/EEC); the 1976 Equal Treatment in Working Conditions Directive (76/207/EEC); and the 1979 Equal Treatment in Social Security Directive (79/7/EEC). The Equal Pay Directive was the easiest and most obvious extension of EC gender policy. The Defrenne cases were working their way through the EC legal system, member states were enhancing their own equal pay legislation (both the UK and France established equal pay acts in 1970 and 1972), and the women's movement and issues were becoming increasingly important. Stimulated by the desire to clarify the scope and implications of Article 119, the directive met with little resistance. The devil, as usual, was in the detail. The original Commission proposal was surprisingly weak and did not include the essential extension of equal pay for 'work of equal value' demanded by the Article 119 Group and the trade union representatives in the ESC. Despite some complaints from Denmark, Germany and the UK, the directive passed smoothly through the Social Affairs

Council in December 1974 and was adopted in early 1975 (Hoskyns, 1996: 86–9).

Overall, the directive functioned primarily as an extension and clarification of Article 119. Article 1 of the directive did expand the definition of equal pay to include 'the same work or for work to which equal value is attributed', required 'the elimination of all discrimination on grounds of sex with regard to all aspects and conditions of remuneration', and provided that any job classification scheme 'must be based on the same criteria for both men and women and so drawn up as to exclude any discrimination on grounds of sex'. The remaining provisions were concerned with the implementation of the directive and the responsibilities of the member states. Although it had taken nearly twenty years for the first substantial piece of gender policy to develop, it represented the first in a series of rapidly maturing developments.

The 1976 Equal Treatment in Working Conditions Directive was the logical progression of gender policy. From its foundation in equal pay provisions, gender policy was easily extended to the other area of acceptable social policy, working conditions. The original proposals for an Equal Treatment Directive were quite radical and consequently divisive. The original Commission proposal went through nine revisions. The final Commission proposal required equal treatment in employment access, vocational training, promotion and working conditions (including pay and social security). Equal treatment was defined as: 'the elimination of all discrimination based on sex or on marital or family status, including the adoption of appropriate measures to provide women with equal opportunity in employment, vocational training, promotion and working conditions' (Article 1/2).[8]

The mention of 'appropriate measures' was particularly important in this proposal since it implied the possibility of 'positive action' by the EC and the member states to correct existing inequalities. Another key element of this early proposal was its emphasis on the creation of legal norms that would facilitate the entry of women into the labour market. This approach fitted both the free-market logic of the common market and the demands for greater market access and equality by a number of women's movements. Both the Parliament and the ESC supported the proposal. The ESC went even further by encouraging the proposal to cover self-employed women, develop 'family policies' on issues such as childcare and paternity leave and address discriminatory implications of national taxation systems, and argued for a reversal of the burden of proof requirements in relation to sex discrimination cases (Hoskyns, 1996: 104). Many of these demands would later be taken up by the EC and developed into policy proposals and instruments. However, at the time, the Council, dominated by conservative governments and struggling with the economic difficulties of the mid-1970s, was very reluctant to radically expand the equal treatment provisions. After a number of debates and amendments, the directive emerged from the December 1975 Council meeting in a substantially weakened form. Article 1 of the directive reaffirmed and built upon the basic orientation of the Equal Pay directive. Member states would need to implement the equal treatment principle regarding access to employment, promotion and vocational training and potentially also to social security provision. Article 2 defined equal treatment as follows: 'the principle of equal treatment shall mean that there shall be no discrimination whatsoever on grounds of sex either directly or indirectly by reference in particular to marital or family status'.[9]

The final form of the directive further reduced the scope of the Commission proposal and ESC demands. Requirements for equal treatment in social security were removed, the concept of 'appropriate measures' was eliminated, the right of member states to define economic sectors was excluded from the directive, and maternity policies were reinstated. Nevertheless, the directive was a substantial achievement, broadening EC gender policy, creating a European level of female legal rights and establishing the parameters for future EC gender debate. Later, most of these early Commission and ESC demands for including social security issues, developing an EU family policy, promoting positive action to promote equality, reversing the burden of proof in discrimination, and even issues of paternal leave would return to the EC/EU agenda.

The 1979 Equal Treatment in Social Security Directive was both the least innovative and most controversial of the three. As the socio-economic changes of the 1960s and 1970s began to alter the position and role of women and the traditional family, the traditional social security systems (which were often biased towards supporting the traditional family) were increasingly perceived as blatantly discriminatory to women and their ability to access the labour market (McCrudden, 1987). The Equal Treatment in Working Conditions Directive raised these issues, but left their resolution to separate and more detailed EC legislation. Upon passage of that directive, the Commission began its preparations for the Social Security Directive. Its choices were, first, to propose a radical extension of equal treatment by demanding that social security benefits be 'individualized', ignoring the marital and/or family status of the individual. While taking a substantial step towards addressing the discriminatory orientation of a variety of national security schemes, this approach would have been extremely controversial in its intrusion into delicate family policies of the member states, and also potentially very expensive. Alternatively, it could pursue the more conservative approach of challenging the discriminatory nature of the existing system, while providing enough qualifications and derogations to leave the basic social security systems unaffected. Not surprisingly, the Commission chose the latter course.

Realistically, the Commission could have done little else. By the time the proposal reached the Council in November 1978, the EC was beginning to move into its 'Eurosclerosis' phase and the political opposition to European intrusions into family policy, together with the implied costs, would have killed the policy immediately. Even the Commission's moderate proposals were substantially weakened by the Council. In its final form, the directive committed the member states to the 'progressive' implementation of equal treatment in social security and the elimination of both direct and indirect discrimination in this area. However, the directive did not apply to the entire field of social security (limiting itself to employment-related social security and social assistance benefits), covering only the 'working population' of the EC, applying only to benefits listed in the directive, and excluding certain aspects of employment-related social security benefits. Finally, due to the complexity of the issues raised and their obvious reluctance to deal with such issues, the member states were given an unusually long period (six years) to implement the directive.

As the 1970s came to an end, despite the failure of larger and more radical proposals, women's activists could take credit for a substantial amount of EC legislation and activity. As various commentators noted (Docksey, 1987; Vogel-Polsky, 1985), a developed legal and legislative framework on gender equality had been created. Moreover, individual women and women's groups were increasingly entering the EC bureaucracy and legislative processes. During the 1970s, DGV established its Women's Bureau (later renamed the Equal Opportunities Unit) and DGX founded the Women's Information Service. The Parliament and ESC established and enhanced their committees for dealing with women's issues. Furthermore, the ECJ took an active role in expanding the definition and scope of gender equalization policy. As Beverly Springer summarized: 'The scope and ambition of the EC policy working women developed in the 1970s is quite remarkable. The policy contains both legal measures to ban discrimination and non-legal measures to facilitate the social and psychological changes necessary for true equality' (Springer, 1992: 68–9). The EU had taken substantial steps towards promoting *de jure* equality. The difficult part would be putting these legal guarantees into practice and extending them to non-market-oriented arenas.

The 1980s and 1990s

Consolidation and expansion in a difficult climate

As discussed in chapter 2, the 1980s were not particularly propitious for EU social policy development. For EU gender policy this was both true and false. In the major policy documents, gender policy was not mentioned until the Social Charter and Social Dimension in the late 1980s. It was not included in the Single European Act and related White Paper and only two new gender directives were created during the decade. However, despite a certain inertia, the activities of the European women's groups, the Commission and the ECJ were creating a foundation for impressive developments in the 1990s.

The most visible indicator of this groundwork was the development of the Commission's Action Programmes on Equal Opportunities. In 1981 the Equal Opportunities Unit of DGV (aided by the newly created Advisory Committee on Equal Opportunities for Men and Women) created the First Action Programme, covering the years 1982–5 (Commission, 1981). This Programme promised to maintain the EC's 'longstanding commitment to the improvement of the situation of women' and developed legislative strategies for enhancing the individual rights of women and non-legislative strategies for promoting equal opportunities. On the former, it proposed new laws on equal treatment for women in occupational social security schemes (extending the 1979 directive), on equal treatment for self-employed women and women in agriculture (expanding the 1976 directive), on parental leave and enhancing the opportunities of working parents and on the rights of pregnant women. On the latter, it called for the creation of a number of 'equality networks' to help promote equal opportunities, to develop the application of the equality directives, to examine the position of women in the labour market and to explore local employment initiatives for women.[10] Furthermore, the Action Programme urged the EC to extend its vocational education policies to encourage female employment, particularly in new technological sectors.

The fate of the legislative proposals during this First Action Programme (1982–5) was predictable. The EC was in the depth of its 'Eurosclerosis' phase and with the pro-market, anti-social policy Thatcher government in Britain capable of blocking any social policy proposal, nothing significant was passed during those years. Nevertheless, in 1984 two pieces of EU 'soft law' legislation were passed: Recommendations on the Promotion of Positive Action for Women (84/331/EEC) and on Combating Unemployment among Women (84/

161/EEC). Although these had little immediate impact, combined with other developments they created an 'atmosphere' or 'dense network' of influence that eventually promoted these policy areas.[11] Similarly, while ECJ did not make any major equal treatment decisions during this period, a number of major cases were initiated. As Ostner and Lewis (1995: 167) pointed out, while there were relatively few equal treatment cases in the 1970s, over forty cases had reached the ECJ during the following decade. Clearly, the willingness of EC women to press for equal treatment cases and the institutional structures to support such cases were both developing in the early 1980s.

In 1986 two major gender policies developed directly out of the First Action Programme: the Directives on Equal Treatment in Occupational Social Security Schemes (86/378/EEC) and on Equal Treatment of the Self-Employed (86/613/EEC). While neither of these was particularly forceful or progressive, both emerged out of perceived limitations of the earlier equal treatment legislation. The 1986 Social Security Directive was originally proposed in that of 1979 and was a direct attempt to expand its coverage into occupational social security provision. The 1986 Social Security Directive merely codified the growing legal changes at the member-state and EC level. The ECJ actively expanded the boundaries of 'pay' – and hence the areas covered by Article 119 – in such cases as: *Worringham and Humphreys v. Lloyds Bank* (Case 69/80), where men and women were required to join the company pension scheme at different ages; *Liefting and others v. Universiteit van Amsterdam* (Case 23/83), where married civil servants' pensions were calculated together rather than as individuals; *Newstead v. Department of Transport* (Case 129/85), where a single civil servant was required to contribute to a general widow's pension scheme; and *Bilka v. Von Hartz* (Case 174/84), which gave different benefits to full-time workers (mostly male) and part-time workers (mostly female). The 1986 Social Security Directive confirmed this expansion, and attempted to clarify the boundaries of Article 119 and EC competencies. The diversity and complexity of social security provisions at the member-state level made this a particularly complicated matter, and an area of continued dispute and discussion. Similarly, the 1986 Equal Treatment for the Self-Employed Directive was intended to expand equal treatment rights to the self-employed and those working in agriculture. Driven by women in the agricultural sector, its original provisions were quite radical (COM (84) 57 final), calling for equal treatment not only for the self-employed, but for 'helper spouses' (those whose work, directly or indirectly, benefits the work of the spouse). However, in the conservative context of the mid-1980s and unanimous voting in the Council, these provisions were quickly watered down and key sections, especially on helper spouses, were reduced to 'undertakings to examine'. In the political and economic context, it was impressive that the legislation was passed at all.

As the 1986–90 Second Action Programme (OJ C 203, 12.8.1986) emerged during the end of the Eurosclerosis period, it proposed no substantial new or expensive legislative policies, but rather re-empha-sized the legislative demands of the First Action Programme. As Springer noted: 'the emphasis on cheap psychological campaigns rather than on programs which would require large budgets probably resulted from the EC being on the verge of bankruptcy at the time' (Springer, 1992: 71). Mirroring a concern with costs and the impacts of policy on the business environment, the Commission even inserted the claim that equal opportunity 'may be achieved without imposing any unreason-able burden on industry or on small- and medium-size enterprises in particular' (quoted in Springer, 1992: 71). Despite these obvious con-straints, in other ways the programme was a bold document. It stressed that gender discrimination was a much deeper and more damaging problem than had been assumed and argued that the EC would have to go beyond simple legal changes, if it was going to tackle *de facto* as well as *de jure* inequality. Instead, the EC would have to begin chang-ing attitudes and norms, particularly in regard to the sharing of family responsibilities. In order to begin to address these challenges, the programme set up a number of new 'equality networks', including positive action on enterprises, equal opportunities in broadcasting, childcare, equal opportunities in education, and the women's training project. Other issues mentioned included sexual harassment of women at work, violence against women and the special needs of migrant women. The key legislative importance of this document was that many of its proposals were subsequently taken up and integrated into more general social policy initiatives such as the Social Dimension, the Social Charter and the 1989 SAP.

When Delors and others (Venturi, 1988) began to promote the idea of the Social Dimension in the mid- to late 1980s, gender was a main area of concern. The Social Charter reflected this by stating that:

> Equal treatment for men and women must be assured. Equal opportuni-ties for men and women must be developed. To this end, action should be intensified to ensure the implementation of the principle of equality be-tween men and women. . . . Measures should also be developed enabling men and women to reconcile their occupation and family obligations.

In the 1989 SAP the Commission confirmed its support for the Second Equal Opportunities Action Programme and for the development of

the Third Action Programme. It expressed its support for three proposed directives (parental leave, burden of proof and retirement age)
which had been blocked by the Council throughout much of the 1980s,
and stated that it would work towards the development of a directive
on the protection of pregnant women at work, a recommendation concerning childcare, and a recommendation concerning a code of good
conduct on the protection of pregnancy and maternity.[12] Although
Delors' social dimension was primarily related to labour policy issues,
the advanced position of EU women's issues made them easy to integrate into the larger proposals. By the end of the 1980s gender policy
was not only a core element of EC social policy, but had a firm base in
the treaties and EC legislation, a substantial network of experts and
women's groups to develop and support legislation, and a growing
number of EC soft law and judicial decisions to back it up. These
factors combined to make gender equalization policy one of the most
successful areas of EU social policy in the 1980s.

Legislative and legal developments

Following the success of the previous decade, there was a substantial
increase in and development of EU gender policy in the 1990s. Causal
factors included the improving EU social policy context, the evolution
of the Equal Opportunities Action Programmes, the continued legal
developments in gender policy and advancements for women's organizations and influence, and the creation of the concept of 'mainstreaming'
gender equalization policy.

   With the revival of the EU and social policy in the late 1980s and
early 1990s, gender policy was well positioned for further gains. All of
the major EU social policy developments outlined in the Maastricht
Treaty, in both the Green Paper and the White Paper for the Medium-
Term Social Action Programme (1995–7), the Amsterdam Treaty and
the 1998–2000 Social Action Programme included gender policy components.

   First and foremost, the changes in the Maastricht Treaty and the
creation of the Social Protocol represented major enhancements for
gender policy. The creation of the Social Protocol as a strategy to get
around the militant opposition of the British government opened up
significant opportunities for gender policy development. More precisely, Article 2 of the Social Protocol created QMV, subject to the
British opt-out, in the Council for policies relating to the creation of
'equality between men and women with regard to labour market opportunities and treatment at work'. Article 6 of the protocol restated

Article 119 (on equal pay for equal work) of the Treaty of Rome and added that: 'This Article shall not prevent any Member State from maintaining or adopting measures providing for specific advantages in order to make it easier for women to pursue a vocational activity or to prevent or compensate for disadvantages in their professional career'. This statement validated programmes for 'positive action' for women and seemed to legitimize 'positive discrimination' as well.[13] Other areas of QMV created by the social protocol such as 'working conditions', 'information and consultation of workers' and 'integration of persons excluded from the labour market' also became potential avenues for gender policy development. Finally, the promotion of the social dialogue between the social partners as a strategy for surmounting social policy blockages in the Council created a new opportunity for gender policy. Overall, the Maastricht Treaty did much to enhance the fundamental treaty foundations of gender equalization policy.

Reflecting this enhanced role of gender policy, the 1993 Commission Green Paper on Social Policy, after emphasizing the 'longstanding track record [of the EU] in promoting equal opportunities', argued that three main issues needed to be addressed: '(i) the reconciliation of employment and family responsibilities; (ii) the desegregation of the labour market – vertical and horizontal; (iii) an increase in women's participation in decision-making' (Commission, 1993: 57). As potential solutions, the Commission listed a broad range of proposals, including encouraging flexibility in careers and family responsibilities, promoting childcare facilities, vocational training for women, and elimination of direct and indirect discrimination. These developments clearly took the Commission beyond the traditional labour market equalization strategy of earlier gender policy and towards open and direct advocacy of gender policy in areas of family policy and national-level political structures.

The responses by the member states and European NGOs to gender issues outlined in the Green Paper were much more positive than to other areas of social policy. Most responses to the Green Paper recognized the importance of integrating women into the labour market, promoting equal opportunities, encouraging greater participation of women in economic and political decision-making, and changing societal and cultural attitudes to the question of gender equality. The majority of respondents urged action on the following equality issues:

(i) appropriate implementation and monitoring of existing directives and recommendations; (ii) adoption of draft directives on parental leave and leave for family reasons; social security and other rights of atypical

workers, burden of proof; (iii) modification of national and social systems so as to encourage unemployed women to undertake training and
seek employment; (iv) European legislation to combat sexual harassment at the workplace. (Commission, 1995: 14)

However, there were obvious differences of opinion over the need for
and range of new legislation. As the UK government response suc-
cinctly stated: 'The legislative framework to ensure the principle of
equality between men and women in the Community is now in place
with a number of binding Community instruments. Further Community legislation in this area is neither necessary nor desirable' (Commission, 1995: 151). Although additional strong opposition to further
gender legislation came from UNICE, there was broad support for
further action.

A key indication of this willingness can be found in the 1994 Commission White Paper entitled *Growth, Competitiveness, Employment*.
In that document, the Commission urged member states to develop
strategies for:

(i) eliminating any potentially discriminatory fiscal and social protection policies which can discourage women's equal participation in the
formal labour market; (ii) improving **existing career opportunities** for
women, thereby generating demand for support and technical assistance services such as child-care and vocational training; (iii) ensuring
that taxation and social security systems reflect the **fact that women
and men may well act as individuals in seeking employment and reconciling family and working life**. (Commission, 1994: 150; emphases in
original)

This passage was particularly important both for the breadth of its
commitment to gender issues and for the linking of these issues to
broader economic and employment policies. The Commission was not
only encouraging further policies to enhance female labour market
participation, but supporting childcare and vocational training, as well
as the individualization of social security and taxation systems. These
proposals were substantially beyond the Commission position of just
ten years earlier. Equally important, the Commission was integrating
these imperatives into one of the most central documents for determining the future of the EU. Because this document otherwise
downplayed the role of EU social policy, choosing to stress the importance of competitiveness and labour market flexibility over social rights
and legislation, the inclusion of gender policies and concerns demonstrated their vitality and influence in the early 1990s.

The 1995–7 Medium-Term Social Action Programme reiterated the recommendations of the Green and White Papers and the positions of the *Growth, Competitiveness, Employment* document and outlined a number of new initiatives. These included the creation of a Fourth Equal Opportunities Action Programme, a framework proposal to be discussed by the social partners for the 'reconciliation of family and professional life', more proposals for extending equal treatment in occupational and general social security schemes, the adoption of a code of practice on equal pay for work of equal value, a draft recommendation for measures and actions to promote the participation of women in political decision-making, a report on the 'dignity of men and women at work', and a debate on the individualization of rights in the member states' social protection systems. This list of proposals is notable not only for its extensiveness, but for its exploitation of a new legislative strategy. Two legislative issues, the proposed Parental Leave Directive and Burden of Proof Directive, were transferred to the consultation process between the social partners outlined in the Maastricht Treaty's Social Protocol. The Commission's choice of gender issues to be among the first to be put into the social partner consultation process reflected both the importance of the gender issues and the likelihood of potential agreement.

'Mainstreaming' gender policy

Before discussing the most recent EU gender policy developments, it is necessary to take a brief step back to the Third and Fourth Equal Opportunities Action Programme. These were particularly important for establishing the 'mainstreaming' of EU gender policy. From the perspective of the substantial gender policy developments in the early 1990s, the Third Equal Opportunities Action Programme (1991–5) (COM (90) 449) was a somewhat cautious document. Although a number of specific legislative proposals and initiatives were included, most had been developed earlier and were either working their way through or had become blocked in the legislative process. The lack of proposals was not surprising given the difficulties in passing gender legislation in the pre-Maastricht/British opt-out period. At a broader level, however, the document illustrated a new bifurcated strategy towards gender policy. The main aims of the programme were, as Susan Cox argued: 'to entrench equality policy as an integral part of the Community's economic and structural policies, and to promote women's full participation in economic and social life' (Cox, 1993: 56). These aims would be achieved, not through new legislation, but through mainstreaming and a broader information and integration campaign.

Mainstreaming was a concept for developing and improving gender policy without creating new policies. The idea, as stated in the programme, was that 'equal opportunities policy must not be treated as a separate policy but as an integral part of other policies, underpinning their effectiveness' (cited in Rees, 1998: 63). What this meant was that gender issues transcended the specific areas of gender policy. Thus, if the goal of gender equalization was going to be promoted, then other policy areas and actors would have to integrate gender concerns into their policy activities and developments. In essence, gender policy would have to be mainstreamed into the policy development of virtually every other EU area. The obvious advantages of this strategy were that it avoided direct legislative confrontations with the British and the Council, promoted a broader interpretation of EU gender policy and brought it into the agenda-setting level of major EU policies, and gave a financially constrained EU a way of promoting gender equalization policies without expensive new programmes. Linked to the strategy of mainstreaming was the promotion of the role of women in political and economic life, reflecting the 'broadening' approach of the Third Action Programme. Consequently, a number of proposals were made to encourage the member states to promote the integration of women into the labour market and to improve the status and influence of women in society (particularly in decision-making processes).

In the wake of the Third Action Programme, a number of important legislative and legal developments occurred. Only one directive was passed between 1991 and 1995, the 1992 Pregnant Workers Directive (92/85/EEC), which intended to improve standards of protection in the workplace for pregnant women and new mothers. It also established minimum standards for maternity leave, the right of pregnant workers to take leave from work without loss of pay for ante-natal examinations, the right not to be dismissed for reasons relating to their pregnancy, and other basic employment rights. Because this directive came under a broad definition of health and safety, it could be passed using QMV in the Council, a successful combination of gender with health and safety issues in order to get both through the British veto in the Council.

A number of 'soft law' developments occurred as well. In 1990 the Council passed a resolution designed to protect the dignity of men and women at work (Resolution 90/C 157/02) and in 1992 the Commission passed a recommendation on Code of Practice (92/131/EEC) 'to promote greater awareness of the problem of sexual harassment' and 'provide practical guidance to employers, trade unions and employees with a view to clamping down on sexual harassment' (Commission, 1996b: 253). Also in 1992 the Council passed its first Recommendation on Childcare (92/241/EEC), which was designed 'to reconcile family obligations arising from the care and upbringing of children and parents' employment, education and training' (Commission, 1996b: 250). This encouraged the member states to develop childcare provisioning, ensure appropriate, safe and accessible childcare, integrate childcare into working life and promote 'a more equal sharing of parental responsibilities between men and women' (Commission, 1996b: 251). Finally, in 1995 the Commission issued a proposed Recommendation on Balanced Participation of Women and Men in Decision-Making (COM (95) 593), accepted by the Council in 1996 (96/694/EC), which mirrored the Action Programmes' demands for a better balance between men and women in political and economic life, for raising awareness of the issue and for encouraging NGOs to promote this balance.

As mentioned above, the number of gender cases had grown substantially in the 1980s and 1990s. Two of the most noteworthy were the Dekker case and the Webb case. The 1988 Dekker case (Case C-177/88) had a substantial impact on the rights of pregnant women. Mrs Dekker applied for a training job in a Dutch youth centre. She was three months pregnant and, despite being chosen as the best candidate for the job, was refused it on the grounds that the youth centre's insurer would not reimburse the centre for her maternity allowance. The ECJ ruled that this was impermissible direct discrimination due to the condition of pregnancy. In the Webb case (Case C-32/93), Ms Webb was dismissed from a temporary job, but one which was expected to become permanent, when she became pregnant. Her employer cited her inability to do the job and linked her dismissal to her being 'unavailable' (or sick) during a critical period. The ECJ rejected the linkage of pregnancy to illness and reaffirmed the rights of Ms Webb to continued employment in the firm. Clearly, the ECJ had helped to enhance gender equalization in social security and pregnancy rights. However, it is important to recognize that not all of the cases went in a feminist direction. As Catherine Hoskyns argued:

> improving the situation of women has never been a prime objective of the Court, and that its rulings only have that effect if the interests of women coincide with other objectives being pursued. Nevertheless, some of the rulings have been beneficial, and have certainly gone well beyond what governments might have expected; others, viewed from a feminist perspective, have been restrictive. (Hoskyns, 1996: 159)

Finally, it is important to mention that the Third Action Programme continued in the tradition of creating and enhancing women's 'networks'. These included the 1990 Women in Decision-Making Network, the 1990 New Opportunities for Women programme (NOW), and the 1995 Families and Work Network. Also in 1990 the Commission directly supported the development of a European women's interest group, the European Women's Lobby (EWL), which by early 1999 had co-ordinated the activities of over 2700 member organizations, performed a variety of research tasks on the position of and policies towards women, and actively lobbied for more, improved, EU gender legislation. Furthermore, over 85 per cent of the EWL's funding comes from the Commission, an obvious extension of earlier support for women's networks that benefits DGV and the Commission itself in a variety of ways. DGV can use the EWL as a research base, a political barometer, a policy innovator and as a pressure group for more gender and general social policies.

The Fourth Equal Opportunities Action Programme (1996–2000) (COM (95) 381 final) was both a continuation of the general mainstreaming approach and a recognition of the new limitations on policy development. Despite the institutional advances of the Maastricht Treaty, it became obvious in the early 1990s that radical and expensive new legislative proposals would be frowned upon not only by the Council, but by the Commission as well. The Fourth Action Programme recognized these new limitations and redirected gender policy towards a thorough mainstreaming approach. As summarized by the Commission: 'The aim of the programme is to promote the integration of equal opportunities for women and men into the preparation, implementation and monitoring of all policies and activities of the Union and Member States, while respecting their specific responsibilities' (Commission, 1996b: 248). The programme then went on to specify how gender mainstreaming would be carried out in the following six ways: by integrating equal opportunities into all policies and actions; by mobilizing groups who support equal opportunities; by promoting equal opportunities in 'a changing economy'; by reconciling family and working life for men and women; by promoting balanced participation of women and men in economic and political decision-making; and by enabling people to exercise their right to equal opportunity. Most of these strategies and proposals were well established, being present in the Third Action Programme, and did not require expensive new legislation or budgetary requirements. To implement these proposals, the Fourth Action Programme stressed the importance of developing 'good practice', monitoring of relevant policies and further studies, and the rapid dissemination of new information and policy strategies.

Some feminists and gender policy supporters were appalled at the lack of legislation and budgetary demands in the Fourth Action Programme. As J Field argued, 'if the first three Action Programmes were relatively modest, the fourth Programme, for 1996 onwards, promises positive humility' (cited in Rees, 1998: 65). On the other hand, during my interviews with EU social policy actors in early 1998, it became obvious to me that the mainstreaming approach for gender policy had been quite successful at integrating gender issues and demands into a number of divergent policy areas. A progress report from the Commission on the mainstreaming of gender issues into EU policy (Commission, 1996g, 1998d), citing the successful mainstreaming of gender issues into the 1998 Employment Guidelines, the development of the Euro, the *Agenda 2000* policy proposals and the EU's human rights policy, confirmed my interpretation. Finally, according to a recent interview with Padraig Flynn, the Structural Funds after 1999 will adopt a much more gender-oriented approach to policy and programme developments. As he stated: 'the (mainstreaming) approach takes a wide-ranging view on the causes of gender inequality – and consequently far more thorough approach to its cures. In the future, Structural Fund programmes will have to do much more than finance specific initiatives for women' (*Women of Europe Newsletter*, no. 78, March–April 1998: 1). In the context of stringent legislative and financial constraints at the EU level in the 1990s, gender policy mainstreaming has been a successful strategy for putting gender issues and strategies at the heart of EU developments, and could be credited with making EU gender policy the most successful area of EU social policy.[14]

Before concluding this chapter, I should briefly mention a few of the most recent EU gender policy developments. In terms of legislation, three 'new' policies have been adopted in the period of the Fourth Action Programme: the 1997 Atypical Workers, the 1996 Parental Leave and the 1997 Burden of Proof Directives. The Atypical Workers Directive, as discussed in chapter 4, was an attempt to improve the rights and conditions of part-time workers. It was not directly linked to Article 119 in the Treaty of Rome, but had substantial implications for gender policy since the majority of part-time workers were (and still are) women. Despite its weaknesses, when it was eventually passed in 1997, it was seen as a major step forward for the rights of part-time female employees.

The 1996 Parental Leave Directive (96/34/EC) had a much more direct gender policy orientation. The original proposal for a directive on parental leave emerged in 1983 in the wake of the First Equal Opportunities Action Programme and was concerned with the amount of maternity leave that parents would receive after the birth of a child. In order to encourage fathers to take maternity leave as well, the draft proposed that each parent would have a *non-transferable* (thereby encouraging men to take the leave as well) three-month entitlement to leave (Hoskyns, 1996: 146–8). Not surprisingly, these expensive and egalitarian demands were rejected by the British government (and others) and the proposal was not adopted. Nevertheless, it continued to be reasserted in the various Equal Opportunities Action Programmes and by European women's organizations. In the aftermath of the Maastricht Treaty, the Commission brought the issue back on to the legislative agenda by setting it before the Social Partners. In December 1995 the Social Partners made an agreement on this topic, which the Council accepted in March 1996. Again, despite complaints over the weaknesses of the legislation (the non-transferable entitlement demands were dropped), the directive did create a number of basic rights for parents such as minimum requirements for parental and urgent family leave, three-month minimum parental leave, and the maintenance of social security rights during parental leave (ETUC, 1997).

In 1997 the Burden of Proof Directive (97/80/EC), also directly related to gender issues, emerged from legal as well as legislative developments. Up until the early 1990s the ECJ generally ruled that in principle the burden of proving the existence of sex discrimination in pay rested with the complainant. However, European women's groups, the Commission and even the ECJ recognized that this often put an intolerable burden on female complainants. In the mid-1980s the Second Equal Opportunities Action Programme demanded that the burden of proof be shifted from the complainant to the defendant. In 1988 the Commission proposed a directive shifting the burden of proof towards a more balanced degree of responsibility between the complainant and defendant, and this indeed was reflected in ECJ judgements in the late 1980s and early 1990s. In the 1988 Danfoss case (Case C-109/88), the ECJ ruled that pay structures had to be transparent in order for workers to know and be capable of demonstrating that they were suffering from discrimination. In the 1992 *Enderby v. Frenchay Area Health Authority* case (Case C-127/92), the ECJ argued that in certain situations, where claimants appeared to be victims of discrimination, the burden of proof could shift to the defendant. With this legal and political momentum, in 1996 the Commission revived its earlier burden of proof proposal. Having again failed to pass through the Council in mid-1996, the proposal was transferred by the Commission to the Social Partners to be discussed through the Maastricht Treaty's consultation procedure. Despite the failure of the Social Partners to reach an agreement, the proposal was again referred back to the Council in mid-1997, was eventually passed in December 1997 and extended to the UK in July 1998 (Council Directive 98/52/

EC). Under this new directive, once a person can establish before a court that he or she has been directly or indirectly discriminated against, then the burden of proof falls on the employer to prove that there has been no discrimination. In general, the directive was seen as a positive development for gender rights. However, it was criticized by the European Women's Lobby (*Women of Europe Newsletter*, no. 77, February 1998) and the ETUC for its unwillingness to go beyond existing ECJ decisions and weak interpretation of indirect discrimination.

Gender policy has indeed remained at the centre of EU social policy development. In the 1997 Amsterdam Treaty, the importance of gender equalization policy was reiterated in Article 137 (previously Article 118), which outlined five main areas of social policy that would receive special attention and fall under QMV in the Council. The fifth was the promotion of 'equality between men and women with regard to labour market opportunities and treatment at work'. Furthermore, in Article 141 (previously Article 119) the Treaty specifically allowed member states to create and maintain 'measures providing for specific advantages in order to make it easier for the underrepresented sex to pursue a vocational activity or to prevent or compensate for disadvantages in professional careers'. More generally, Article 13 gave the Council, using UV procedures, the ability to 'take appropriate action to combat discrimination based on sex (and other forms of discrimination)'. Hence, the Treaty opened the door to further gender policy legislation by giving it QMV status and guaranteeing the rights of member states to pursue positive discrimination in order to redress past unequal treatment. The 1998–2000 Social Action Programme reaffirmed the recent Equal Opportunities Action Programmes and committed the Commission to develop proposals combating sexual harassment in the workplace, promoting gender-balanced participation in decision-making, and focusing on the problem of violence against women. In May 1998 the EU hosted its first conference on women's employment and was attended by women's ministers from ten member states.[15] Reaffirming the demands of the Fourth Action Programme, the three key issues of this conference were increased access to childcare, promoting family-friendly employment policies and further mainstreaming of EU gender policies. EU gender policies had come a long way since their distant beginnings in Article 119 of the Treaty of Rome.

As argued in the introduction to this chapter, despite its unfavourable beginnings gender policy has become one of the most successful areas of EU social policy, having expanded rapidly from the 1970s onwards with the growth of second wave feminism, changes in family structure and occupational arrangements as well as the activities of the ECJ, the

Commission and Parliament. This expansion manifested itself in legislative developments, both 'hard' (directives, etc.) and 'soft' (recommendations, etc.), and a panoply of ECJ decisions. The overall success of EU gender policy was also illustrated by three other factors: the achievements of mainstreaming; the influence of EU women's organizations; and the growing range of gender policy. Mainstreaming increasingly integrated gender policies and issues into the core of EU policy-making. The success of EU women's organizations, particularly the EWL, provided the political muscle to keep gender issues under the spotlight. Consequently, gender policy areas have continually expanded in the 1990s to include issues of gender and power in EU health institutions (Commission, 1997e), gender roles in childcare (Commission, 1994c), work and childcare (Commission, 1996k), women's health in the EU (Commission, 1997e), gender relations in political institutions (Commission, 1996f), and the position and role of black and migrant women (Parliament, 1995).

As some gender policy experts point out, this success merely mirrors the changes that have occurred at the national level; it is not particularly innovative, and remains wedded to the core labour market orientation of the common market strategy. On the other hand, compared with other EU social policy areas, gender policy development has been tremendous. Furthermore, the success of gender policy, its strength in the EU treaties and ECJ decisions, its political strength at the EU level and continued development at the member-state level make it very likely to continue to be one of the primary areas of EU social policy activity, to deepen its influence in labour market-oriented policy, and to push the boundaries of that labour market orientation. Although these developments may be slow, difficult and uneven, gender policy is one area where all of the political, institutional and legal factors appear to point in the same general direction.

6

The Structural Funds and the European Social Fund

Paying for EU Social Policy

> In order to improve employment opportunities for workers in the
> common market and to contribute thereby to raising the standard of
> living, a European Social Fund is hereby established.
>
> *Article 123, Treaty of Rome, 1958*

The Structural Funds, and the European Social Fund (ESF) in particular, compose the financial backbone of EU social and regional policies.[1]
For the funding period 1994–9 the various Structural Funds will have
allocated a total of 138 billion ECUs, about a third of the total EU
budget. Of that total, the ESF will have allocated around 42 billion
ECUs, a little over 30 per cent of the Structural Funds. In terms of the
EU as a whole, these are relatively minor amounts. The total EU budget
represents only about 1.4 per cent of EU GDP, while the funds cover
only about 0.4 per cent. On the other hand, for less developed member
states and regions of the EU, where this funding is concentrated, these
amounts are quite substantial. In the early 1990s, the Structural Funds
support to Portugal equalled 3.5 per cent of Portuguese GNP (Springer,
1994: 128). Ireland received over 350 ECUs per person from the funds
during the 1994–9 period (Commission, 1996d: 95). More specifically,
from the ESF alone during the 1994–9 period, Ireland was allocated
over 2.1 billion ECU, nearly 1000 ECU per working age Irish adult,
and nearly 10,000 ECU per Irish unemployed person (a primary target
group for the ESF) (Commission, 1998h: 28). Thus, for the deprived
member states and regions of the EU and for disadvantaged and/or ex-

cluded groups, this is a substantial pot of accessible money. The size of the funds and the determination of their application has spawned a growth industry in EU-level lobby groups from the regions and member-state interest groups (Greenwood, 1997: chapter 9).

Obviously, the Structural Funds and the ESF are important, but are they, in fact, social policies? From the very beginning, they have played a variety of roles in the EU, all of which have shifted over time. Do the funds constitute EU regional policy? Are they member-state regional policies paid for by the EU? Are they bribes to keep weaker member states and interest groups committed to the larger integration project? This chapter attempts to address these questions through a review of the historical evolution and application of the funds, paying particular attention to the ESF.[2]

The ECSC: buying off losers and creating markets

The Structural Funds evolved out of the distinctive vision of the Schuman Plan. As opposed to the limited trade liberalization strategies of the OEEC (the predecessor of the OECD), Robert Schuman, the French Foreign Minister, suggested a much deeper integration strategy for the ECSC: 'in the light of the disparate conditions of production prevailing in the member countries, certain transitional measures must be taken, such as a production and investment plan, a mechanism for equalising prices, and *an amortisation fund to facilitate the rationalisation of production*' (my emphases).[3] Schuman's statement implied that this fund could be used to help weaker member states adjust to the new arrangements, to help workers who might be threatened by them, and eventually to create more rational and efficient European coal and steel sectors. The ECSC's Treaty of Paris reflected all of these concerns. Article 2 spoke of the need for 'safeguarding continuity of employment'. Article 5 emphasized that the ECSC would 'place financial resources at the disposal of undertakings for their investment and bear part of the cost of readaptation'. More precisely, Article 56 stated that:

> If the introduction . . . of new technical processes or equipment should lead to an exceptionally large reduction in labour requirements in the coal or the steel industry, making it particularly difficult in one or more areas to re-employ redundant workers, the High Authority . . . may facilitate . . . the financing of such programmes as it may approve for the creation of new and economically sound activities capable of reabsorbing the redundant workers.

Furthermore, the High Authority 'shall provide non-repayable aid towards: the payment of tideover allowances to workers; the payment of resettlement allowances to workers; the financing of vocational retraining for workers having to change their employment'. Finally, Article 69 encouraged member states, when confronted with a labour shortage in the coal and steel sectors, to 'facilitate the re-employment of workers from the coal and steel industries of other Member States'. All of these commitments to protecting employment, encouraging economic modernization and adaptation, promoting 'new and economically sound activities', aiding workers suffering from the restructuring of the industries, and enhancing vocational training and international mobility implied substantial responsibilities and funds. Clearly, these elements of the ECSC were not only designed to be market-creating, but were also essential to convince sceptical workers and trade unions of the benefits of the ECSC project. As Doreen Collins aptly summarized: 'the ECSC was a social system intended to buffer the worker against the responsibility of bearing the cost of changes and *to win his acceptance of them*' (Collins, 1975: 39, my emphases).

How were these early treaty commitments carried out in practice? Luckily, for the emerging ECSC, the early 1950s was a boom period for the coal and steel industries. Demand for coal and steel remained high during the first half of the 1950s, spurred on by the forces of recovery from the Second World War and the Korean War. Hence, in the beginning, the ECSC did not play much of a role in unemployment assistance. On the other hand, in line with strategies for creating a common market and increasing the efficiency of European firms, the ECSC began to develop schemes for promoting worker mobility between declining and emerging industrial areas. In 1954, in co-operation with the French government, it attempted to transfer 5000 French miners from declining coal fields in Centre-Midi to the Lorraine area. The operation was expected to cost nearly 1 billion francs, split evenly between the ECSC and the French government. The result was a disaster. The miners did not want to leave. The towns that depended on the miners were enraged. After three years and tremendous effort and expense, only 500 miners had been moved (Collins, 1975: 40–1).

The dramatic failure of this transfer approach led to a fundamental shift in ECSC strategies. The main lesson learned was that geographic mobility of workers, even within their own nation-state, could not be assumed. The problems of declining areas could not simply be solved by moving the workers out of that area and into an emerging area. Instead, as the conclusions of a special intergovernmental conference in October 1960 emphasized (Collins, 1975: 43), the much more difficult task of attempting to revive the declining area had to be addressed. This led the ECSC into several new policy areas. First and foremost, it prompted the ECSC to move strongly into regional policy, rather than mobility policy. Thus, unemployment aid to workers would be directed more towards retraining than towards mobility grants. Furthermore, in response to the complaints of the French miners, the ECSC began to develop its own housing policy. The Second World War had devastating effects on European housing stocks. A key element of the ability to keep workers in, or attract them to, a given area was the availability and quality of the housing stock.

As the coal and steel sectors started to go into their slow declines in the late 1950s and early 1960s, the ECSC began to develop substantial policies in all of these areas. From 1960 onwards the ECSC began to offer a substantial number of regional development loans to coal and steel firms in declining areas. Between 1961 and 1968 over 33,500 coal and steel workers had obtained new or alternative jobs with the help of the ECSC. Of workers laid off as a result of closure measures, between 50 and 80 per cent (depending on the member state) had received aid from the ECSC by 1965. In the decade 1960–70 over 75 million units of account had been spent in readaptation aid for unemployed coal and steel workers. This aid was divided into two main forms: direct aid to make up redundant workers' incomes; and indirect aid to help workers take other jobs (Collins, 1975: 45–53). Between 1954 and 1971 Michael Shanks (Director-General of DGV in 1973–6) estimated that over £206 million had been spent to aid 440,000 coal and steel workers (Shanks, 1977: 1). Finally, the ECSC also developed a substantial housing policy. From 1950 to 1970 over 110,000 houses and flats had been built with ECSC aid.[4]

With the creation of the EEC and the subsequent formation of the ESF and Structural Funds, the activities of the ECSC have been greatly overshadowed and its housing policy wound down. However, direct and indirect aid to redundant coal and steel workers has remained one of its principal activities. Between 1980 and 1994 over 3 billion ECU had been spent on helping over 800,000 ECSC workers (Commission, 1994: 3). The ECSC's lasting significance was the foundation that it laid for further social and regional funding development. A clear indication of this founding activity was the modification of Article 56 of the ECSC Treaty. In its 1951 version, the article committed the ECSC to respond (with direct and indirect aid) to unemployment due to 'new technical processes or equipment' attributable to the creation of the common market. In theory, only common market developments, not external shocks, were the ECSC's responsibility. In 1960 the article was modified and expanded, whereby any 'fundamental changes' that increased unemployment would trigger ECSC action. The discussion below shows how this broader interpretation was directly integrated into the ESF and Structural Funds.

The Treaty of Rome and the early years of the ESF and European Investment Bank

Following in the footsteps of the ECSC, early discussions on the formation of the EEC spoke of the creation of two major funds for European integration. After the 1955 Messina Council meeting, the Council declared that if the member states were to create a new common market, they would need to develop a 'European Investment Fund' for the 'joint development of European economic potentialities and in particular the development of the less developed regions of the participating states' and 'a readaptation fund' for encouraging unemployed workers to obtain new skills and/or move to areas of low unemployment.[5] Its rationale was a combination of self-interest and belief in the benefits of a common market strategy. By the mid-1950s it was becoming increasingly obvious that Germany, and to a lesser extent France and Belgium, were suffering from a labour shortage. Their economies were booming, labour was in short supply and labour-related production bottlenecks were becoming increasingly obvious. At the same time, Italy, particularly southern Italy, had a substantial oversupply of primarily agricultural labour. Improving underdeveloped regions and moving unemployed southern Italians into the booming German, French and Belgian economies became the primary strategies of the EEC funds.

These calls for the two funds were translated into the creation of the ESF and European Investment Bank (EIB) in the Treaty of Rome. The ESF was founded in Articles 123–8. Its objective was to 'improve employment opportunities for workers in the common market and to contribute thereby to raising the standard of living . . . [by] rendering the employment of workers easier and of increasing their geographical and occupational mobility within the Community' (Article 123). The fund was to be administered by the Commission, which would be assisted by a special committee composed of member-state, trade union and employer representatives (Article 124). Moreover, the ESF would cover half the cost (the other half being paid by the member state which applied to the ESF) of two types of projects:

a) ensuring productive re-employment of workers by means of vocational retraining [and] resettlement allowances; b) granting aid for the benefit of workers whose employment is reduced or temporarily sus-

pended, in whole or in part, as a result of the conversion of an under-
taking to other production, in order that they may retain the same wage
level pending their full re-employment. (Article 125)

On the surface, the ESF as proposed was quite radical. It created an
EEC obligation to support and improve employment opportunities,
encourage mobility and vocational training and contribute to unemployment benefits. The ESF was aimed at encouraging workers and
trade unions to accept the common market strategy and its potential
costs. The creation of the ESF committee and the inclusion of trade
unions on that committee was obviously a further inducement to the
unions to sign on to the EEC.

From the outset the ESF was strongly oriented towards retraining
and resettlement. During its first fifteen months, the ESF spent 5.8
million units of account, 4.7 million on retraining. By 1970 the ESF
was spending 37 million units of account, 36.3 million on retraining.
For the EEC as a whole, between 1960 and 1973 the ESF had paid out
327 million units of account, 316 million for retraining and 10 million
for resettlement, benefiting nearly 1 million workers from retraining
funding and 715,000 from resettlement funds. Over 1.1 million of the
total 1.7 million workers who were assisted by the ESF came from
Italy (Collins, 1975a: 67).

Contrary to its stated objective, providing a buffer for unemployment was not a significant ESF activity during its early years. In the
1960s unemployment was not a substantial problem in Western Europe. Labour shortage problems were much more acute. Moreover,
unemployment provision remained the job of the member states. The
emerging strategy of the ESF was to enhance the functioning of the
common market and to encourage the movement of mostly southern
Italians to Germany and France. At the time, the ESF's role was also
seen as a redistributive policy between the member states. This was
based on the privileged position of Italy not only in that its citizens
were by far the largest beneficiaries of the ESF, but in the budgetary
contributions to the ESF as well. Of the larger member states, during
the 1960s Germany, France and Belgium all agreed to higher than
average contributions; Italy was required to pay only 20 per cent
(Collins, 1975a: 267). Thus, the early ESF was a mixture of market-
enhancing strategies, indirect redistribution and mechanisms for encouraging labour to view the common market strategy more positively.

However, a number of problems and complications with the ESF
quickly emerged. First, soon after the ratification of the Treaty of
Rome, it became apparent that the Council had a much more re-
strictive interpretation of the scope and obligations of the ESF than

was implied in Article 123 (Collins, 1975a: 63). Unemployed workers had to be over eighteen years old (with some exceptions), not in the public sector, and not self-employed. Further, as mentioned above, the commitment to maintaining wage levels of the unemployed was never implemented and, despite the treaty implications, remained the responsibility of the member states. Second, all the ESF payments to the member states were made *retroactively*. The member states would develop a particular scheme, implement and pay for it, and then apply to the Commission to have half of the costs covered by the ESF. As a result of the retroactive payments, the member states dominated the development and implementation of the programmes and would merely submit as many project applications to the ESF as they had been allocated, making the EEC a completely passive participant in the development and allocation of ESF-funded projects. This passive position was enhanced by the inability of the Commission to reject schemes or withhold funding from member-state projects that met the basic technical criteria. Third, therefore the Commission could not use the ESF to develop new and/or innovative programmes and relied completely on member-state initiatives. The result was a clumsy, marginally redistributive, bureaucratic mechanism for essentially doing work that the member states were, most likely, going to do anyway. It was not long before demands for reform of the ESF were made by the institutions and member states of the EEC.

Before exploring these reforms, passing mention needs to be made of the European Investment Bank (EIB). Reflecting the general weakness of EU social policy and the emphasis on redistribution as a member-state concern, the Treaty of Rome did not have a specific provision for regional policy or a clear redistributive strategy. As just discussed, redistributive elements were built into some policies, but they were generally cloaked within a rhetoric of market-making and enhancing strategies. The EIB is a case in point. After its emergence in a 1955 Council proposal for the European Investment Fund, its framework was established by Articles 129 and 130 in the Treaty of Rome. Using its own resources and access to the private capital market, the EIB was supposed to:

> operate on a non-profit-making basis, grant loans and give guarantees which facilitate the financing of . . . (a) projects for developing less developed regions; (b) projects for modernising and converting undertakings . . . (c) projects of common interest to several Member States which are of such a size or nature that they cannot be entirely financed by the various means available in the individual Member States. (Article 130)

Here again was the combination of regional/social policies for less developed regions, with compensation policies for firms under pressure from common market competition, wrapped up in a market-creating envelope of cheap finance for trans-European projects. The weaknesses of the EIB were similar to those of the ESF. Funding for the EIB was relatively small and the only benefits of EIB loans was a lower rate of interest. Moreover, the member states dominated the selection of loans, hence the development of new and innovative projects was determined by the member states (Tsoukalis, 1997: chapter 9). Together with the Structural Funds, the EIB was to develop a much more influential presence. However, its initial weakness and contradictory goals reflected the limitations of social policy funding and financing during the early years of the EEC.

The first wave of reform: the ESF and ERDF in the 1970s

From its inception, the ESF was fraught with debate. A key struggle developed between the member-state governments who were not interested in relinquishing control of the ESF and the EU Parliament and Commission who were intent upon developing a more common European policy approach with it. This was a classic 'intergovernmentalist' versus 'supranationalist' struggle. In 1963 the Parliament and Commission began to argue that the ESF should be used to develop a common vocational policy and extend its coverage to the self-employed, and that the EU should be able to initiate its own pilot programmes (Collins, 1975a: 72). Despite these proposals, little changed. The EU was soon in the midst of its 'empty chair' crisis and in this atmosphere an extension of Commission control over the ESF was unthinkable. A small victory for the Commission did occur in 1968, when it was allowed to establish a new Regional Policy Directorate (DG XVI) in response to the growing demand for and interest in the EU regional dimension.

By the late 1960s, several change-inducing factors came to bear upon the ESF. First, due to the shifting economic developments of Western Europe in the 1960s, the ESF was becoming increasingly 'unbalanced' in its distribution of funds. The old bias towards aid to Italy for training and moving southern Italians to the workplaces of Germany and France was being replaced by German development of ESF-funded vocational training programmes for its own nationals. The result was that by 1967–8, Germany became the largest recipient of ESF funds (Commission, 1998: 13). This unsettled the agreement between the member states over the structure and allocation of the ESF and opened the door to intervention by the Commission and Parliament. Second, Article 126 of the Treaty of Rome contained a requirement for a twelve-year review and revaluation.

As 1969 approached, the Commission and Parliament took the opportunity to demand changes in the structure and functioning of the ESF. They proposed that the ESF should be directed towards helping workers adapt to changing employment needs, particularly in the rapidly declining agricultural, textiles and coal and steel sectors (Collins, 1975a: 72). Also, to develop a coherent EU level strategy, the Commission had to be given some influence over the type and scope of ESF-funded projects. The Intergovernmental Conference at The Hague, which took place in December 1969, was a watershed. The need to reform the ESF was agreed upon, and the Council meeting of July 1970 adopted the reforms which were finally passed in November (Council Decision 71/66/EEC).

The new ESF was based on the Commission proposals and a key member-state compromise. First, the resources of the ESF were substantially enhanced. The budget for the first two years of the new ESF's operation (1972–4) was larger than the total from the preceding twelve years. Second, the retroactive nature of the ESF project funding was replaced by a pro-active funding structure which could evaluate projects before they began their operations. Third, the Commission was given the right to develop innovative pilot projects which could be funded by the ESF. Fourth, private sector actors could now directly bid for ESF funding rather than just member-state governments. Fifth and last, two new ESF priorities were developed: Article 4, backed by the labour-importing Germans, was designed to support general EEC policies and/or to improve the balance of supply and demand of labour within the common market as a whole; and Article 5, supported primarily by Italy with its less developed southern regions, promoted employment in certain economic sectors (agriculture, textile, coal and steel) and for certain groups (handicapped, elderly, women and young workers) in less developed regions. This combination of priorities was an obvious compromise between the interests of Germany and Italy. In 1972–4 Italy seemed to be the definite winner since the majority of ESF funding went to projects in the second group, which primarily aided southern Italy (Collins, 1975a: 75). On the other hand, by 1974, following the OPEC oil shock and the subsequent economic downturn and increase in unemployment, the Germans had lost interest in promoting further labour migration to Germany and the projects outlined in Article 4.

For the rest of the 1970s only relatively minor modifications were made to the ESF. As the economic difficulties, particularly unemployment, of the early 1970s continued and deepened in the mid-1970s, the EC responded by expanding the categories of workers eligible for funding under Article 4 to include migrant workers and their families (Council Decision 77/803/EEC), women over twenty-five (Council Decision 77/804/EEC) and the unemployed under twenty-five (Council Decision 77/802/EEC). Furthermore, in response to the growing attention being paid to EC regional disparities and the integration of the three new member states (UK, Ireland and Denmark) the Council adopted Regulation (EEC)/2895/77 for increasing the ESF's regional orientation, giving greater priority to less developed regions (southern Italy, Northern Ireland, Ireland, Greenland and French Overseas Departments). Finally, during the 1978 Council meeting in Bremen, the Council passed Regulation (EEC)/3093/78, directed primarily towards job creation and employment strategies for the young. Overall, the ESF was developing a much more European profile with a strong orientation towards vocational training. Its key weakness remained its limited resources and the problem of additionality.

Before exploring these weaknesses in the ESF, it is essential to mention the other main regional/social policy development, the creation in 1975 of the European Regional Development Fund (ERDF). Confronted with the growing economic difficulties of the early 1970s, some member states and EC actors grew increasingly aware of the need for a coherent EC regional policy. During the golden age of the 1950s and 1960s, an EC-level regional policy was relatively unimportant. With an expanding economic pie in all of the member states, it was relatively easy to redistribute parts of that pie to less developed regions. When that golden age came to an end, regional demands were amplified. Recognition of the importance of regional policy was also linked to the potential creation of the European Monetary Union (EMU). When EMU was first proposed in the early 1970s, it was quickly realized that it could have substantial regional effects. Thus, if EMU was to develop, the EC had to develop a substantial regional policy. Unrelated to these changes were the demands of the new member states, UK, Ireland and Denmark. In particular, the UK argued that due to its efficient agricultural sector, the costs of the Common Agricultural Policy (CAP) for the UK were onerous, and demanded some form of repayment for the costs of the CAP (George, 1990). The British demands, the EMU and changes in the European economic climate came together to provide the political impetus for the ERDF.

The ERDF developed problems and limitations similar to those of the ESF. Original funding was limited, and member states retained substantial control over the projects that were funded. Furthermore, the fund was not very redistributive, since each member state was allocated a certain percentage or quota of the total.[6] The EC controlled and hence could allocate only 5 per cent of the ERDF. Thus, only limited redistribution occurred between member states and the EC could do little to promote regional strategies. Moreover, the EC could never be sure that the member states were spending the ERDF money *in addition to* money that they would already be allocating to a particular region or project. This uncertainty became known as the 'additionality problem' and undermined the whole concept of an EC regional policy. Until the reforms of 1983–4, the structure of the ERDF remained basically unchanged.

The Structural Funds in the 1980s: from stagnation to consolidation

The early 1980s were not a particularly progressive period for the Structural Funds. Deep in the throes of Eurosclerosis, the EC had little interest in or political will for expanding and strengthening the funds. On the other hand, with the accession of Greece in 1981 and Spain and Portugal in 1986, the EC added three new member states with over 60 million inhabitants who were at a level of economic development substantially below that of the first nine member states (average per capita GDP for the new member states in 1984 was half to two-thirds of the EC average). Given these conditions, if the Structural Funds were going to address these new developments they would have to be radically expanded and restructured. As discussed below, the Single European Act (SEA) provided the impetus for these changes and laid the foundation for the radical consolidation and expansion of the funds in 1988.

Initially, despite the accession of Greece in 1981, there were only limited changes in the ESF and the ERDF. A special fund for Greece was created in 1984, totalling 120 million ECUs and aimed primarily at strengthening vocational programmes in the Athens area. However, this was never strictly integrated into the Structural Funds. Other minor changes were made, including the accentuation of the regional focus of the ESF in 1985 in response to the forthcoming accession of Portugal and Spain, the development of a system of grants for small and medium enterprises, and the creation of an 'Integrated Mediterranean Programme' in 1986 to help the region adjust to the accession of the new member states. A more central concern for the ESF in the early 1980s was the disturbing rise in youth unemployment in the EC. In that year, 10.5 million EC workers were unemployed, 42 per cent of them under the age of twenty-five (Commission, 1998: 15). At the time, 44 per cent of all of the beneficiaries of ESF funds were under twenty-five, largely through vocational training schemes. In its 1982 review of the ESF (COM (82) 485), the Commission argued that the ESF's goal should be to 'provide support for the implementation of a training guarantee for all young people'. The Council responded by stating that by 1984 75 per cent of all ESF beneficiaries should be young people, predominantly through vocational training, particularly in less developed regions (Council Decision 83/516/EEC). Finally, funding for the ESF expanded substantially at this time: between 1982 and 1986 annual allocations for the ESF grew from 155.6 to 237 million ECU. However, these increased funds were immediately consumed by the higher demands generated by high European unemployment, stagnant European growth, and the accession of three relatively poor new member states, the demand for the funds rapidly expanded.[7] *Hence, relative to the increasing needs, the ESF expansion was actually a reduction.*

Similarly, there were no substantial changes within the ERDF during this period. However, it did undergo a number of minor modifications that enhanced the European elements of basic administration and orientation. The ERDF grew annually, but in terms of the increasing economic difficulties and demands of the new member states this made minimal impact. More significantly, the structure of the ERDF was revised in 1984 (Armstrong, 1985; Commission, 1987) to counter the perceived weaknesses in the management and effectiveness of the fund. These changes included: a transformation of the earlier 'quota scheme'; a shift from 'project assistance' to 'programme assistance'; the creation of 'integrated development programmes'; and the promotion of small and medium-sized enterprise development. Before these reforms the ERDF allocated funds to the various member states along strict quota lines. For example, the UK would receive 23.8 per cent of the ERDF. In essence, the EC had virtually no say in the general allocation of the fund. The reforms did not eliminate the quota system, but made it much more flexible by implementing an 'indicative range' or bands between which the EC could choose to allocate funds. Thus, after the reforms, the UK was granted an indicative range between 21.42 per cent and 28.56 per cent of the ERDF. Above its minimum band, the member state had to convince the Commission of the viability of its projects and thereby greatly strengthened the role of the Commission. Before 1984 95 per cent of all ERDF funds were allocated through 'project assistance'. The member state would propose a project that fit ERDF criteria and the EC would be obliged to provide assistance to it with virtually no input. The remaining 5 per cent of funds was allocated to 'programme assistance', which was much more broadly defined and allowed the EU to play a much larger role. After 1984 'project assistance' strategies were reduced to 80 per cent of ERDF funds, while 'programme assistance' strategies were expanded to 20 per cent. Moreover, similar to the ESF, the ERDF began to develop 'integrated development programmes' for regions (rather than just member states) and to promote the development of small and medium-sized enterprises. Although the changes in the ESF and ERDF in the early and mid-1980s were not overwhelming, they substantially strengthened the role of the EC in the management and allocation of the Structural Funds and set the stage for the radical reform of the fund in 1988.

The SEA created the legal and political base for the transformation of the Structural Funds. Articles 130a to 130e, under 'Title V Economic and Social Cohesion', set out the framework for and orientation of the Structural Funds. Article 130a required that the EC should use the Structural Funds to promote 'overall harmonious development . . . [the] strengthening of its economic and social cohesion . . . [and] reducing disparities between the various regions and the backwardness of the least-favoured regions', while Article 130b outlined the funds that would compose the Structural Funds (ERDF, ESF, EAGGF and other small instruments) and Article 130d required the Commission to draw up a plan for co-ordinating the various funds. Article 130d specified that the Council would have to vote unanimously on the plan within one year. However, when the plan was accepted, the Council would then enact decisions relating to the ERDF on a qualified majority basis. The importance of the creation of qualified majority voting for the ERDF was obvious. The ERDF was the largest fund and with the ESF, which was also voted on a QMV basis, the substantial majority of the funds would now be decided along QMV lines. This not only opened up opportunities for more efficient policy creation, but gave the EC an opportunity to increase its role in the allocation and operation of the funds. In 1988 the Commission's plans were complete and the new format for the Structural Funds was ready to be put into place.[8]

The 1988 revision of the Structural Funds was radical in a number of ways. It more than doubled the size of the funds for 1989–93 to total over 63 billion ECUs for the project period while the basic division of monies between the funds was left relatively unchanged (ESF 31.7%, EAGGF 17.9%, ERDF 47.6%, other 2.8%). Administratively, the revision was based on four new principles: concentration, programming, partnership and additionality. Concentration was applied in a variety of ways. First, instead of each fund having its own priorities, five core 'objectives' were created for each fund to address:

Objective 1, the development of the least prosperous regions; Objective 2, aid to regions hit by industrial decline; Objective 3, combating long-term unemployment; Objective 4, encouraging employment pathways for young people; and Objective 5, aid to agricultural and rural areas. The ESF was involved in all these areas, the ERDF primarily in Objectives 1, 2 and 5, and the EAGGF in 1 and 5. Second, the funds were also increasingly concentrated on areas of lower development. Of the five objectives, nearly 60 per cent of the funding went to Objective 1, 12 per cent to Objective 2, 20 per cent to Objectives 3 and 4, and under 10 per cent to Objective 5. In relation to Objective 1 a region was defined as having an average per capita GDP of less than 75 per cent of the EU average per capita GDP. Areas of low development thus began to receive the substantial majority of Structural Fund monies, making the policy truly redistributional by regional policy.

The second strategy of the 1988 reforms, programming, was intended to enhance the planning aspect of the various funds. Instead of merely accepting the various plans and projects for the member states or local authorities, the programming strategy demanded that each member state applying for the funds would have to create plans detailing and explaining the use of the funds and how those funds would be integrated into national- and regional-level strategies. Ultimately, the Commission would then draw up a Community Support Framework for the region which would describe the EC's role and its linkages to national and regional plans. From this larger EC-level plan, particular regional strategies would develop.

Linked to this was the third strategy, partnership. The obvious point here was that the EU was no longer a passive player in the allocation and development of the funds and the projects which it supported. It was a full partner with national and regional governments. As such, it had the right and obligation to set criteria for success and failure, to monitor the development and to take part in the implementation of projects funded by the Structural Funds.

The fourth strategy, additionality, addressed the continuing effort of the EU to force member states to use the Structural Funds in addition to existing national funds. The intention was that the greater programming and partnership would make it easier for the EU to evaluate the nature of the member-state plans and whether they were reducing state expenditures in response to the Structural Funds received by certain regions.

A final key element of the reforms was the creation of the EC's own initiatives under the Structural Funds (Commission, 1998h: 21). These programmes were designed specifically by the Commission and were oriented towards policy areas which the EC saw as particularly im-

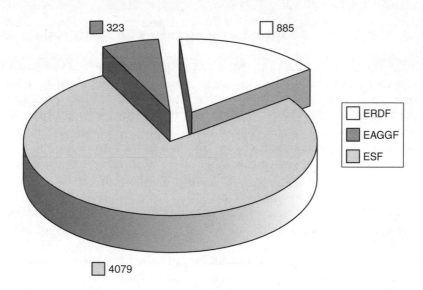

Figure 6.1 Breakdown of Community initiatives by Structural Fund, 1989–93
1997 prices in ECU millions

portant. It was also an opportunity for the EC to develop new, innovative and European-level projects. The total funding for the EC initiatives for 1989–93 was 5.3 billion ECU and was taken from the various funds (see fig. 6.1). Those policies with a strong social policy orientation were generally allocated to the ESF. The three initiatives with the largest funding from the ESF were EUROFORM (a vocational training and employment opportunities programme), which received 300 million ECU (1989–93), HORIZON (to improve the employment opportunities of the disabled), which received 300 million ECU, and NOW (New Opportunities for Women, promoting equal opportunities), which received 156 million ECU (Commission, 1998h: 21). In 1989–93 the ESF also contributed over 125 million ECU to the social policy aspects of thirteen other European-level initiatives. Overall, this new ability to create its own initiatives, though limited by a relatively small budgetary allocation (only 8 per cent of the total Structural Funds), greatly strengthened the influence and opportunities of the EU in its relationship to the member-state governments. The EU was actually making strides, albeit small ones, towards exercising fiscal control over the substantial Structural Funds.

The 1990s: expansion, restructuring and uncertainty

With the basic outline of the structural funds in place by 1988, major changes in the funds did not occur until the development of EMU and the approach of the 1993 review. As discussed above, one of the central elements of the Maastricht Treaty was the creation of the European Monetary Union (EMU). This implied a substantial leap in economic integration and was rightly seen as a major economic challenge to the less developed member states and regions in the EU. In order to assuage their fears and encourage their successful development and integration into the EMU, the EU agreed to the creation of a new Cohesion Fund aimed solely at easing the transition of less developed member states into the EMU, more than doubling the size of the Structural Funds.

Article 130d of the Maastricht Treaty called for the creation of a Cohesion Fund, 'to provide a financial contribution to projects in the fields of environment and trans-European networks in the area of transport infrastructure'. Later, in the attached Protocol on Economic and Social Cohesion, it was stated that the Cohesion Fund would provide aid only to those countries with a per capita GNP of less than 90 per cent of the EU average and which had plans for meeting the economic convergence criteria of EMU. Under these requirements, the fund concentrated its 15 billion ECU resources (in 1993–9) on the member states of Greece, Ireland, Portugal and Spain (Council Regulation (EEC) 792/93). The fund was allowed to cover up to 85 per cent of given projects and was not subject to the additionality criterion (Commission, 1996j). Keeping this in mind, the fund was clearly to be used by those member states that were expecting to be forced to make substantial public debt and government budget cuts in order to meet the EMU criterion. Although the fund was supposed to be used only for 'trans-European networks' (as referred to in Articles 129b–129d in the Maastricht Treaty) and environment projects, without the additionality criterion, it would have been easy for the member states to receive the Cohesion Fund monies and allocate them into projects which their governments would have funded regardless. In this way, they could use the fund to lessen and reallocate national burdens of adjustment to the EMU criteria.

More importantly, under the new provisions,[9] total Structural Fund allocations grew from 63 billion ECU for 1989–93 to 138 billion ECU for 1994–9 (see table 6.1). The ESF grew from 20 billion ECU to 42 billion ECU, while the ERDF grew from 30.1 to 71.5 billion ECU. The Structural Funds had now become nearly 33 per cent of the EU budget.

Table 6.1   Comparison of Structural Fund allocations by objective, 1989–1993 and 1994–1999

	1989–93 *(current prices in ECU million)*	*1994–9* *(1994 prices in ECU million)*
Objective 1	42818	94000
Objective 2	61281	15400
Objectives 3 and 4	6670	15200
Objective 3	–	12900
Objective 4	–	2300
Objective 5a	4100	6113
Objective 5b	2231	6859
Objective 6	–	700

Source: Commission, 1998h: 23

Even the funding abilities of the EIB were expanded: during 1993 it granted nearly 20 billion ECU in loans (more than the activities of the World Bank) to the poorer areas of the EU, the prime beneficiaries being Spain, Portugal and Italy. The overall division of the funds stayed basically unchanged. However, the number and orientation of the objectives was altered. Objectives 1 and 2 remained unchanged, focusing respectively on least developed regions and those adapting to industrial decline. Their funding allocation was substantially expanded and continued to consume the lion's share of the Structural Funds. A new Objective 3 was created which combined the old Objectives 3 and 4 (combating long-term unemployment and integrating young people into work). In addition to these two traditional areas, the new Objective 3 was also directed to support projects that promoted equal opportunities between men and women and to promote the employability of those individuals at risk of social exclusion. The new Objective 4 was aimed directly at providing vocational training and support for workers facing 'changes in production'; it did not have a regional specification and could be applied throughout the EU. Objective 5 was expanded, slightly increasing its allocation for aid to agriculture and fisheries and substantially increasing its aid to rural areas. However, its basic structure and orientation were left unchanged. Finally, a small Objective 6 was added to the group in 1995, following the accession of Sweden and Finland as new member states. When Sweden, Finland and Norway were seeking admission to the EU in 1994, they argued that their sparsely populated northern regions would be unduly pressured by European economic integration. Moreover, due to their unique economic structure (heavily subsidized by southern urban centres), they would not be adequately covered by the existing Structural Fund objectives. Hence, in order to protect these areas, and gain the support of the northern voters for the membership referendum in these countries,[10] the EU agreed to establish Objective 6 for the 'development of sparsely populated areas' (population density less than eight persons per square kilometre) and allocated 600 million ECU from 1995 to 1999.

The geographic spread of the funds is clearly demonstrated by Map 1. The main beneficiaries of the funds remained Greece, Portugal, Ireland and Spain. The entire countries of Greece, Portugal and Ireland, as well as southern Italy, were covered by Objective 1 status. The major new area covered by Objective 1 was the former Eastern Germany. The UK also benefited from the designation of Northern Ireland, northern Scotland and the Merseyside region as Objective 1 regions. As the map demonstrates, the other objectives tended to be much more regionally linked. Rather than entire nations being covered, only particular regions within the member states were included. This gave these objectives a much more regionally specific orientation and increased the ability of the EU to influence the development of projects in those regions by dealing directly with them, rather than through the member-state central governments (Anderson, 1995).

Building upon this development, combined with the growing volume of funds and number of applications, the EU began to adopt much more detailed rules and criteria for the functioning and development of the various funds and objectives. A key example of this change could be seen in the development of the ESF. For the new ESF (Council Regulation (EEC)/2085/93), the EU made ESF support conditional on project plans that were clear and coherent. The plans were intended to complement national strategies, to be innovative, to promote the principle of equal opportunities, to exploit potential synergies with other Structural Fund projects, to involve the social partners in the development of the project, and to include adequate financial control and monitoring and evaluation systems. Projects meeting these criteria would receive grants from the ESF covering, generally, 50 to 75 per cent of their costs in the regions of Objectives 1 and 6 or 25 to 50 per cent of their costs in other regions. The four main priorities of the ESF were: to improve the quality of education and vocational training, as well as access to it, particularly for young persons; to fight unemployment and encourage competitiveness through training; to fight long-term unemployment and social exclusion through forming 'pathways to integration'; and to promote equal opportunities.

The second and third of these priorities were of particular interest. Emerging out of the work of British academics and local groups, particularly in the Merseyside region (Commission, 1996i), the 'pathways' concept was based on the importance of integrating local groups and demands in order to enable individuals and groups in deprived regions to find their own way out of social and economic exclusion. Pathways strategies included: strengthening the role of the voluntary sector and community organizations; integrating input from the local social partners; and 'localizing' development strategies. The success of the pathways approach was demonstrated by its integration into the ESF criteria and to the recent discussions by the EU over its potential expansion within the ESF and to the other Structural Funds (Commission, 1998c). The promotion of equal opportunities was also of importance in its reaffirmation of how successful European women's groups had been in embedding their criteria into the ESF structure. As discussed in chapter 5, women's groups were particularly successful in 'mainstreaming' equal opportunities policies and strategies into a variety of EU policy areas. Following the recent changes in the Structural Funds, 'the principle of equal opportunities is observed across all measures' (Commission, 1998h: 30). This meant all ESF projects had to take account of the impact of their actions on the equal opportunities situation in their areas. Thus, despite only a small specific allocation within the ESF for promoting equal opportunities, the development of equal opportunities strategies became one of the main ESF priorities. Possibly more important, applicants for ESF funding began tailoring their projects to reflect this growing equal opportunities orientation (Lefebvre, 1998). Finally, the regulations of 1993 renewed the Commission's ability to create and promote its own initiatives, and expanded funding for these initiatives to 9 per cent of the Structural Funds budget. This further confirmed the growing role of the Commission and the EU in the direction and operation of the Structural Funds. Consistent with the focus of the funds, the Commission grouped these various initiatives into five main themes:

- cross-border, transnational and inter-regional co-operation;
- rural development;
- extremely remote regions;
- employment and development of human resources;
- and management of industrial change.

A major example of Commission initiatives during the 1994–9 programme was the EMPLOYMENT initiative (Commission, 1998f). It allocated nearly 2 billion ECU and co-ordinated the employment strategies of several programmes, including NOW (promoting equal opportunities), HORIZON (promoting pathways to employment for those at risk from exclusion), YOUTHSTART (integrating those under twenty into the market), INTEGRA (promoting employment for immigrants, refugees and others) and ADAPT (helping workers adjust to industrial change).[11]

Since the mid-1990s the direction of the Structural Funds has been increasingly shaped by the continued problem of unemployment. Following on the conclusions of the 1994 White Paper *Growth, Competitiveness, Employment*, the European Council meeting at Essen that December made five recommendations: greater investment in vocational training; more flexible work organization; a reduction in non-wage labour costs; a move from passive to active labour market strategies; and increased support for unemployed and excluded groups to return to work. The Structural Funds, particularly the ESF, were already focused on these strategies, but the growing strains of unemployment and the need to respond to it highlighted their importance. In 1996, following the detailed tripartite consultations between the EU and social partners, the Commission presented a 'Confidence Pact' for reducing European unemployment (Commission, 1996), which encouraged the member states to allocate additional resources to the employment problem, to promote the employment-creating activities of small and medium-sized enterprises, to encourage the development of innovative human resource programmes, to strengthen local development initiatives and to develop more local initiatives and locally based 'Territorial Employment Pacts' (Commission, 1997k). These suggestions were supported at the Dublin Council meeting in December 1996 and elements of this approach were integrated into the Amsterdam Treaty revisions in summer 1997 and the Employment Guidelines of the Luxembourg Council meeting in November 1997.

Debates over the future: the 1997–1999 reform process

The most recent proposed reforms concerning the future of the Structural Funds, particularly after 1999 when the current project period ends, are contained in the Commission's *Agenda 2000*, published in 1997. The basic strategies and funding of the Structural Funds remained unchanged. However, the size, allocation and control of funds was substantially modified by the document. If these changes are accepted, which is likely (final agreement is unlikely before the end of 1999), it will be a substantial transformation in the direction and functioning of the funds. What made change necessary, and what specific changes are proposed?

The three main contextual reasons for the proposed transformation of the funds were the continuation of the European unemployment crisis, the increasing economic difficulties of the German economy and German unification, and the challenges of integrating the new Central/East European member states. Despite innumerable national efforts and the increasing attention of the EU, the unemployment crisis in the EU continued to drag down the European economy. Unemployment rates remained stubbornly high, averaging between 11 and 12 per cent of the EU workforce (nearly 20 million individuals), while the USA was experiencing an unprecedented economic boom and record-breaking low unemployment. At the EU level, the response to this crisis was substantial. Following in the footsteps of the White Paper entitled *Growth, Competitiveness, Employment* and the various Employment Summits, the Structural Funds were increasingly seen as key ameliorative policy tools. It appears likely that responding to this crisis will become one of the main pillars of the Structural Funds. A related problem was the continuing difficulties of the German economy and German unification. In 1989 and 1990 the German Chancellor Helmut Kohl had promised that the unification process would be short and that extra funds would not be necessary to bring the two Germanys together. After nearly nine years of phenomenal effort, the former Eastern Germany continues to suffer from massive under- and unemployment, with 25 to 30 per cent of the working population receiving state support. German willingness to continue to act as the major contributor to the EU budget was increasingly undermined by poor economic performance and high transition costs. Increasingly concerns were expressed over the costs of maintaining the EU budget, the lavishness of the Structural Funds, and the inefficient use of the funds by the Commission. Finally, with the end of the Cold War and the fall of the USSR, East European countries were quick to ally themselves with the EU and NATO. EU membership applications were swiftly lodged by every Central/East European country and it became apparent that some would be allowed to join in the near future. The obvious difficulty was that these countries had per capita GNPs of between a quarter and half of the EU average; furthermore, the potential of having over 100 million new EU citizens would create enormous demands on the Structural Funds. The contradictory pressures of these three developments set the stage for the reforms of 1997, which could be described as strategies to define expenditure limits for, increase the control over, and intensify the impact of the Structural Funds.

These funds had steadily expanded throughout the 1980s and early

1990s. *Agenda 2000*, on the other hand, set out a number of clear limits to the expansion of the Structural Funds. First, it set an upper limit on the total amount of funding of no more than 0.46 per cent of EU GNP, about 275 billion ECU in 1997 prices for the project period 2000–6. At first glance, this seemed to allow for further expansion to nearly twice the prior amount. However, there were a number of limitations. First, of the 275 billion ECU, 45 billion ECU was allocated to the new member states (which were later announced to be Poland, Hungary, the Czech Republic and Slovenia). This was obviously appropriate because their needs would be substantial, but it reduced the total available for the existing fifteen member states. Second, to limit the total amount of transfers to the new member states, a cap in total aid was established so that no member state would be allowed to receive more than 4 per cent of national GNP in EU aid (under the previous programme period, Portugal received a little over 3.5 per cent of its GNP through EU aid). Third, when comparing the total amount of funding for the 2000–6 period with the 1994–99 period, it must be remembered that the earlier period went from twelve to fifteen member states by adding three very wealthy countries, while the forthcoming period will probably increase the membership from fifteen to nineteen, adding four relatively poor countries. Finally, the forthcoming period is one year longer than the previous programme. Thus, minus the funds for the new member states and the Cohesion Fund, 210 billion ECU are (would be) left for the fifteen. As demonstrated in table 6.2 and as stated in *Agenda 2000*, 'over the new period average annual funding for EUR 15 will fall slightly from the 1999 level' (Commission, 1997: 22). This may be a reasonable strategy in the face of European economic developments and the expansion of the EU, but it is a substantial change from the member-state allocation growth of the 1980s and 1990s.

During the 1994–9 programme period, the Structural Funds became increasingly diverse and complicated. There were seven main objectives (including 5a and 5b), four major funds and thirteen Community initiatives, which created over 400 specific programmes and consumed 10 per cent of the Structural Funds. Furthermore, the project allocation and development process had become increasingly complex. Member-state governments, social partners, regional authorities and local groups were all supposed to be integrated into the projects. Often, the Commission had neither the staff nor the expertise to deal with this growing complexity. Furthermore, there was growing political opposition from the member-state governments to the complicated and expansionary nature of the Commission's control over the funds.

In response to these complaints, *Agenda 2000* outlined strategies

Table 6.2 Projected Structural Fund expenditure, 1999–2006 (1997 prices in ECU billion)

	1999	*2000*	*2001*	*2002*	*2003*	*2004*	*2005*	*2006*
Community of 15								
Structural Funds	31.4	31.3	32.1	31.3	30.3	29.2	28.2	27.3
Cohesion Fund	2.9	2.9	2.9	2.9	2.9	2.9	2.9	2.9
New member states[a]	–	0.0	0.0	3.6	5.6	7.6	9.6	11.6
Pre-accession aid	–	1.0	1.0	1.0	1.0	1.0	1.0	1.0
Total	34.3	35.2	36.0	38.8	39.8	40.7	41.7	42.8

[a] Including participation in the Cohesion Fund.
Source: Commission, 1997: 74

for concentrating, simplifying and enhancing the funds. First, the total number of objectives would be reduced from seven to three. Similar to its predecessor, the new Objective 1 would continue to receive the majority of the Structural Funds, around two-thirds of the total, and would concentrate on aiding less developed regions, those with a per capita GDP of less than 75 per cent of the EU average. However, it would try to improve the concentration and focus of the funds. More stringent criteria would be used to determine an Objective 1 area. As *Agenda 2000* stated: 'In future, the threshold of a per capita GDP of 75% of the Community average should be applied strictly' (Commission, 1997: 22). Regions redefined as being just over the threshold would be given short-term support to ease the transition away from EU aid. Furthermore, aid would be applied in a more integrated fashion, co-ordinating all of the components of the Structural Funds with member-state governments and regional authorities.

Allied with the new Objective 1, the new Objective 2 would be a combination of the former Objectives 2, 5 and 6, providing support for regions 'suffering from structural problems . . . [including those] undergoing economic change, declining rural areas, crisis-hit areas dependent on the fishing industry or urban areas in difficulty' (Commission, 1997: 23). Similarly, the application of the fund will be concentrated and simplified through the creation of stricter EU-established criteria, combined with the member-state responsibility of creating a single programming document for each region. For both Objectives 1 and 2, the Commission's strategy is to reduce the total amount of the EU population covered by the new objectives from 51 per cent to 35–40 per cent.

The new Objective 3 would concentrate on reproducing the former Objectives 3 and 4, but would also co-ordinate the human resources elements of all of the former objectives. Mirroring the developments of the ESF and strongly influenced by the European Employment Strategy set out in the Amsterdam Treaty (Title VI), the new Objective 3 was designed to respond to the needs of regions not covered by Objectives 1 and 2. New Objective 3 would be based on a common EU framework for the promotion of human resource development, but would be flexible enough to apply to the different member-states' circumstances. It would promote activity in four key areas: economic and social change; lifelong education and training systems; active labour market policies to fight unemployment; in combating social exclusion, it would mirror the four core themes of the Employment Guidelines, employability, entrepreneurship, adaptability and equal opportunities (Commission, 1997).

Mirroring demands for greater concentration of effort and simplification, the *Agenda 2000* document demanded that the thirteen existing Community initiatives be reduced to three, 'where the value added by the Community is most obvious'. These included cross-border, transnational and inter-regional co-operation, rural development and human resources development. The overall budget allocation for these initiatives was dramatically reduced to 5 per cent of the Structural Funds and innovative and pilot projects were encouraged to concentrate on 'significant projects'.

Clearly, the member states wish to reassert control over and limit the scope of manoeuvre for the Commission in the development and management of the funds. This purpose was emphasized by the push for greater concentration, simplicity and openness in the activities of the Structural Funds. It was hoped that the greater concentration of the funds would have a larger 'multiplier effect' on depressed regions. This effect would also be promoted by using fewer grants and more indirect means of support, requiring more private–public co-operation such as interest rate subsidies, loan guarantees and venture capital holdings, making the increasingly limited funds more cost-effective. With more simplicity and openness, member states would be required to develop multi-year and annual plans to co-ordinate the Structural Funds with their own development strategies and National Employment Action Plans. In essence, the member states would be more responsible for the running of the actual regional projects and would be required to 'systematically . . . account directly for the use made of the Structural Funds' (Commission, 1997: 26). On the other hand, the document required the member states to work in partnership with the Commission and the local regions and to provide stringent checks and verification of the results of the funds. Finally, the Commission will retain a 'reserve' of at least 10 per cent of each project's funding which may be allocated only after a successful review of the 'good performance' of a given project. In short, the Commission was moving towards a more passive role in the administration of the funds, but at the same time demanded greater capabilities to oversee and indirectly influence the operation of the funds.

Overall, the proposed changes are quite substantial. They reflect the realities of continued unemployment, growing member-state resistance to Structural Fund expansion, and the massive needs of the new Eastern European member states. A key feature has been a return of detailed control over the application of the funds to the member states. From an institutionalist perspective, control has been taken from the Commission and returned to the member states. The cost of this transfer has been the requirements of greater project openness, more responsibility for the member states and continued oversight by the Commission. For some actors in the Commission, this transfer of responsibility to the member states has a number of advantages.[12] In a period of fiscal constraints and limited manpower, it lifts a substantial administrative burden from the Commission. At the same time, the Commission maintains overall influence over the funds through its central criteria formation and the required openness and responsiveness of the member states. Clearly, the proposed new system is not a return to the member-state dominance of the 1970s, but a new balance of administrative co-ordination between the member states and the EU. Without increased administrative resources and facing substantial political criticism of its role in the operation of the funds, the Commission had little choice but to adopt a more balanced approach.

This chapter began with an inquiry into what was and is the role of the Structural Funds. Do they cover regional or social policy, or are they just bribes for the weaker member states to keep them committed to the larger integration projects? As with other areas of EU social policy, the Structural Funds are a complicated mix of policies and strategies. From their earliest beginnings in the ECSC, the Structural Funds were used as a cushion against the demands of the common market. Buffering weaker regions, supporting worker mobility and subsidizing the living standards of workers threatened by the creation of the common market were all original objectives. With the creation of the EIB and the ESF, the Treaty of Rome followed in the footsteps of the ECSC. During the golden economic years of the 1950s and 1960s the ESF and EIB did much to encourage labour mobility and training, primarily for unemployed southern Italians to move to and work in

France and Germany. In this early period, the funds were administered as a regional policy (aiding southern Italy, France and Germany), an employment and social policy (for southern Italy in particular) and a market-creating strategy (creating labour mobility and easing regional tensions). However, there were weaknesses and contradictions in all of these strategies. The regional policy element was weakened by the control of the member states over the funds and pre-set regional allocations. The employment and social policy aspects were undercut by the lack of the additionality principle and the possibility that any EU-allocated monies were merely being subtracted from national funds. The market-creating element was limited by the dominance of one particular group (southern Italians) who benefited from the funds.

With the economic and institutional difficulties of the 1970s, the funds went through a major transformation. Through the ERDF a major regional policy was established. However, it shared problems and limitations with the ESF. The member states retained primary control over the funds and were not very redistributive. The additionality criterion was not firmly applied. Moreover, relative to the emerging economic difficulties, the size of the funds was quite small. Substantial revision, reorganization and expansion of the funds took place in the 1980s. With the addition of Greece, Spain and Portugal and the creation of the Single European Act and the Social Dimension, the EU brought together the various funds in one co-ordinated package. Using concentration, programming, partnership and additionality, the EU managed to expand the funds, increasing their regional policy aspect, to establish the additionality principle, to develop innovative employment-oriented social policies and to buffer certain groups and regions from the impact of the common market enhanced by the Single European Act. The 1993 review, following in the footsteps of the Maastricht Treaty and the development of EMU, furthered these trends. The funds were expanded, regional policy elements strengthened, social programmes encouraged, and employment-generating strategies strengthened. The most recent proposals for the future of the funds followed these basic trends while trying to continue to deal with the problem of unemployment, German economic and unification difficulties, and the substantial demands of the new Eastern European member states. Distinctively, the most recent changes reduced the growth of the funds and shifted their control away from the EU Commission. Nevertheless, the basic regional policy, employment-based social policy and market-creating strategies remained. The future proposals would strengthen the regional impact of the funds, particularly in favour of the new member-state entrants, intensify their employment enhancing orientation,[13] and continue their 'buffering' strategies, particularly in relation to the burdens of joining and maintaining EMU.

Hence, the answer to the question is, yes, the Structural Funds cover regional, social and market-creating policy. Their effectiveness and form have changed with varying demands and time, but these basic elements have remained. At present, the member states and EU have reached a new balance over the control of the funds that retreats from the trend of the early 1990s towards greater EU control, but does not return to the structures of member-state dominance in the 1970s. This new balance reflects the current limits of integration strategies, and the ability of member states to reassert their dominance over the policy process. It also shows the increasing complexity and interrelatedness of the 'multi-level' EU. Consequently, balancing local, regional, national and European demands results in a variety of contradictory and complementary policy developments.

7

Expansion and Extensions I

The European Union must make a major effort to study and combat new forms of social exclusion. These should not be analysed solely in quantitative terms, as a component of long-term unemployment for example, but as social phenomena of a new kind which need to be dealt with in new ways.

Portuguese Economic and Social Council, 1995[1]

More than 57 million people in Europe live below the poverty line. An increasing number of these are suffering the poverty in part as a result of racism in its many forms. . . . Marginalisation and social exclusion together with racial discrimination in Europe must be addressed as a priority in all European institutions and legislation.

European Anti-Poverty Network, 1997[2]

The Community's role in public health has increased over time and especially with the ratification of the Maastricht Treaty. It gave the Community a particular role in promoting health protection and disease prevention. . . . Developments in the last two years . . . have contributed to a new and greater awareness of the importance of health policy at Community level.

Commission, 1998[3]

As the above quotations demonstrate, the boundaries of EU social policy are broadly interpreted by pro-social policy member-state governments, interest groups and the Commission. Issues of poverty, race, health and the multiple ways in which these areas interact are all included. However, despite the wishes and demands of these social policy supporters, at present these areas remain primarily ones of potential, rather than existing, EU social policy, none of which has a long history in EU policy development. Most emerged in the mid- to late 1980s through the Social Charter and the Social Dimension. Moreover, many of the European-level interest groups in these areas are not particularly influential or powerful and are often subsidized and sustained by the EU Commission.

I have combined these areas because they deal broadly with social issues, while the social policies for the elderly, the disabled and youth focus on particular social groups and are discussed in chapter 8. Each of these policy areas has its own particular history and dynamics. Nevertheless, all have several common features at the EU level. They are struggling to emerge with only relatively weak bases in the treaties and are poorly funded and institutionalized within the EU system. The interest groups that promote them are young, weak, and intimately linked to the Commission and Parliament. In the future, they are likely to progress, but very unlikely to do so rapidly. This chapter attempts to provide brief introductions to these policy areas and concludes with an exploration into their similarities and differences. They are all the offspring of core EU social policy areas. How well they will survive and expand will depend greatly on their ability to integrate into the core areas and establish themselves within key institutions and legal structures.

Anti-poverty policy: from poverty programmes to promoting social inclusion and combating exclusion

In general, concerns with issues of poverty were not directly related to core EU activities.[4] We have already seen that early EU social policy was relatively limited and primarily revolved around promoting and enhancing the development of the free-market aspects of the EU, overall employment, and assuaging and subsidizing groups and regions threatened by market integration. Articles 2 and 3 of the Treaty of Rome spoke of promoting 'economic and social cohesion and solidarity among Member States' and 'strengthening economic and social cohesion'. However, these concepts were primarily related to regional inequalities and were to be addressed through employment, training and mobility schemes via the various Structural Funds, particularly the European Social Fund. Poverty was only a concern when it threatened the cohesion of the EU and overall employment levels. The early EU did pursue a variety of policies, including vocational training, housing and economic development, that would have had an impact on poverty. However, they were justified not in terms of alleviating poverty, but as a way of promoting employment, development and the underlying integrative strategies of the EU.

There were a number of reasons for this initial lack of attention to poverty at the European level. First, during the 1950s and 1960s the member states were in the middle of the postwar economic golden age. Growth rates were high. Inflation was low and stable. Most importantly, unemployment was negligible. Poverty did exist, but with the emergence of the welfare state and the creation of full employment it was seen as being adequately dealt with at the national level and, if the good times continued, might be eliminated as a major policy concern. Second, the ECSC/EEC was not interested in, and/or was not capable of, expanding beyond its early market-creating orientation. Poverty alleviation was clearly linked to the national level and the ECSC/EEC lacked the political will to force itself into that issue during those years. Third, during the early years of the EU the balance of political forces was oriented towards the right in the member states, which were more antagonistic to and/or sceptical of substantial poverty alleviation policies.

The earliest direct attempts to address poverty issues in the EU emerged during the changed economic and political circumstances of the early 1970s. With the collapse of the golden age of West European economic growth in the late 1960s and early 1970s, followed by the end of the dollar link to gold and the beginning of the OPEC oil crisis, in the early 1970s substantial economic crises and 'stagflation' began to develop. Unemployment soared and concerns about poverty quickly began to rise. At the same time, under pressure from the Social Democratic government in Germany and an increasingly activist EC Commission, anti-poverty proposals began to emerge in the 1974 Social Action Programme (SAP).

The creation of the poverty programmes

The first SAP focused on an expansion of typical EC social policies (i.e. greater vocational training, mobility and employment promotion to deal with the growing unemployment problem), but also attempted to include programmes for general poverty alleviation. These programmes were passed by the Council in July 1975 and created the first two-year 'programme to combat poverty' (75/458/EEC). Through this action, the Council agreed to allocate 5.4 million units of account into twenty-one Commission pilot or action projects that would 'test out new methods of combating existing or potential poverty . . . [and would] be drawn up and implemented in collaboration with persons served by the schemes . . . [and] be of interest to the Community as a whole' (Commission, 1976: 8). This programme was subsequently extended by a Council Decision (77/779/EEC) in 1977 for another three years. It extended the life of many of the existing programmes and gave the Commission the ability to develop new ones. A key element of the first 'poverty programme' was its research element. In essence, the EC was attempting to explore and evaluate the new form of poverty and to examine the role, as distinct from its traditional training and employment promoting strategies, that it could play in alleviating it.

When the first poverty programme came to an end in 1980, the EC was in the grips of its 'Eurosclerosis' period. Member states had turned strongly inward in pursuit of ways of dealing with the economic difficulties of the 1970s and European integration came to a standstill. As a result, the poverty programme was allowed to expire. It was not until 1984, during the first glimpses of a revival of the EC under the French Presidency, that it was revived. The second poverty programme was created in 1984 for the period 1985–8 with a total budget of 25 million ECU. In 1986, 4 million ECU were added to the programme to extend it to cover the new member states, Portugal and Spain. The second poverty programme was very similar to the first. It created sixty-five action/research projects covering such issues as single parent families, the homeless, migrants, the elderly, youth and urban poverty, intending to promote research, integrate affected groups and encourage co-operation between the various member states. Perhaps the most interesting and earliest predecessor of the comprehensive nature of the later social inclusion approach could be found in the 'integrated urban action programmes' which promoted a broad and comprehensive approach to the needs of the poor in urban environments (Hantrais, 1995: chapter 8).

Despite this programmatic activity and the renewed integration activity brought on by the Single European Act, neither the Social Charter nor the broader Social Dimension specifically mentioned anti-poverty policies. This was probably due to the reluctance of the Commission to promote these contentious areas. However, these developments greatly expanded the sphere of EC social policy and widened the scope for the development of anti-poverty policies. By 1989 the Third Poverty Programme (Council Decision 89/457/EEC) had been created in their shadow. This followed the basic pattern of the previous two, but again, on a larger scale; 55 million ECU were allocated for 1989–94. The Council Decision specified that the programme must concentrate on 'attacking the structural causes of this economic and social exclusion . . . [and] foster the economic and social integration of groups in society at risk of becoming economically and socially less privileged'. In order to carry out these tasks the Council demanded that the programme should: 'ensure overall coherence between all

Community operations' impacting upon the less privileged; develop 'preventative measures' and 'corrective measures' to help the less privileged and poor; develop a 'multidimensional viewpoint' for the reintegration of the poor; and promote further research and exchange of member-state experiences on poverty policies. Linked to the Third Poverty Programme was the creation of the Observatory on National Policies to Combat Social Exclusion (Room et al., 1991, 1992) and, recognizing the importance of the voluntary sector, the European Anti-Poverty Network (EAPN, *Network News*).

What is particularly important about the Third Poverty Programme is its redefinition of anti-poverty policies to include strategies to combat social exclusion and promote social inclusion. By the late 1980s traditional anti-poverty policies were increasingly unpopular and the nature of poverty appeared to be changing. Poverty had become much more complicated and intractable than during the 1950s and 1960s. Experts, inspired by French approaches to social inclusion, began to note that individuals and groups were being excluded not only from the labour market, but from an entire array of basic social and economic institutions (Room, 1995b). To make a difference, EC policy had to go beyond its traditional employment-creation orientation and take a much more inclusive approach. Doing so opened the door of EC anti-poverty policy to a whole new range of policy areas, responsibilities and especially costs also encouraging the development of a network of supportive social policy voluntary organizations.

The Maastricht Treaty was ambiguous towards this broader interpretation of anti-poverty policy. The fundamental importance of training and vocational education was re-emphasized in Article 126 and in the restructuring of the European Social Fund. Economic and social cohesion were re-emphasized. More importantly, in the Protocol on Social Policy (adopted by the eleven), Article 1 stated that the 'combating of exclusion' was a major objective and that the EU should 'support and complement the activities of the Member States in . . . the integration of persons excluded from the labour market' (Article 2). On face value, this would seem like a clear victory for the broader anti-poverty strategies. They were now written into the basic treaties and would hereafter have a sound foundation in EU policy formation. However, the actual wording did not guarantee the broad interpretation of anti-poverty policy. In fact, with its emphasis on exclusion from the labour market, the provisions of the treaty mirrored the traditional training, education, mobility and employment generating approach of EU policy. As discussed below, this limitation continued to constrain the parameters of anti-poverty policy throughout the 1990s.

From Maastricht to Amsterdam: limiting anti-poverty policy

Following in the footsteps of the integration of anti-exclusion state-ments in the Maastricht Treaty, the Commission and particularly the DGV moved quickly to build upon and expand the EU's commitment to broader anti-poverty legislation. In 1992 the Commission adopted a Communication entitled 'Towards a Europe of Solidarity: Intensifying the Fight against Social Exclusion, Fostering Integration' (COM (92) 542) which restated the basic aims of the existing Third Poverty Pro-gramme and presented the basic guidelines for further EU action. In June 1993 the Commission sponsored a conference on social exclusion which it hoped would sketch out new policy areas and proposals, raise awareness of the exclusion issue and generate political support for it. Following this conference, the Commission unveiled its proposal for a new, dramatically expanded, 1994–9 Fourth Poverty Programme (COM (93) 435) with more than double the previous programmes' funding, from 55 million to 121 million ECU. However, the basic orientation of the programme remained substantially unchanged, and emphasized the research and experimental nature of the particular programmes, recog-nized the 'multidimensionality' of the problems of exclusion, promoted 'partnership' with member states and local government, and encour-aged 'participation' with regional and local organizations and the vol-untary sector. It also provided for the EU to grant joint funding to 'model actions' at the local, regional and national levels and to pro-mote the establishment and development of 'transnational networks' of anti-exclusion projects. In essence, using the traditional structure, the Commission was encouraging the EU to step beyond its traditional anti-poverty policy boundaries to directly confront the challenges of promoting social inclusion and combating social exclusion.

In many ways, it was a bold step. Nevertheless, with the publication of the earlier Commission document and support from the confer-ence, the Commission felt confident that the programme would pass. As Delors had argued time and time again, if the EU was to develop, it had to have a social as well as an economic side. With the EMU and its strict economic criteria set to develop in the near future, it seemed clear that the EU had to show that it was doing something to help those who might bear the brunt of the transition to monetary union. The poverty programme and fight against social exclusion would be-come a cornerstone in the drive to develop social Europe and soften some of the sharper impacts of EMU. Moreover, the Commission pro-posal was strongly supported by the Parliament and by the Economic and Social Committee. The final hurdle was the Council.

Unfortunately, the climate in the Council had become very chilly by the time the Fourth Poverty Programme appeared before it in April 1994. This was due to a number of factors. First, Euro-enthusiasm had suffered a beating during the near rejection of the Maastricht Treaty during 1991–2. Substantial EU policy expansion would be much more difficult to sell to sceptical electorates. Second, both the EMU and the EU's finances had suffered severe setbacks. In 1992 and 1993 international financial speculation sent shock waves through the EU and future plans for EMU, and plunged the EU member states into varying degrees of economic crisis. At the same time, the Council rejected the expansive Delors 2 package for substantially expanding the financial resources and taxing capabilities of the EU. Hence, by 1994 both the fiscal and political constraints on the EU and the member states were substantially higher than they had been. Consequently, the Fourth Poverty Programme received a chilly reception in the Council. In the preparatory stages to the April 1994 Social Affairs Council meeting a number of member states expressed doubts over the need to more than double the programme's funding during the forthcoming period. Others demanded that the Council should have more control over the various elements of the programme. Finally, when the Germans openly challenged the justification for the entire programme, arguing that the policy area was best dealt with at the national level and invoking the need for subsidiarity, the Fourth Poverty Programme proposal was completely blocked (Pochet et al., 1994: 235–6).

Since that time, the expansion of anti-poverty policy has been redirected towards the more traditional areas of vocational training, mobility enhancement and employment promotion. The 1993 social policy White Paper raised the issue of social exclusion and how the EU should fight it. The national responses to the document were lukewarm at best (Commission, 1995). The Germans reiterated the importance of subsidiarity to social policy development. The British argued that there was not even a common definition of social exclusion. The French and Italians stressed that future social policy should be in line with the 1994 Commission White Paper, *Growth, Competitiveness, Employment*, which did not mention social exclusion. Reflecting a growing emphasis on employment strategies, the 1994 Commission White Paper, *European Social Policy*, mentioned the fight against poverty and social exclusion only in passing, stating that the Commission would continue to try and pass the Fourth Poverty Programme and work towards the creation of a 'solemn public declaration against exclusion'. It also mentioned the need to avoid the exclusion of the disabled and the elderly. However, the Commission's subsequent Medium-Term Social Action Programme 1995–7 offered no new anti-poverty proposals. Clearly, the Commission began to sense the shifting political winds and abandoned broader anti-poverty strategies. Instead, it concentrated on the traditional areas of employment promotion and the reintegration of excluded individuals into the labour market.

Since 1995 EU anti-poverty policy has become increasingly integrated into training and employment strategies. The Fourth Poverty Programme has not been adopted. In 1995 the Commission did manage to provide 5 million ECU of credit to extend the life of the Third Poverty Programme and supported the creation of the organization of 'European Businesses against Social Exclusion'. In 1996 despite continued pressure from the Parliament, social policy NGOs and the Committee of Sages, no major new initiatives for combating social exclusion were initiated by the Commission. In 1997 the Commission's *Agenda 2000* argued that the primary means of promoting social and economic cohesion in the EU would be through the Structural Funds' strategies of generating employment and integrating the labour market. Anti-poverty policy and strategies to combat exclusion outside the Structural Funds should be primarily advisory: 'Beyond the targeted use of Structural Funds and other Community instruments, the Union can play a supporting role by encouraging best practices and facilitating co-operation in the fight against social exclusion and all forms of discrimination' (Commission, 1997: 20). This position was confirmed by the 1997 Amsterdam Treaty. Article 136 (consolidated treaties) stated: 'The Community and the Member States . . . shall have as their objectives . . . the development of human resources with a view to lasting high employment and the combating of exclusion.' The 'combating of exclusion' was directly linked to training and employment policy. Article 137 (consolidated treaties) outlined five areas where the EU 'shall support and complement the activities of the member states'. One of these areas was 'the integration of persons excluded from the labour market'. With the creation of this article, anti-poverty policy gained QMV status within the treaties. However, to gain this position, anti-poverty policy had to be subsumed within employment and training strategies.[5] This was starkly confirmed in the 1998–2000 SAP, which stated in its section on 'Promoting Social Inclusion' that:

> despite the successes of Europe's social model, poverty and social exclusion remain significant problems in the EU. The new employment strategy . . . will contribute to overcoming these problems by targeting those at risk of exclusion from the labour market and by encouraging the reform of social protection systems to enhance people's employability. (Commission, 1998e: 15)

The multi-faceted problems of social exclusion would now be solved with one simple solution, reinsertion into the labour market.

However, a variety of actors are still trying to promote a broader anti-poverty/ social inclusion strategy. From over thirty interviews with EU social policy actors in September 1997 and January 1998, it became clear to me that the various social policy NGOs, Parliament, particularly the Social Affairs Committee, and actors in the Commission were continuing the struggle, subject to two major constraints: no new money and no direct policy tactics. Even in the most pro-EU social policy circles it was accepted that greater funding of EU social exclusion policy was off the agenda and the Fourth Poverty Programme was reluctantly accepted as being completely dead. Moreover, following the latest treaty changes, direct calls for a broader anti-poverty policy to combat social exclusion have been abandoned, leaving less direct methods as the only instruments left. These indirect strategies have taken two directions. First, in the aftermath of the November 1997 Employment Summit, one Parliamentary actor argued that 'the only way to pass social policy now is via employment'. In other words, the best social policy promoters can hope for is to use employment and labour market policy as a 'Trojan horse' for broader anti-poverty policies. Second, using recent EU statistics to point out that poverty was more than just a lack of employment,[6] supporters argued that anti-poverty policy should be mainstreamed, similar to gender policy.

However, neither of these strategies is likely to be very successful. As seen in other social policy areas, the 'Trojan horse' strategy can lead to some legislative gains, but they are generally slow and partial. Moreover, passing proposals that direct substantial funding to broader anti-poverty policies will probably remain extremely difficult.[7] Furthermore, despite some successes in developing a network of voluntary organizations that support social inclusion strategies and strong support from the Commission, Parliament and some member states, the political will to mainstream social exclusion strategies is likely to remain weak for the foreseeable future.[8] Thus, broader developments in EU anti-poverty policy may be found only in covert attachments to employment and vocational strategy, rather than through Commission action programmes.

EU anti-discrimination policy against racism: from policy laggard to promoter

For the first twenty years of its development, racism was not an issue for the EU.[9] The founding treaties, despite forbidding discrimination based on gender (Article 119) and nationality (Article 48), made no mention of racial discrimination. There were several reasons for this. First, despite the racist horrors that emerged during the Second World War, racism as a political issue was not prominent during the early postwar years. Second, the predominant economic orientation of the ECSC/EEC precluded it from developing an anti-discrimination policy against racism. Primarily, anti-discrimination policy was often considered a human rights issue and, therefore, best addressed at the level of the United Nations and Council of Europe and implemented at the national level. Hence, it was not until the late 1960s and mid-1970s that responses to racism began to emerge on the EC policy agenda. Early elements of an anti-discrimination policy against racism began to emerge through the struggle for 'migrant rights' in the 1974 Social Action Programme. As that document argued: 'The migrant population live and work in conditions substantially inferior to those of the indigenous population. Discrimination against migrant workers exists in various forms throughout the Community, in such matters as social security, housing and rights to participate at different levels of decision making' (Commission, 1974: 23).

The 1974 Social Action Programme never directly discussed racism, nor did it deal directly with the rights of third country nationals in the EC (Turks in Germany, Algerians in France, etc.) However, since many of the EC migrants were non-white, non-Europeans who were encouraged to emigrate and join the booming labour markets of the 1950s and 1960s, the question was deeply intertwined with the issue of migrant rights. As the West European economies began to move into recession in the mid-1970s and unemployment re-emerged, re-patriating third country nationals was one of the easiest solutions. At the time, the general position of the EC was to defend and promote the rights of legal migrants and ignore and/or downplay the rights of non-legal migrants, who often came from non-white Third World countries (Geddes, 1995).

Early developments: racism becomes an issue

During the 1970s and 1980s, most of the EC member states had begun to struggle with and implement policy on racial issues. In 1972 France established early anti-racist laws and Denmark incorporated the UN's Declaration on the Elimination of All Forms of Racial Discrimination into Danish law. Italy incorporated the UN declaration in 1976. Britain passed its Race Relations Act in 1976, while Belgium passed an anti-racism law in 1981.[10] These were often extremely bitter political struggles in which the EC had no role or influence. EC actors seemed reluctant to interfere with issues that were so socially explosive, politically divisive and nationally distinct. For example, it was not until 1977 that the EC finally issued a Joint Declaration supporting and respecting the 1950 European Convention for the Protection of Human Rights and Fundamental Freedoms.

By the mid-1980s this reluctance had begun to yield. Responding to a growing awareness of anti-racist issues and concerns and the political success of racist and far right political parties in the 1984 elections to the EC Parliament, the socialist-dominated leftist majority in the Parliament created a committee of inquiry within the Parliament to study the rise of fascism and racism in Europe. This committee, unsuccessfully challenged by Jean-Marie Le Pen representing the Group of European Right (Parliament, 1991: 11), published an impressive report in December 1985 documenting the disturbing rise of European fascism and racism (Parliament, 1985). In the wake of this report, the EC passed a Joint Declaration against Racism and Xenophobia which committed the EC to:

> 1. vigorously condemn all forms of intolerance, hostility and use of force against persons or groups of persons on the grounds of racial, religious, cultural, social or national differences; 2. affirm their resolve to protect the individuality and dignity of every member of society . . . ; 3. look upon it as indispensable that all necessary steps be taken to guarantee that this joint resolve is carried through. (Commission, 1997n: 12)

Committing the EC to the fight against racism was an impressive step, but went little beyond words. No money was allocated and little legislation and policy ensued. It was an easy way for member-state governments to show concern without committing themselves to major legal or policy changes. Similarly, the 1989 Social Charter held that 'it is important to combat every form of discrimination', but did not go on to specify particular measures to combat racial discrimination. The subsequent Action Programme to implement the Charter did not directly mention remedial policies and demanded only the creation of a memorandum on the social integration of migrants from non-member countries. In short, the EC was committed to the elimination of racial discrimination and encouraged the member states to actively eradicate it, but remained reluctant to develop its own anti-discrimination policies against racism.

The importance of the Parliament in promoting anti-discrimination policy

Following an increase in racist and hate crimes in the late 1980s, the Parliament, once again, took the lead on the issue of anti-discrimination policy. A new Committee of Inquiry, created in 1989, published an elaborate report in 1991 on the state of racism and xenophobia in the member states and provided a detailed list of seventy-seven recommendations (Parliament, 1991). Further, pressured by the Parliament, the Council passed a Resolution on the Fight against Racism and Xenophobia in 1990 (Commission 1997n: 35), which called upon the member states to ratify all major international agreements against racism and resolutely apply their anti-discrimination laws, but merely committed the EC itself to developing an 'effective information and education policy'. This was a clear demonstration of the predominantly advisory and educative limits of EC anti-discrimination policy against racism.

Anti-discrimination activities and policies against racism at the EC level expanded considerably during the early to mid-1990s, attributable primarily to the growing importance of the issue at the member-state level, the continued activities of the Parliament, the increasing activities of European-level anti-racist interest groups and, most important, as a response to a series of racist atrocities which occurred in the early 1990s and kept the issue at the top of the political agenda. It was constantly mentioned in the Presidency Conclusions of the European Council; for example those of June 1990 (Dublin) noted the EU's 'deep revulsion at recent manifestations of anti-Semitism, racism and xenophobia', while the December 1991 (Maastricht) Council expressed its concern that 'manifestations of racism and xenophobia are steadily growing in Europe' (Commission, 1997n: 47–8). The result of these Council conclusions was the implicit development of anti-discrimination policy against racism in the Maastricht Treaty. With its emphasis on the creation of European citizenship and mobility rights, the treaty had to deal with the rights of third country migrants (often from non-white races and non-European ethnic backgrounds) and in Title VI (Provisions on co-operation in the fields of justice and home affairs) committed the EU to complying with the 1950 European Convention for the Protection of Human Rights and Fundamental Freedoms.

During the various struggles over the ratification of the Maastricht Treaty, the Parliament created a continuous stream of anti-discrimination proposals and strategies. In 1991, in response to a proposal in the Parliament's 1991 Inquiry on Racism and Xenophobia (Ford Report), the EC created and funded the EC Migrants Forum to give a voice to the estimated 18 million migrants and to promote strategies of inclusion and migrant rights.[11] In 1993 the Parliament passed two further resolutions (Commission, 1997n: 28–32) re-emphasizing many of the key recommendations of the 1991 Ford Report, and calling on the Commission to develop an action programme to create 'practical measures to combat racial prejudice ... measures to strengthen the legal instruments existing in this field, ... [and] campaigns to raise awareness throughout Europe' (Commission, 1997n: 18).

In response to these developments, the Commission integrated anti-discrimination strategies against racism into its 1993 Green Paper on social policy and requested proposals for 'comprehensive anti-discrimination legislation'. At the June 1994 (Corfu) European Council meeting, the French and Germans proposed to create a 'consultative commission' charged with making recommendations for 'encouraging tolerance and understanding of foreigners', for developing a 'global strategy' to combat racism and xenophobia and for promoting training for officials dealing with these issues at member-state level (Commission, 1997n: 49). Shortly thereafter, the Commission's 1994 White Paper on social policy committed the Commission to promote the development of 'systems to monitor incidents of racial harassment', to increase 'existing financial support for anti-racism projects' and to involve the social partners in the development of 'a code of good employment practice to combat racial discrimination'.

The late 1990s: growing soft law and a treaty base

In 1995 further developments of EU anti-discrimination policy activity were initiated with the publication of the Commission's Medium-Term Social Action Programme 1995–7, which highlighted three main areas of Commission activity: the creation of an action plan against racism, the designation of 1997 as the European Year against Racism, and the promotion of the social partners' code of conduct to combat racial discrimination. During mid-1995, the Parliament passed three resolutions pushing for greater anti-discrimination policy development (Commission, 1997n: 27–32). These promoted:

● the Commission's plans for an anti-discrimination action plan;
● the Franco-German consultation committee on race and xenophobia;
● the proposed European Observatory on Racism and Xenophobia;
● the integration of anti-discrimination legislation into the EU treaties;
● the anti-discrimination activities of the social partners;
● the continued financial support for anti-discrimination initiatives and interest groups;
● and a variety of other activities and policies.

In response, the Council adopted two resolutions in mid-1995 which encouraged the member states to co-operate on and extend a variety of anti-discrimination policies and strategies with a primary focus on the role of educational systems in the fight against racist and xenophobic attitudes (Commission, 1997n: 35–43). In October 1995 the social partners presented their Joint Declaration on the Prevention of Racial Discrimination and Xenophobia and Promotion of Equal Treatment at the Workplace (Commission, 1997n: 103–8). Finally, in December 1995 the Commission presented its action plan on racism and xenophobia (COM (95) 653), outlining its guiding principles, means and key actions for combating racism. The guiding principles rested on three key strategies: developing universal co-operation; prevention; and the principle of subsidiarity. The key tools for the fight against racism were the European Social Fund, particularly its EMPLOYMENT-INTEGRA, HORIZON and URBAN initiatives, the EU policies on education, training and youth, for example Socrates, Leonardo da Vinci and Youth for Europe, and continued support for anti-discrimination pilot projects and interest groups. Other areas for action included the linkage between inclusion strategies and anti-racism policies, prevention of racial discrimination in the workplace, raising public awareness of racism, preventing racist behaviour and monitoring racist crime. Finally, the Commission called for 'a general non-discrimination clause' in the EU treaties.

This legislative and policy movement was easily carried into 1996 and 1997. In July 1996 the EU agreed to promote judicial co-operation between the member states to combat illegal racist activity and to make 1997 the European Year against Racism (Barnard, 1996: 530). The December 1996 European Council meeting agreed to the development of the European Observatory of Racism and Xenophobia. During 1997 nearly 5 million ECU was allocated to 178 projects in four general categories (everyday racism, racism in working life, legislation and awareness-raising) to combat racism during the European Year against Racism. Annual funding for specific anti-discrimination projects against racism in the late 1990s averaged nearly 16 million ECU (Kohli, 1998: 179).

Even more important were the results of the 1997 Amsterdam Treaty negotiations. After extensive debate, the member states agreed to include a new Article 13 (consolidated treaties) which stated that:

> Without prejudice to the other provisions of this Treaty and within the limits of the powers conferred by it upon the Community, the Council, acting unanimously on a proposal from the Commission and after consulting the European Parliament, may take appropriate action to

combat discrimination based on sex, *racial or ethnic origin*, religion or belief, disability, age or sexual orientation. (my emphases)

This new Article expanded the responsibility and scope for action of the EU in anti-discrimination policy against racism. Not only was the EU committed to an anti-discrimination policy through its earlier declarations, but it now had the potential to create significant EU-level anti-discrimination law. The member states were careful to build limitations into this Article, stressing the importance of other provisions of the treaty, the limitations of the Council, and making legislation based on unanimous voting procedures in the Council. Nevertheless, a substantial opening for further EU-level anti-discrimination policy was created. Perhaps most important, with the considerable number of resolutions and declarations creating a 'soft law' base, this increasingly clear treaty commitment to non-discrimination could open the EU legal system to litigation from individuals and/or groups who suffered under racism in the member states. As Jitinder Kohli summarized:

> Not only does it [the treaty] allow the Commission to proceed with work in the field of racism and xenophobia without having to justify links to other areas on which it has competence, but it also allows for the passing of an anti-discrimination directive . . . [which would] allow all ethnic minorities resident in the Union (regardless of their citizenship status) the right to challenge cases of discrimination in the European Court of Justice. (Kohli, 1998: 185)

Although EU anti-discrimination policy against racism continued to make progress, it remained hostage to the fate of the Amsterdam Treaty. In 1998 the European Monitoring Centre for Racism and Xenophobia opened in Vienna, a proposed anti-discrimination directive by the Starting Line Group was drafted and the Commission's Social Action Programme 1998–2000 was published, all indicating that the Commission was ready to propose new legislation to combat racial discrimination as soon as the Amsterdam Treaty was ratified. Finally, in mid-1998 the Commission published its Action Plan against Racism (COM (1998) 183 final) which, although reasserting that 'the prime responsibility for combating racism lies with Member States', proposed a four-pronged strategy for further action:

● paving the way for further action;
● mainstreaming the fight against racism;
● developing and exchanging new models;
● and strengthening information and communication.

The document did not make specific legislative proposals, but launched a 'wide debate on the possible application of the non-discrimination clause [Article 13] . . . with a view to ensuring that concrete proposals are on the table for adoption before the end of 1999' (Commission, 1998i: 10). It also encouraged the mainstreaming of anti-discrimination policy against racism in a variety of areas, including the Employment Guidelines, the Structural Funds, education, training and youth programmes, public procurement and external relations.

In general, EU anti-discrimination policy against racism has tended to trail member-state legal and political developments. The politically sensitive nature of the issue, the need for unanimity in the Council, and its legal and financial implications, have all acted as a continual brake. Against this resistance, actors in the Parliament, Commission and member states, and social interest groups have pushed for a greater commitment by the EU to anti-discrimination policy. It may be poised for substantial expansion in the near future, depending on the success of such groups as the European Migrants Forum, the Starting Line Group, and Migration Policy Group, continued pressure from the Parliament and Commission and the new basis for anti-discrimination policies in the Amsterdam Treaty; allied to this is the potential for individuals and groups to take anti-racist issues to the EU court system based on a future EU anti-discrimination directive and 'soft law' developments. On the other hand, if the Council is unwilling to implement Article 13, if member states continue to oppose the development of anti-discrimination legislation at the EU level and if legal blockages are put in the way of anti-discrimination cases, EU anti-discrimination policy could remain primarily small programmes and 'cheap talk'.

Public health policy: from occupational to general health policy

As demonstrated in chapter 3, the EU has a lengthy history in occupational health and safety policy and related workplace health policy activities. Despite this record, during the 1950s, 1960s and 1970s the EU made no major attempts to expand beyond its strict orientation towards workplace health and safety issues. Health policy and national health services/systems were seen as predominantly national institutions which did not have a significant European dimension. Further, the EU had no base in its treaties for developing a substantial public health policy. There were bits and pieces here and there, for example the right to limit worker mobility (Article 56) and the free movement of goods (Article 36) as well as the demand for improving the 'standard of living' (Article 2) indirectly implied responsibility for public health matters. Nevertheless, public health issues and policy areas remained firmly in the hands of the member states until the late 1980s.

Early steps and the Single European Act

The early steps to a more direct EU public health policy grew out of the larger integration dynamic that emerged from the Single European Act (SEA).[12] As discussed above, the SEA and associated White Paper were primarily devoted to creating and opening the single market. Many labour and social policy interest groups feared that this new market would undermine economic and social rights in the member states through the process of 'social dumping' and that member states with less regulation and lower health standards would undermine those with higher standards. The activist Delors Commission, taking advantage of these social concerns, was able to argue for and insert a variety of social policy elements and implied guarantees into the treaty revisions. One of these elements was the promotion of public health. Article 100A committed the Commission to 'take as a base a high level of protection' in matters relating to health, safety, the environment and consumers when proposing legislation to create the single market. More explicitly, Article 130R of the SEA (under the Title 'Environment') stated that 'action by the Community relating to the environment shall . . . contribute towards protecting human health'. Neither of these articles provided a clear treaty base for public health policy. Nevertheless, they were an improvement on the previous situation and demonstrated the growing awareness of health issues at the European level.

In the aftermath of the SEA, substantial progress was made in the area of occupational health and safety, but only a few developments occurred within the field of public health. In later proposals for the Social Dimension and the Social Charter, health policy issues were noticeably absent. In 1988 a small budget was allocated to this new policy area and DGV established a new public health division. Like many other emerging social policy areas, the primary foci of EC public health policy after the SEA were to increase information, support European research, promote trans-European projects and concentrate on a few key issues with a clear European dimension. A main example of this approach was the 1990–4 'Europe against Cancer' Action Plan (Council Decision 90/238). The plan was allocated 50 million ECU and developed a small programme for promoting public information, training health care workers, and for research. Linked to the plan were several proposals to reduce smoking in Europe. In 1989 the Council agreed to harmonize health warnings on tobacco products (Directive 89/622/EEC, later amended by Directive 92/41/EEC), while the Commission presented its proposal for harmonizing the advertising of tobacco products (COM (89) 163). In 1990 the Council passed a directive on maximum tar yields in cigarettes (90/232/EEC). Overall, these were small-scale projects and legislative proposals were aimed at easy targets. The Commission was clearly feeling its way into this area and was reluctant to move beyond the more technical and non-political areas of public health policy.

Maastricht and the expansion of public health policy

The hesitant approach to public health policy within the EU was transformed by the Maastricht Treaty. Article 3(o) and, more importantly, Article 129 explicitly recognized its role and importance. Article 129 maintained that national health systems remained the concern of the member states. However, it asserted that the EU 'shall contribute towards ensuring a high level of human health protection' by encouraging co-operation between the member states, promoting international co-operation between the member states, the EU and such bodies as the World Health Organization, and co-ordinating EU policy with member-state policy. Article 129 also provided a strong focus for EU public health policy: 'Community action shall be directed towards the prevention of diseases, in particular the major health scourges, including drug dependence, by promoting research into their causes and their transmission, as well as health information and education.' In essence, this article reinforced the existing information/research orientation of public health policy and intensified its strategy of concentrating on a few key issues and only a few diseases. Further, the treaty changes broadened the remit of EU public health policy, implying that attaining a high level of human health protection, as outlined in Article 3(o), applied to all areas of EU policy which have an impact on health.[13] Finally and perhaps most important, Article 129 gave public health proposals QMV status within the Council. Overall, the treaty did not substantially modify the emerging EU public health policy, but rather greatly legitimized and strengthened it by giving it a firmer base within the treaty.

In the wake of the Maastricht Treaty, the Commission moved quickly to expand and deepen its activities in the field of public health. In 1991 the Council accepted the 'Europe against AIDS' Action Programme for 1991–3 (Decision 91/317/EEC) which concentrated on increasing public information and awareness of AIDS, promoting research into a cure, and promoting and co-ordinating member states' efforts in dealing with the syndrome. In 1992 the first European Drug Prevention Week was announced, with a strong campaign to distribute information. More significantly, in 1993 the Commission adopted its first Public Health Action Programme (COM (93) 559), which focused on eight main areas: cancer, drug dependence, AIDS and other transmittable diseases, health promotion, health monitoring and research, pollution-related diseases, injury prevention and rare diseases. It was accepted in the Council in 1994.

From the action programme, the Commission developed and obtained budgeting for the first five main health policy programmes. The existing cancer programme was extended with a further Action Plan (1996–2000) (COM (95) 131). The anti-drug dependence policy resulted in the creation of a new Action Plan (1996–2000) (COM (94) 233), which aimed to reduce demand for illegal drugs and combat trafficking on a global scale (COM (94) 243); also a new European drugs and drug addiction monitoring centre was established. The Europe against AIDS Action Programme was extended for 1994–5 and again for 1996–2000 (COM (95) 209). The Community Action Programme on Health Promotion (1996–2000) (COM (95) 138) was also accepted. In June 1997 an agreement was reached on the creation of a health monitoring programme. All these separate strands of EU public health policy were adopted independently and had distinctive budgetary allocations, which increased in the second half of the 1990s.[14] Finally, the remaining three sub-policy areas identified by the 1993 programme (on pollution-related diseases, injury prevention and rare diseases) were submitted by the Commission in 1997 and in mid-1999 were awaiting final decisions in the Council.

With its policy success in these areas, public health policy became increasingly integrated into core EU social policy proposals in the mid- to late 1990s. The direction and role of EU public health policy was mentioned in the 1993 Green Paper on social policy. Although the general response from the member states was that national health systems were primarily their concern, the existing areas of EU public health policy did not generate substantial comment or opposition. Consequently, the 1994 White Paper on social policy included a section on public health policy which reiterated the demands of the 1993 programme. These demands were echoed in the 1995–7 Medium-Term Social Action Programme and, as mentioned above, five of its major health policy proposals had been adopted by 1997.

All in all, public health was quite a successful policy area in the 1990s. AIDS, drugs and cancer were all clearly trans-European (as well as global) problems. Developing programmes to combat them was not politically divisive, nor particularly expensive. The programmes helped to give the EU a way of promoting its 'human face' in a period when economic difficulties and EMU were focusing most Europeans' attention upon the EU's strict monetary orientation and criteria. Moreover, with the development of these programmes a number of groups concerned with health issues began to establish themselves at the EU level and take an active role in public health policy. These ranged from general health promotion organizations such as Health Action International and the European Public Health Alliance to organizations with more specific concerns, for example EUROCARE, which aims to prevent alcohol abuse.

Recent developments: mainstreaming public health

The 1997 Amsterdam Treaty did little to alter the basic focus of EU public health policy. On the one hand, Article 152 (consolidated treaties) reaffirmed the basic orientation of public health policy towards 'complementing national policies', 'fostering co-operation' and addressing the established problems (drugs, AIDS, etc.). On the other, it specifically requested the EU to develop 'measures setting high standards of quality and safety of organs and substances of human origin, blood and blood derivatives'. More importantly, in response to the results of a 1996 ECJ case,[15] the article stated that: 'a high level of human health protection shall be ensured in the definition and implementation of all Community policies and activities'. This implied that policies on the environment, transport, consumers and agriculture, must take into account the impact of their actions on health in the EU. In other words, public health policy had to be mainstreamed into all relevant areas of EU policy-making. Annual reports have already been created on the health implications and requirements in some of these policy areas (COM (98) 230).

Two major Commission documents have already begun to sketch out the future of EU public health policy. The 1998–2000 Social Action Programme reiterated the Commission's commitment to the existing public health programmes and pressed for the adoption of its outstanding proposals for programmes against rare diseases, pollution-related diseases and accidents and injuries. It also stressed that the Commission would continue to develop its strategy for combating tobacco consumption and 'deepen the exchange of experience on efforts to improve the efficiency, cost-effectiveness and quality of health systems' (Commission, 1998: 17). In 1998 the Commission outlined the underlying strategies for the future development of EU public health policy:

> A Community public health policy should have several characteristics. It should make the best use of the limited resources available at Community level. It should emphasise the improvement of health and health gain and concentrate on a limited number of priorities. It should be sufficiently flexible to respond promptly to new health threats and developments. Most importantly, the policy should take up the concerns of Community citizens and be credible and convincing so that they are aware that effective arrangements exist at Community level to attain a high level of health protection. (Commission, 1998: 11)

This excellent summary captures the basic parameters of EU public health policy. Given recent fiscal constraints, the policy cannot expect more resources. With these limits and its existing focus on key areas, it must continue to concentrate on a limited number of priorities. At the same time, in light of the experience with the BSE crisis in the UK in 1997 and the growing debate over genetically modified foodstuffs, the policy needs to be able to respond to new health crises and challenges as well. Moreover, for reasons of general EU legitimacy and the Commission's own interests in maintaining and expanding its policy area, health policy actors must concentrate on pursuing policies and actions that the general public will see and appreciate. Finally, reflecting these parameters, the document outlined three key 'strands of action':

- improve information for the development of public health;
- reacting rapidly to threats to health;
- and tackling health determinants through health promotion and disease prevention.

Overall, EU public health policy has come a long way in a very short time. From a virtually untouched activity (with the exception of occupational health and safety) and resting on a weak base in the treaties, public health policy has become a significant new area of EU social policy activity. The Maastricht and Amsterdam Treaty changes have given it a firmer base, with general support from the member states, and there is increasing EU-level interest-group activity in this area. Above all, following recent ECJ decisions, public health policy has been mainstreamed, particularly within the EU areas related to agricultural and consumer policy. Linked to continued trading and economic interdependence, the growing responsibilities of the EU for consumer protection (see Article 129a in the Maastricht Treaty) and the expansion of European-level public health organizations (European Public Health Alliance), one would expect to see the development of increased competencies and policies in these areas. On the other hand, the member states and the Commission are hesitant to push EU public policy into the areas of national health systems and services, and its minimal budgetary allocation and small Commission staff virtually guarantee that only limited developments will occur in the near future. In sum, where the EU has staked out its areas of health policy competence (information and research, specific disease-related programmes, and promoting co-operation between the member states and responding to health crises), it should easily defend and possibly expand these areas, perhaps developing one or more new specific disease-related health programmes while continuing its active role in new health crises. However, it will certainly not be able to invade the massive areas of national health policies and, reflecting its fiscal and institutional constraints, it will probably exercise a relatively minor influence on overall European public health policies.

Not surprisingly, the development and fate of the three policy areas differ in detail, but show a number of similarities as well. First, all three were dependent on larger developments in EU social policy. Social inclusion policy emerged out of the revival of EU social policy under the 1974 Social Action Programme. Anti-discrimination and public health policy developed in tandem with the Social Dimension. Hence, the success or failure of these and similar policy areas may be substantially dependent on general social policy development. Second, the main opposition to development of these policy areas could be found in the Council and key member states. Social inclusion policy was halted in 1994 by Council and German opposition. Anti-discrimination and public health policy proposals have often been diluted by the Council. Moreover, future developments (particularly for anti-discrimination policy) greatly depend on the willingness of the Council to take advantage of new treaty provisions. Third, the Parliament, Commission and social policy interest groups remain the main supporters of these three policy areas. The Parliament was absolutely essential to the birth of anti-discrimination policy, while the Commission was the key to the foundation of anti-poverty and public health policy. More recently, social policy interest groups (linked strongly to the Commission) have developed an increasingly important role in promoting these policy areas. Finally, all three demonstrate the need for policy actors to be flexible and adaptable in the EU policy system. Following the German rejection of the 1994 Fourth Poverty Programme, anti-poverty policy promoters shifted towards a focus on employment in order to maintain some of its programmes and policy elements. For anti-discrimination policy promoters, the next step is to develop an anti-discrimination directive that is legally enforceable. Meanwhile, public health policy promoters are currently attempting to expand their particular programmes through a mainstreaming approach.

Overall, despite these general similarities, there is no clear model to explain their distinctive development. As argued in chapter 2, each area displays its own dynamics of development which can not be easily captured by classical theories of integration.

8

Expansion and Extensions II

Yes, Europe moves forward, but social Europe advances at a different pace, particularly with regard to older people.

Maurice Bonnet, *Eurolink Age Annual Report, 1997*

Mainstreaming the disabled in the EU policy process and structural funds is a good idea, but we still have different specific needs. If we were incorporated into the mainstream labour market, we would probably drown.

European Disability Forum, 1998

There is a big difference between the EU's youth policy and an ideal one.

Youth Forum, 1998

As EU social policy has developed, it has expanded not only into new policy areas, but also into 'new' social categories. The elderly, disabled and young have always been groups within the EU. However, it was only from the 1970s onwards that they were recognized as legitimate EU social policy recipients. Reflecting the Commission's desire to expand the arenas of social policy and social policy developments at the member-state level, during the 1980s EU policies on the elderly, the disabled and youth began to make legislative and programmatic advances. By the 1990s all of these groups were mentioned in the treaties, to some degree, and each was supported by a growing number of European-level interest groups. However, as is clear from the above quotations, none of the representatives from these three NGOs was completely happy.

Despite some similarities between the three areas, the development of each and its potential for future expansion vary significantly. The weakest of the three policies is that for the elderly, who were an insignificant concern in EU social policy in the 1950s and 1960s and were not even recognized as an important social category until the 1974 Social Action Programme (SAP). From the mid-1970s to mid-1980s EU policy towards the elderly was little more than the occasional reference in the policy areas of social inclusion, social protection and pensions. The 1988 Social Charter and 1989 SAP brought the elderly back on to the EU agenda and led to the creation of a small action programme and some related legislation, but neither the Maastricht nor the Amsterdam treaties did much to enhance the breadth or role of policy on the elderly.

Similarly, the disabled were ignored in the early years of the EU. Some programmes were established in the late 1960s and the European Social Fund integrated some needs of disabled workers into its programmes. The role of the disabled was first highlighted by the 1974 SAP and resulted in the creation of a series of action programmes throughout the 1970s and 1980s. By the time the disabled were integrated into the 1988 Social Charter and the 1989 SAP, there were already several programmes for them. During the early 1990s action programmes continued to develop, particularly those integrating the disabled into the labour market, but there was little legislative progress. The disabled were ignored by the Maastricht Treaty, but briefly mentioned in the Amsterdam Treaty and the 1997 Employment Summit. Despite similar weak beginnings, policy towards the disabled has developed a stronger base in the treaties and more funding from the EU than that towards the elderly.

By contrast, youth policy has played a noticeable role in EU social policy since the earliest treaties. Young workers were mentioned in the 1958 Treaty of Rome. By the 1970s and 1980s, youth policy in the areas of vocational training, education and employment promotion had established a firm base in the Structural Funds and received substantial economic resources for their programmes. In the 1990s these three areas of youth policy were directly addressed in Title VIII of the Maastricht Treaty, making them among the most 'mainstreamed' and entrenched areas of EU social policy. However, outside these three areas, youth policy saw virtually no movement at all.

Policy on the elderly: failed entrenchment

As a social category, the elderly played a minimal role in EU social policy development in the 1950s and 1960s. They were not specifically mentioned in either the Treaty of Paris or the Treaty of Rome. At most they were expected to be beneficiaries of the ECSC and EEC and were affected only indirectly. For example, Articles 51 and 121 of the Treaty of Rome, designed to promote freedom of movement, did call for the elimination of discrimination in social security benefits (including pension rights) for internal EEC migrants, which would have provided some benefits for elderly migrants. Nevertheless, as a specific social group with distinctive needs they remained unseen at the European level. This was in stark contrast to the growing voice of elderly people and the increasing pension rights, health care and social protection which they were obtaining at the national level within Western Europe.[1]

The earliest references to the elderly in EU policy were generally as an aside to other issues and concentrated on the position of the elderly in the labour market. In the early 1960s the development of the European Miner's Charter called for increased pension provisions and seniority protection. In other areas such as social security and social provisioning, the growing rights of migrants to equal treatment on pensions, health care, old-age benefits and so on reflected a desire to promote free movement and to improve the conditions of older workers. By the mid-1960s, studies initiated by the ECSC began to demonstrate that older miners were having the most difficulty with new jobs in mining or in other fields. Consequently, they remained unemployed for longer periods of time and, early documents argued, should be granted preferential allowances (Collins, 1975: 50–2). This work, and the growing political influence of the elderly, was increasingly integrated into the functioning of the European Social Fund in the early 1970s. Following the reform of the ESF in 1970, it was given two main priorities: to support general Community policies and to help particular groups and areas experiencing economic distress. Included within the later priority area were proposals to help distressed regions and industries and 'the rehabilitation and specialised training of groups such as the handicapped, elderly, women and young workers' (Collins, 1975a: 74), thus making the elderly a distinctive category of worker with specific needs at the European level.

This focus on the needs of the elderly as workers was enhanced and expanded by the 1974 SAP. The Council Resolution which empowered the programme encouraged the Community 'to seek solutions to the employment problems confronting certain vulnerable categories of persons (the young and the aged)' (Commission, 1974: 8). However, in the SAP drawn up by the Commission a much broader interpretation of elderly policy was embraced. Strategies for co-ordinating social security schemes and eliminating discrimination against internal European migrants were developed. Furthermore, linked to plans for the continued 'erasing of pockets of poverty and hardship', the programme proposed the extension of 'social protection' to those individuals 'not covered or inadequately provided for under existing schemes' (Commission, 1974: 27). This proposal, attached to a related call for 'action against poverty', was to form the basis of the anti-poverty programmes which included the elderly as an important category. Moreover, the Commission proposed the 'dynamization' of social security benefits. This was a bizarre label for indexing social security benefits to inflation, which in the early 1970s was eating away at the value of pensions and threatening to push more and more elderly into poverty. The Commission proposed to convene a group of experts to discuss the problem and bring proposals to the Council by 1975. Finally, the Commission was concerned with 'the number of elderly workers who face premature retirement or down-grading to lower paid activities' (Commission, 1974: 29). The proposed solution was to integrate the needs of the elderly into the ESF and to consider later initiatives to support the elderly and other threatened groups.

On the one hand, the 1974 SAP had made the elderly a recognizable category in EU social policy. They could obtain support from the ESF, a significant and growing pot of EU money. Their poverty and social exclusion were highlighted, and special employment and labour market needs had been recognized. On the other, the elderly were largely assimilated into existing policy strategies rather than being perceived as an independent policy concern. Social security and pension issues were primarily a matter of freedom of movement. Problems of unemployment of the elderly remained a question of training policy. Elements of poverty of the elderly were the concern of anti-poverty policy. This contradictory balance between traditional market-oriented EU policy arenas and the extension of those arenas into social fields, as in other areas, was neither particularly coherent nor effective. It reflected the hopes of the Commission to expand the field of EU social policy, the lengths to which they had to go to justify that expansion, and the entrenched resistance of the member states to that expansion.

As with other social policy areas, elderly policy came to a near standstill from the mid-1970s to the late 1980s. The 1979 directive on equal treatment in matters of social security (Directive 79/7/EEC) had some implications for the pension rights of elderly women. In 1982 a Council Recommendation (82/857/EEC) developed standards for EC policy on retirement age. In the mid-1980s the Parliament continued to push resolutions on services for the elderly (OJ C 88/17, 14.4.1986) and to otherwise improve their situation (OJ C 148/61, 16.6.1986). However, beyond these areas little was accomplished. Even the 1983 reforms of the ESF were more concerned with growing youth unemployment and did little for the other end of the age spectrum.

Like most other 'extensions' of EU social policy, elderly policy was reborn in the 1988 Social Charter. Section 10 on social protection stressed that:

> Every worker of the European Community shall have a right to adequate social protection and shall . . . enjoy an adequate level of social security benefits.
>
> Persons who have been unable either to enter or reenter the labour market and have no means of subsistence must be able to receive sufficient resources and social assistance in keeping with their particular situation. (Commission, 1990: 15)

These minimum rights to social protection, security and assistance were of genuine significance. Furthermore, the Charter also included a distinctive section on the elderly which again concentrated on establishing their basic retirement, social protection and social assistance rights:

> Every worker of the European Community must, at the time of retirement, be able to enjoy resources affording him or her a decent standard of living.
>
> Any person who has reached retirement age but who is not entitled to a pension or who does not have other means of subsistence, must be entitled to sufficient resources and to medical and social assistance specifically suited to his needs. (Commission, 1990: 19)

If interpreted rigidly and fully implemented, these rights could have had a substantial impact on the lives of millions of European pensioners and elderly people, but at a significant and politically unacceptable cost. In attempting to develop a policy towards the elderly, the Delors Commission had to perform a delicate balancing act between developing meaningful proposals that would attract the support of elderly Europeans, and avoiding proposals that were too expensive and would be rejected in the Council.

Not surprisingly, the subsequent SAP fell well short of these rather grandiose social rights claims and returned to the traditional areas of training and employment oriented programmes for poverty alleviation. In the area of social protection, the 1989 SAP began by emphasizing that: 'The social security schemes vary greatly in nature . . . [and] reflect the history traditions and social and cultural practices proper to each Member State. . . . There can therefore be no question of harmonising the systems existing in these fields' (Commission, 1989: 27). Recognizing this diversity the Commission called for a new recommendation that would promote the 'convergence of objectives' of social protection rather than harmonization. How this convergence was to be accomplished and its consequences for the elderly was left undefined by the Commission! A second recommendation was proposed by the Commission for funding the fight against social exclusion, but again, how this should be done and paid for was left rather vague. However, in that proposal, the Commission did argue that the Community should 'take an initiative to assist the least advantaged citizens of the Community and the elderly in particular' (Commission, 1989: 28).

Similarly, in the section of the 1989 SAP which dealt directly with the elderly, the Commission recognized that the Community had paid little attention to the elderly in the past, because 'most action in this area falls within the direct responsibility of the Member States at national, regional or local level' (Commission, 1989: 51). Nevertheless, it proposed to develop an action programme for the elderly and promote 1993 as the European Year of the Elderly. Finally, to reiterate the primarily advisory nature of the EU's elderly policy, in the section on new initiatives the Commission stressed that 'it is not a question of the Commission's adopting legislation in an area in which approaches, traditions and culture vary greatly from one Member State to another' (Commission, 1989: 52). Overall, the Social Charter and 1989 SAP demonstrated that the Commission was determined to elevate the elderly within the categories of EU social policy. However, the Commission was also very careful not to tread on the national traditions of elderly policy, nor threaten hard-pressed member states with expensive new legislation or obligations to their elderly citizens. Elderly EU citizens were given a commitment of certain basic rights, but this was not supported with economic resources or legislative instruments.

From this limited foundation, elderly policy developed in a number of directions in the early 1990s. In 1990 and 1991 the Commission presented and the Council accepted a proposal for Actions for the Elderly (1991–3) (COM (90) 80 final). These were given three objectives (to develop preventative strategies for dealing with the problems of an ageing population, to strengthen solidarity between the generations, and to promote the potential of elderly citizens) and based on three main strategies (exchange of information, studies and database creation, and the creation of a European network). Salient actions included the creation of the European Observatory on Ageing and Older People for monitoring the demographic development of the EU and highlighting issues of the elderly and the designation of 1993 as the European Year of the Elderly and of Solidarity between Generations. With a small budget of 13 million ECU and no legislative agenda, these actions were likely to have minimal effects on the welfare of elderly Europeans.

The Maastricht Treaty did little to enhance the position of elderly policy in the EU. The elderly were not specifically mentioned in the treaty and the Social Protocol was the only area in the treaty which dealt with some areas that directly affected them. Article 2 of the Protocol encouraged the EU to develop policies to promote the 'integration of persons excluded from the labour market' (which included the elderly) and gave these proposals QMV status in the Council. However, Article 2 (section 3) reaffirmed that issues of 'social security and social protection of workers' would still be covered by UV procedures in the Council, and Article 7 required the Commission to make annual reports on the 'demographic situation' in the EU. Once again, social policies that affected the elderly were not designed with them in mind, but were offshoots of other traditional policy areas.

In the early 1990s EU policies which affected the elderly continued to develop, but not an EU elderly policy as such. In response to proposals made under the 1989 SAP, the Council passed two recommendations for the convergence and 'sufficient funding' of social protection objectives (91/442/EEC and 92/442/EEC). These recommendations emphasized the diversity of EU social protection regimes, but encouraged the member states to develop systems that led to convergent outcomes and to allocating sufficient resources to fund them. Regarding the elderly, these outcomes included guaranteeing a minimum level of resources, preventing social exclusion, providing basic working rights and decent pensions, and adapting pension systems to demographic changes. These were praiseworthy goals, but no money was allocated to support them, and beyond making further studies, encouraging information exchanges and making regular reports, no further action was promised. One exception to these general policy pronouncements was the creation of a programme called TIDE (technology initiative for disabled and elderly people) (Decision 93/512/EEC), which allocated 35 million ECUs during 1993–4 to promote 'rehabilitation technology' to enable the elderly and disabled to live more independently.

The 1993 Green Paper on social policy discussed issues of the ageing of European society and concerns over the growing pensions burden, but did not attempt to lay out any particular policy proposals other than vague references to 'intergenerational solidarity' and the need for flexible pensions. Unsurprisingly, there was little mention of elderly policies in the national responses to the Green Paper. Of the major member states, France was the only country to clearly state its support for a convergence of social protection policies. On the other hand, in a section addressing poverty, the elderly and the handicapped, the French argued that in these areas 'the main responsibility falls on Member States and local authorities' and that 'Community action needs to be co-ordinated around clear-cut objectives and programmes' (Commission, 1995: 73–4). Thus, even traditionally strong EU social policy supporters, like France, were unwilling to see substantial development of elderly policy at the EU level.

Consequently, the 1995–7 Medium-Term Social Action Programme offered no new proposals for elderly policy development, focusing instead on the general area of social protection and an extension of the existing action programme for the elderly. The 1995–7 programme reaffirmed the basic co-ordinating and facilitating nature of EU policy for social protection, noting the success of, and the Commission's continued support for, the MISSOC programme (mutual information on social protection), which was set up to develop a comparative database and to exchange information on national social protection systems. It reiterated the basic conclusions of the Commission's 1995 report on social protection (COM (95) 457 final), which was primarily a consultative document and did not offer any distinctive EU policy proposals. Furthermore, it reaffirmed the Commission's support for a second group of 'actions in favour of older people' (COM (95) 53 final). Stressing measures to support transnational activities and partnerships to promote the exchange of information and 'best practice', this second set of 'actions' was intended to build upon the activities of the 1993 European Year of Older People and Solidarity between Generations and support the development of European-level organizations concerned with the elderly. It had a proposed budget of 25 million ECUs for 1995–9, but with no QMV basis in the treaty, the proposal needed a unanimous vote in the Council in 1996. It was rejected and put into legislative limbo, similar to the fate of the 1994 anti-poverty programme.[2]

Most recently, the weakness of EU elderly policy was underlined by the Amsterdam Treaty and the 1998–2000 SAP. On the positive side, the treaty's Article 13 (consolidated treaties) gave the EU the ability to 'take appropriate action to combat discrimination based on sex, racial or ethnic origin, religion or belief, disability, *age* or sexual orientation' (my emphasis). However, as discussed in the previous chapter, the article did not have a direct effect or create a right to anti-discrimination, and confirmed that actions to combat discrimination must be based on a unanimous vote in the Council. A more important defeat occurred in the rewriting of Article 118 (Article 137, consolidated treaties). An early proposed version of the article, which lists policy areas that merit special attention and QMV status, included a reference to the elderly and disabled. Had it been approved, elderly policy would have obtained a firm QMV basis in the treaty. However, German and other member-state fears that this would lead to expensive claims on national and European resources resulted in the removal of the references to the elderly and disabled. Finally, the 1998–2000 SAP barely mentioned the elderly as a specific group. Under the section labelled 'An inclusive society', the document focused on the need to further EU efforts on promoting convergence in European social protection systems, and referred to its recent communication on the topic (COM (97) 102 final). Moreover, with the recent success of integrating demands for combating social exclusion and fighting discrimination into the Amsterdam Treaty, the document mentioned the elderly in the context of the development of programmes in these areas. However, no mention was made of the 1995 'actions in favour of older people', which remained in limbo. Most likely, the Commission will attempt to integrate the proposals in that document into the strategies for combating social exclusion and discrimination. It is unlikely that they will develop quickly or make a substantial impact in the near future.

Elderly policy remains one of the weakest areas of EU social policy. It began as an adjunct to traditional policy areas such as freedom of movement and employment policy and has only succeeded in expanding its influence by becoming an adjunct to social inclusion and anti-discrimination policy. Issues of social security have been kept off the EU agenda by firm resistance from the majority of member states. Undoubtedly, elderly policy is more visible than in the first three decades of EU integration, and EU-level organizations for the elderly have become increasingly vocal and influential (for example, Eurolink Age). Nevertheless, for the foreseeable future EU elderly policy will continue to be a weak adjunct to more successful policy areas, rather than a coherent policy area on its own.

Disability policy: partial 'mainstreaming'

Despite similarities between the early development of elderly and disability policy, in the 1980s and 1990s the disabled have been more successful at maintaining economic support for their programmes and entrenching disability issues within the EU policy process. This success has allowed them to partially mainstream disability issues within the EU policy process and maintain access to the ESF. However, EU disabled policy is not a major policy area and remains an adjunct, though an important one, to key policy areas of training and employment.[3]

Similar to elderly policy, EU disability policy was virtually non-existent in the 1950s and 1960s. The treaties of Paris and Rome made no mention of the disabled. As with the elderly, the working disabled, in theory, should have been able to benefit indirectly from the creation of the common market. Early references to the disabled emerged in training and employment proposals in the early and mid-1960s. In 1961 a Commission proposal for the creation of a European vocational training policy explicitly mentioned the disabled as one of several groups that should receive special attention (Collins, 1975a: 55–6). Moreover, studies in the mid-1960s performed by the ECSC confirmed that physically disabled miners had many more difficulties in gaining employment and re-employment (Collins, 1975: 50–1). In May 1963 the Council accepted a new Regulation (47/63/EEC) which broadened the definition of an 'unemployed worker' to include individuals who had lost their jobs due to physical or mental incapacity. This broader definition allowed the handicapped worker to take advantage of significant European vocational training funds. By 1965, 21 per cent of repayments for retraining schemes concerned disabled workers. By 1967, disabled workers were receiving nearly 42 per cent of all aid, while only representing 12 per cent of the total number of workers obtaining retraining.[4] Furthermore, the disabled were singled out for special attention in the 1971 reform of the European Social Fund (ESF) in which one of the two main priorities was 'providing support for . . . the rehabilitation of persons with disabilities' (Commission, 1998h: 14).

Again, similar to the elderly, the first clear reference to the disabled in a major social policy document occurred in the 1974 SAP, in which the Commission argued that 'the handicapped constitute a group which deserve immediate consideration by the Community as a whole' (Commission, 1974: 16). Of the seven 'immediate proposals' for action presented to the Council by the Commission, two (demands for greater assistance from the ESF to handicapped workers and the creation of an action programme for handicapped workers 'in the open market economy') dealt directly with the disabled. Furthermore, the Commission outlined plans for the creation of a 'long-term programme for the social reintegration of handicapped people', including the creation of 'vocational training and special employment facilities', a special programme addressing the 'housing needs of the handicapped' and 'further studies and seminars giving particular attention to local experiments to involve the severely handicapped in the life of the community'. The number of immediate proposals and clear demand for the creation of a long-term strategy indicated that the disabled were already beginning to gain more attention in the EC social policy process than the elderly.

Despite this greater emphasis in the 1974 SAP, disability policy fell prey to the general social policy stagnation during the late 1970s and early 1980s. It was not until 1981 that the first action programme for the disabled was finally adopted (Waddington, 1995: chapter 3). This small action programme (1983–7) concentrated on fostering 'more concerted and more imaginative action at the local level', rather than developing European-level policies to address problems of housing, training, employment and other areas of concern. The next major piece of EC disability policy legislation did not emerge until 1986. Following a memorandum from the Commission (COM (86) 9 final), the Council adopted a non-binding Recommendation and Guideline on the Employment of Disabled People in the European Community (86/379/EEC). The recommendation encouraged member states to 'take all appropriate measures to promote fair opportunities for disabled people in the field of employment and vocational training', to set realistic employment targets for the disabled and to adopt a guideline of positive actions towards their training and employment opportunities. Most important, the preamble to the recommendation asserted that 'disabled people have the same right as all other workers to equal opportunity in training and employment'. Although the action programme was small and the recommendation non-binding, any policy development during this period was a substantial achievement and a clear indication of the strength of disability policy.

The years 1988–9 represented a watershed for EC disability policy. They saw the creation of the second action programme for the disabled (HELIOS), the development of the HORIZON programme in the ESF, and the integration of the disabled into the Social Charter and subsequent Social Action Programme. When the first action programme for the disabled came to end in 1987, the Commission requested, and the Council accepted, its extension in April 1988 (Decision 88/231/EEC), before the acceptance of the Social Charter and 1989 SAP. The programme, titled HELIOS, was to run from 1988 to 1991 and followed closely in the footsteps of the previous programme. In order to 'promote the social integration and independent lifestyle of people with disabilities', it encouraged the fostering and dissemination of 'best practice' towards the disabled, promised to establish new strategies for using information technologies, and committed the EC to developing programmes for disabled women and the integration of disabled school children. Furthermore, during 1988 the Structural Funds were, once again, reformed. The new ESF was given a substantially enhanced role in funding projects for the disabled through the HORIZON programme. From 1989 to 1993, HORIZON allocated over 300 million ECU to programmes for 'improving job prospects for people with disabilities or at risk of exclusion from employment for other reasons' (Commission, 1998h: 21).

More important, disability policy was clearly recognized by the 1988 Social Charter and the 1989 SAP. Reaffirming the growing rights of the disabled, Section 26 of the charter stated: 'All disabled persons, whatever the origin and nature of their disablement, must be entitled to additional concrete measures aimed at improving their social and professional integration. These measures must concern, in particular, according to the capacities of the beneficiaries, vocational training, ergonomics, accessibility, mobility, means of transport and housing.' The subsequent 1989 SAP argued that the EC was already promoting these rights through the existing HELIOS programme and called for the extension and expansion of that programme for 1992–6. Further, it demanded a Council directive for the improvement of travel conditions for workers with disabilities, arguing that 'making it easier for disabled people to travel is an essential prerequisite for vocational training and employment' (Commission, 1989: 54). With the development of the charter and the 1989 SAP the vocational training and employment rights of the disabled were being increasingly entrenched in the EC policy process. Outside those areas, little was happening.

In the early 1990s a number of smaller legislative and programmatic developments occurred. In May 1990 the Council passed a resolution which encouraged member states to 'contribute to the social integration of the disabled through school integration . . . [and] encourage integration of pupils and students with disabilities, in all appropriate cases, into the ordinary education system' (OJ C 162, 3.7.1990). No funding was allocated for this resolution, but a report was to be issued on the progress of the member states in 1992. In early 1991, responding to its commitment in the 1989 SAP, the Commission published its proposal for a Council directive for improving mobility and transport services for the disabled (COM (90) 588 final). It argued that member states had to ensure that transport was 'available and accessible' and as affordable as other forms of public transport. With an eye to British opposition in the Council, it based the proposal on health and safety elements of Article 118a in the pre-Maastricht Treaty. However, this treaty basis was not accepted and the directive became bogged down in the legislative and amendments process.

The Maastricht Treaty was a disappointment for promoters of disability policy. No mention was made of the disabled in either the main body of the treaty or the Social Protocol. At best, the treaty provided some indirect gains. Theoretically, the needs of the disabled could be integrated into proposals for larger groups mentioned in the Social Protocol, such as 'persons excluded from the labour market'. The Commission could use its newly established QMV status in this area to develop disability policy. However, with this weak basis in the treaty and the various difficulties in passing the treaty itself and proposals made under the protocol, any disability policy development in this area was bound to be slow and limited.

However, major developments were occurring in the existing action programme (HELIOS) and the Structural Funds. As promised in the 1989 SAP, the Commission submitted proposals in 1992 for the extension and expansion of the HELIOS programme. In 1993 the Council agreed to support the HELIOS II programme for 1993–6 (Decision 93/136/EEC). HELIOS II was allocated 37 million ECU and given four main objectives: to develop and improve information activities with member states and NGOs, to co-ordinate and increase the effectiveness of existing programmes, to promote member-state policy co-operation and 'best practice', and to co-operate with and encourage European-level NGO activities. Linked to this programme was the development of the HANDYNET (Decision 94/872/EC) system (a computerized network of information for the disabled), the TIDE programme (Decision 93/512/EC), which was given a 35 million ECU budget to stimulate the creation of a European market in rehabilitation technology, and the foundation of the European Disability Forum (EDF). The EDF was funded by the HELIOS programme and designed to act as an umbrella organization and pressure group for the wide variety of NGOs in the EU (Hurst, 1995). Another major development was the 1993 review of the Structural Funds. Following that review, the former HORIZON programme, now labelled EMPLOYMENT-HORIZON, was allocated 730 million ECU for 1994–9, 'to improve the employment prospects of the disabled and other disadvantaged groups' (Commission, 1996b: 60). Overall, for the 1993–9 period, nearly 800 million ECU was to be allocated to the disabled and related groups.

Despite this success in generating economic support, disability policy made few gains in the legislative process through the mid-1990s. In a brief section, the 1993 Green Paper on social policy argued that in order to promote the social integration of the disabled, 'special facilities, institutions and legal rights are obviously necessary, but they should not be an obstacle or an alternative to the principle of 'mainstreaming' – that is to say acceptance of people as full members of society' (Commission, 1993: 48). However, other than reaffirming its commitment to the HELIOS programme, it did not list any new proposals. In the member-state responses to the Green Paper, Germany, Spain, France, Italy and even the UK expressed their firm support for the HELIOS and HORIZON programmes, but no interest in further legislation; only France supported the unresolved directive on transport for the disabled. The 1994 White Paper, though asserting that 'disabled people have the same right as all other workers to equal opportunity in training and employment', did little to go beyond existing programme commitments. Consequently, the 1995–7 Medium-Term Social Action Programme specified few actions for the disabled. With the HELIOS II programme ending in 1996, the Commission promised a thorough evaluation of the programme and a proposal for its continuation. Furthermore, the Commission promised that it would focus on the issue of employment and the disabled in the run-up to the 1997 Employment Summit, develop a code of good practice for employing the disabled, present a communication on the removal of discriminatory barriers, and a recommendation for the creation of disabled parking badges (COM (95) 696 final).

The next major development was the creation of the 1996 Communication on Equality of Opportunity for People with Disabilities (COM (96) 406 final). This proposal reviewed the obstacles to establishing equality of opportunity and presented a 'new' approach that moved away from traditional notions of social and economic compensation for the disabled towards a 'rights-based approach to disability'[5] that emphasized the mainstreaming of the disabled into all relevant areas of policy development. Included in this communication was a draft resolution for the Council and a set of guidelines for member-state action. Member states were encouraged to promote equal opportunity for the disabled through 'empowering' the disabled to participate in society, removing barriers to their participation, opening up 'various spheres of society' (mainly employment) and 'nurturing' public opinion towards the disabled. The resolution, which was approved in 1997 (OJ C 12, 13.1.1997), promoted a new approach to the disabled but did not allocate any further funds for them, nor demand further legislation. While important as an early attempt by the Commission to outline and promote a mainstreaming and rights-based approach to the disabled, in practical and legislative terms it remained limited.

This rights-based approach became a key rallying point for groups supporting disability policy during the Amsterdam Treaty negotiations. Unlike the failure of the Maastricht Treaty to mention the disabled, disability policy activists, particularly the European Disability Forum, were determined to force the rights of the disabled into the Amsterdam Treaty. At first, it seemed that their hopes would be answered. Building on earlier proposals, the Irish Presidency of the Council (July to December 1996) identified the creation of a non-discrimination clause as a priority and wanted it to have 'direct effect', giving it precedence over national law and allowing individuals to bring cases of non-discrimination to the ECJ. The Dutch Presidency (January to July 1997) discussed the possibility of integrating the disabled into internal market legislation in Article 100a and making it a priority of Article 118.[6]

Until the last minute, it appeared that the disabled would see a number of substantial gains in the treaty revisions. However, the final result was much less than they had hoped for, although better than the Maastricht Treaty. The disabled were integrated into the general non-discrimination clause in Article 13 (formerly 6a), which gave the Council (acting unanimously) the power to 'take appropriate action to combat discrimination based on . . . disability'. This was a significant step forwards, but did not imply that the Article had 'direct effect'. Moreover, instead of integrating a disability clause into Article 95 (formerly 100a), which would have put disability rights at the centre of EU policy-making, the member states would only accept a declaration attached to the end of the Treaty, stating 'The Conference agrees that, in drawing up measures under Article 95 (100a) of the Treaty establishing the European Community, the institutions of the Community shall take account of the needs of persons with a disability'. Like the elderly, the disabled were removed from the special categories for action in Article 137 (formerly 118) in the final draft of the treaty. Although included in the definition of groups 'excluded from the labour market', they were not entitled to receive more attention than any other excluded group. Opposition to a radical expansion of the rights of the disabled at the EU level appeared to be widespread, with Germany particularly opposed. Ultimately, the Amsterdam Treaty gave the disabled a deeper foothold in the treaties, but one which required further legislation to entrench a mainstreamed and rights-based approach.

Since the Amsterdam Treaty, disability policy has seen a number of research and programmatic developments, but no substantial legislative ones. In 1996 the European Disability Forum (EDF), supported by the Parliament and DGV, wrote a report entitled *Towards Equalisation of Opportunities for Disabled People: Into the Mainstream?* (European Disability Forum, 1996) to coincide with the 1996 European Day of Disabled Persons. The report provided a detailed review of the situation of the disabled in the EU, argued for a new EU disability programme, a strengthening of EU non-discrimination legislation, and an increased level of research activity from the EU and NGOs. In 1997 the EDF report *Manifesto by Disabled Women in Europe* was published and the PROMISE project, a development of the larger programme, 'Living and Working in the Information Society' (COM (96) 389 final), was created. The main aim of PROMISE was to produce case studies demonstrating how the information society might benefit the disabled and elderly.

In early 1998 the 1998–2000 SAP was presented and the disabled were integrated into the Employment Guidelines. The 1998–2000 SAP reaffirmed the Commission's support for the new 'European Disability Strategy' outlined in the 1996 Council recommendation and did not call for further legislation. The only piece of legislation regarding the disabled that was mentioned in the 1998–2000 SAP was the 1990 proposal for a directive on transport for the disabled, which was mentioned only in passing and was clearly not a priority of the Commission. As a member of the EDF mentioned during an interview in September 1998, the proposed transport directive was put into a 'vegetative state'. More importantly, following the conclusion of the November 1997 Employment Summit, the disabled were integrated into the 1998 Employment Guidelines. Under the section titled 'Strengthening the Policies for Equal Opportunities', Point 79 stated that the member states will 'give special attention to the problems people with disabilities may encounter in participating in working life'. This demand was vague and only one among many, but it was a significant victory for activists attempting to mainstream EU disability policy.[7] Unfortunately, it was rumoured that the position of the section on the disabled was under threat by gender activists who were demanding that 'equal opportunities' refer only to gender and that a second section should be designed for the disabled and other groups.

Finally, the position of programmes for the disabled and EU-level disability NGOs was greatly complicated by the results of the ECJ ruling in May 1998. This put several million ECU of project money for the disabled into legislative limbo; it was not until mid-1999 that a budget could be secured and new funds for the extension of the disability programme allocated. According to the experts in the EDF, the latest proposals from the EU were to consolidate all funding for excluded groups into one central programme, entitled EQUAL. The EDF was very cautious towards this development, fearing that overall spending on social policy programmes would be reduced and that the opportunity for entrenching a mainstreaming rights-based strategy for the disabled would diminish.

Overall, disability policy advanced significantly in the 1980s and 1990s. There are now a number of distinctive programmes to help the disabled and to promote their interests at the European level. Moreover, some progress has been made towards mainstreaming a rights-based approach to disability within the EU. Disabled persons are now mentioned in the treaty, are integrated into various policy areas, have built a substantial base in EU 'soft law', have a well-organized political base for promoting their interests at the European level, and seem well positioned to build on this base. As with other policy sub-areas, however, there is still no central piece of EU legislation, a directive or regulation, that would firmly establish disability rights within the EU, and no immediate prospect for one. Until that is created, the mainstreaming of EU disability policy is likely to remain only partly successful.

Youth policy: always part of the mainstream?

While the elderly and disabled were originally ignored, the founding treaties of the EU did mention the position of the young worker.[8] Early integration visionaries hoped that the young would provide a driving force for European integration (Deutsch, 1957). The Treaty of Paris did not mention the young, but the Treaty of Rome explicitly mentioned them in Article 50: 'Member States shall, within the framework of a joint programme, encourage the exchange of young workers'. This was not a substantial article or commitment to youth policy, but it did directly recognize the role of young workers in the creation of a common market. Other articles, including Article 118 which promoted the development of 'basic and advanced vocational training', and Article 125, which established the 'vocational retraining' priority in the ESF, did not mention the young directly, but would have substantial implications for later youth policy development.

Three related strands of youth policy evolved in the 1960s: vocational training, employment promotion and exchange schemes. Vocational training and employment promotion emerged out of the ECSC and the EEC. By the early 1960s it was becoming increasingly difficult to attract young workers to the coal mining industry. The rising level of education and expectations combined with the growth of new sectors of the modern West European economy led to a significant decline in young coal miners.[9] Although often offset by the employment of foreign or 'guest' workers, youth recruitment remained a concern of the industry during the 1960s. The response of the ECSC was to promote a system of vocational training to encourage the young to return to the mining industry. This emphasis on training did not have a strong foundation in the Treaty of Paris, but was more firmly entrenched in the Treaty of Rome. As early as 1961 the Commission was already sending proposals to the Council for the creation of a European vocational policy (Collins, 1975a: 55). These proposals recognized the diversity of vocational training systems but hoped to promote a more common and compatible approach. The Commission proposals also encouraged special provisions for the vocational training of the young. Despite some weakening, the proposals were accepted by the Council in 1963[10] and led to some early forms of transnational vocational policy creation.

More important, pursuant to Article 50 of the Treaty of Rome, the Commission quickly began to develop an exchange programme for young workers that included vocational training arrangements. The first programme was submitted to the Council in 1962, but confronted significant opposition which did not want to see it develop beyond existing bi-lateral agreements. The final result, which was not implemented until 1965, was a system of exchanges dominated by the member states and with virtually no common European vocational policy element (Collins, 1975a: 60–1). Between 1965 and 1971 over 15,000 young persons took part in various types of exchange schemes, but most of them were based on existing bi-lateral agreements (Collins, 1975a: 62). Other youth policy developments in the 1960s included the creation of a Commission recommendation calling for the establishment of minimum rights for young workers, and directives in 1964 that increased the rights of internal migrants to bring their families and children with them when they migrated and granted the children of migrants the right to be educated and obtain work in their new member-state home.

During the 1970s and early 1980s there were a few developments in youth policy, primarily along the established lines of vocational training, employment and exchange schemes. The 1971 reform of the ESF expanded the funding for vocational and employment programmes for the young. The 1974 SAP reiterated the parameters of existing youth policy. It promoted the extension of young worker exchange programmes and of educational and working rights for the children of migrants, called for the development of Community initiatives to deal with growing youth unemployment, and encouraged the ESF to expand programmes for youth training and employment. In response to these demands and the growing crisis of youth unemployment from the mid-1970s onwards, the EC developed several policies. In 1976 an education policy action programme was adopted (OJ C 38/1, 19.2.1976), encouraging member states to improve educational and training facilities, to promote educational and academic exchanges of individuals and information and to enhance the free movement of teachers, students and researchers. In 1977 a Council Decision (77/802/ EEC) created a special category in the ESF to support unemployed first-time job seekers under twenty-five years old, while a further Council recommendation encouraged the member states to make combating youth unemployment a top priority (Mallet and Milliat, 1997: chapter 8). In 1978 a Council Regulation ((EEC)3093/78) empowered the ESF to provide assistance to workers under twenty-five in jobs which provided training for permanent employment. Following the continued economic difficulties of the early 1980s and worsening youth unemployment, the member states agreed, once again, to restructure the ESF to address this problem (Council Decision 83/516/EEC). In 1982 young people accounted for 44 per cent of ESF beneficiaries. The 1983 ESF reforms required the member states to increase this to 75 per cent and focus their efforts on creating vocational training and work experience for those under eighteen, general vocational training for eighteen- to twenty-five-year-olds and job promotion schemes for the young in deprived regions (Commission, 1998h: 15). One author estimated that nearly 13 million young people benefited from ESF programmes between 1983 and 1989 (Mallet and Milliat, 1997: 228). Unfortunately, despite these efforts, EU policy appeared to have little impact on the major problems of youth unemployment and education needs. However, in a period of 'Eurosclerosis', any policy movement was a significant achievement and an indication of the strength of education- and employment-related aspects of youth policy.

The late 1980s and early 1990s marked a watershed for EU youth policy. In these years youth-related policies continued to expand in the ESF and were integrated into the Social Charter, while youth-related programmes proliferated. In the aftermath of the SEA and the integration of two new member states, the Structural Funds were again reformed in 1988. The result of this reform for youth policy was that among the fund's five main objectives were 'combating long-term unemployment' (which had a large youth component) and finding 'employment pathways for young people'; these two had a combined budget of 6.7 billion ECU for 1989–93. Furthermore, the 1989 Social Charter had a number of youth policy elements. It promised that 'every worker of the European Community must be able to have access to vocational training'. Although young workers were already well served by EU policies in this area, this recognition further enhanced their position. More importantly, the charter made a special note of promoting 'protection of children and adolescents'. These protections included: minimum employment age (not under fifteen); equitable remuneration; special access to training and employment; limited work duration and night work; and 'sufficient' initial vocational training. The subsequent 1989 SAP called for a series of new vocational policy initiatives to improve access to vocational policy, promote a common European vocational policy, and encourage youth exchanges and comparability of job qualifications, and one significant new directive on the protection of young people in the workplace.

Built upon or linked to the proposals in the 1989 SAP, a substantial list of youth-related programmes, primarily linked to employment, exchanges and education/vocational training soon emerged. For 1986–94 these included the following:[11]

COMETT (1986–95) (206.6 mecu)	Programme on cooperation between universities and industry regarding training in the field of technology
FORCE (1991–4) (31.3 mecu)	Action programme for the development of continuing vocational training in the EC
PETRA (1988–94) (79.7 mecu)	Action programme for the vocational training of young people and their preparation for adult and working life
ERASMUS (1987–95) (307.5 mecu)	EC action scheme for the mobility of university students
TEMPUS (1990–4) (194 mecu)	Trans-European mobility scheme for university studies
LINGUA (1990–4) (68.6 mecu)	Action programme to promote foreign language competence in the EC
EUROTECNET (1990–4) (7 mecu)	Action programme to promote innovation in the field of vocational training resulting from technological change in the EC
YOUTH FOR EUROPE (1988–94) (32.2 mecu)	Action programme for the promotion of youth exchanges in the Community – 'Youth for Europe' programme
IRIS (1988–95) (0.75 mecu)	European network of vocational training projects for women

Source: Rees 1998:125

The total funding for the programmes of 1987–95 totalled nearly 1 billion ECU. While most dealt with training, education and employment and not all were aimed directly at the young, within EU social policy these were substantial programmes with significant resources. In 1995 a number of these programmes were subsumed into the Leonardo da Vinci vocational training programme (Council Decision 94/819/EEC), designed to co-ordinate and increase the impact of training policy. It maintained the former programmes' strong youth orientation and was allocated a budget of 620 million ECU for 1995–9. Two other programmes established in 1995 were the 1995–9 Socrates programme

(Council Decision 95/819/EEC), to promote the European dimension in higher education and to fund student mobility grants, and the 1995–9 Youth for Europe III programme (Council Decision 95/818/EEC), to encourage educational and work-related exchange activities.

Despite these impressive programmatic developments and resources, youth policy legislation remained limited outside the areas of education, training and employment. Most outside developments areas were linked to other policy fields, including the creation of the European Observatory on National Family Policies in 1989, the 1992 Council Recommendation on Childcare (92/241/EEC), and the 1996 Daphne initiative 'to combat violence against children, adolescents and women' (COM (98) 335 final). Of these, the first was a small-scale attempt to create an EU family policy, while the second two were clearly linked to EU gender policy. Even youth policy proposals made by the social partners through the social dialogue never stepped beyond traditional boundaries.[12]

The inability to go beyond established areas of youth policy was clearly reflected in the Maastricht Treaty. The term 'youth' was explicitly mentioned in Title VIII, chapter 3, 'Education, Vocational Training and Youth'. However, the subsequent Articles 126 and 127 held to the traditional educational/vocational training approach to youth policy. Article 126 stated that EU actions should be aimed at 'developing the European dimension in education . . . encouraging mobility of students and teachers . . . promoting co-operation' and other basic, well-established and accepted areas of educational collaboration. Article 127 called for an EU vocational training policy that would 'facilitate adaptation to industrial change . . . improve initial and continuing vocational training . . . facilitate access to vocational training . . . stimulate co-operation . . . and develop exchanges of information and experience'. Again, all of these areas were examples of established and accepted vocational policy activity and were given QMV status. Although these articles did little to further youth policy outside its traditional areas, by giving those areas a firm base with the treaties and QMV status they increased the prospects for future development.

Youth policy after Maastricht continued in its established direction, with the major exception of the 1994 Young Workers Directive creating a number of basic labour rights for young people. The 1993 Green Paper did little more than discuss the employment problems, vocational training requirements and educational needs of the young. Consequently, in summarizing the member-state responses to the Green Paper, the Commission duly noted: 'it is generally felt that young people should receive more assistance in the transition from education to working life' (Commission, 1995: 10). These sentiments were also reflected in the 1993 review of the Structural Funds. Again, Objectives 3 and 4 were aimed primarily at the vocation and employment needs of young people, while the budget for these areas was significantly expanded to 15.2 billion ECU for 1994–9. A special initiative within the ESF, entitled Employment-Youthstart, was allocated over 300 million ECU specifically for vocational training and employment development of people under twenty.

A further indication of the strength of the traditional areas of youth policy appeared in the position of youth policy in the 1994 White Paper on EU social policy. Instead of being lumped in with the other categories of social policy recipients at the back of the document, they were brought to the front and linked to key areas of employment and training. The document called for the creation of a 'Union-wide guarantee' of training or education for all people of eighteen and under, the expansion of training and apprenticeship programmes, and a general promotion of vocational training and its status. The 1995–7 SAP reaffirmed the increased status of these traditional areas and the success of existing programmes, but not a single legislative or programme proposal outside these areas was made. On the one hand, the firm treaty foundations and successful mainstreaming of the traditional areas of youth policy made it easy for policy activists to use these areas as an inroad to youth policy development. On the other, with no base in the treaty and little political support, youth policy outside these areas was a dead end. For a proposal to make progress in the EU system, it had to be positioned within the traditional areas.

During the mid- to late 1990s, the uneven nature of EU youth policy continued. Programmes in traditional areas were strengthened as youth policy was increasingly integrated into basic EU employment strategies. New programmes included Learning in the Information Society (COM (96) 471 final), Towards a Europe of Knowledge (COM (97) 536 final) and European Voluntary Service for Young People (COM (96) 610 final). The situation was reaffirmed by the Amsterdam Treaty. With education, vocational training, and youth employment already integrated into the treaty, there was little for the Amsterdam Treaty to add. The new employment section to the Amsterdam Treaty endorsed the existing employment orientation, while no additions were made to the education, training and youth chapter in the treaty. More important, the 1997 Essen Employment Summit put commitments to youth training, employment and easing the transition from school to work at the top of the list for member-state priorities. According to the 1998 Employment Guidelines, member states should provide every unemployed young person with a 'new start' in the form of training or job promotion every six months. Moreover, national school systems should be encouraged to reduce the number of dropouts and encourage the development of skills relevant to the job market. None of these proposals was either divisive or innovative. They all confirmed the importance of traditional areas of youth policy and made no mention of other areas. Finally, the 1998–2000 SAP reaffirmed the traditional areas of youth policy, but hardly mentioned the young outside these areas. Even as a category of the socially excluded, they hardly receive any attention and no legislative proposals in non-traditional areas were made.

To summarize, EU youth policy exhibits a remarkably divergent structure. On the one hand, traditional areas of youth policy, employment, vocational training and education have enjoyed substantial programmatic and legislative success. From only a brief mention in the original treaties, they have been integrated into the mainstream of general EU policy, obtained QMV status, gained substantial funding through the Structural Funds, evolved a broad array of specific programmes and have become the political equivalent of a 'motherhood and apple pie' issue. Different sides of the political spectrum and nearly all member states support these areas. As they prosper, they increasingly act as a cover for proposals from other social policy areas. However, outside these traditional areas youth policy has vanished. Other than as recipients of education, training and/or employment initiatives, the young are not seen as a distinctive category. The EU continues to fund a number of European-level youth organizations, particularly the European Youth Forum. However, these groups have been unable to popularize other areas of youth policy and remain a relatively weak voice in the EU social policy process.

At its founding, the EU paid scant attention to non-labour market social categories. During the 1950s and 1960s there were only occasional references to the elderly and the disabled. The young received more attention, but primarily in regard to their position in the labour market. Early calls for more vocational training, mobility and employment opportunities were easily combined with the basic common market strategy. The 1974 SAP saw the explicit recognition of these three social groups in EU policy. However, only in the traditional areas of youth policy was there significant development during the 1970s and early to mid-1980s. The 1988 Social Charter and the 1989 SAP reasserted the importance of these social categories in EU social policy. Various legislative proposals and programmes were developed, but with a substantial variation in their success and influence. In general, policy on the elderly was the least successful. Though promoted by the Commission and strengthened by growing European-level NGO activity, it never established a firm base in the treaties. Moreover, member states, confronting mounting national pension costs and welfare state burdens, were extremely unwilling to see policy on the elderly develop at the EU level, where the disabled were able to make a few more strides. Disability policy was integrated into the treaty, though weakly, and it continued to receive significant funding for its programmes through the Structural Funds. Further, some smaller legislative proposals were passed. Nevertheless, neither of these two groups obtained the fundamental 'social rights' status which they enjoy in the member states. The promotion of a mainstreaming and social rights approach remains the key strategy of European NGOs concerned with the elderly and disabled. Youth policy reflects a dualistic evolution. On one side, traditional youth policy areas have been main-streamed into the EU policy process, received substantial economic support via the Structural Funds and independent programmes, and have become so deeply entrenched that the 1996 ECJ case which hobbled the action programmes of the elderly and disabled in 1998 could not touch them. On the other, non-traditional youth policies areas have remained completely underdeveloped. In essence, the EU wants the young to be educated, skilled and then employed. Beyond that, it has paid no attention. Overall, of these three groups the elderly appear to be the least likely to benefit from future policy and programmatic developments, while some progress should be made by the disabled. Meanwhile, traditional areas of youth policy should keep their central position in EU social policy, while non-traditional areas show no signs of development.

9

The Future of European Social Policy

And good sense dictates . . . [that] the economy should bring progress to society, not the other way around.

Jacques Delors, *Conference on the Future of European Social Policy, 1994*

EU social policy is a remarkably diverse and complicated area of EU policy and politics. As the title of this book implies, this work is primarily an exploration. Its central strategy has been to map the contours of EU social policy, to update earlier studies and to provide the foundation for further research in this area. In this concluding chapter I briefly summarize the current 'map' of EU social policy, explore some implications of the shape of this map on current debates in EU social policy and discuss the possible future of that policy area.

The 'map' of EU social policy

The following two lists provide a general outline of the main sub-areas of EU social policy. Again, I would like to emphasize that they are not intended to be complete. In fact, the very definition of the boundaries of social policy is fraught with uncertainty. Nevertheless, this selection represents most of the main contours of EU social policy:

	Original base in the treaties	*Selected current base in consolidated treaties*	*Attained QMV status under:*
Free movement	EEC (Art. 3c, 7, 48–51)	Art. 3, 14, 39–42 61–9	SEA (Art. 7)
Health and safety	ECSC (Art. 3, 35) EEC (Art. 117, 118)	Art. 3, 136, 137, 140	SEA (Art. 118a)
Employment rights	No direct reference until Maastricht	Art. 137	Unanimous voting
Working conditions	ECSC (Art. 3) EEC (Art. 117, 118)	Art. 137	SEA (Art. 118a)
Worker participation	No direct reference until Maastricht	Art. 137	Maastricht Social Protocol (Art. 2)
Social dialogue	ECSC (Art. 46, 48) EEC (Art. 193–8 creating ESC)	Art. 136, 139	Maastricht Social Protocol (Art. 4)
Gender	EEC (Art. 119)	Art. 13, 137, 141	Maastricht Social Protocol (Art. 2)
Anti-poverty	EEC (Art. 2, 3)	Art. 136, 137	Maastricht Social Protocol (Art. 2)
Anti-racist discrimination	No direct reference until Amsterdam	Art. 13	Unanimous voting
Public health	No direct reference until SEA (Art. 100a, 130r)	Art. 3, 152	Maastricht (Art. 129)
Elderly	No direct reference until Amsterdam	Art. 13	Unanimous voting
Disability	No direct reference until Amsterdam	Art. 13 and Declaration at end of Amsterdam	Unanimous voting
Youth	EEC 50, 118, 125	Art. 149, 150	Maastricht (Art. 126, 127)

	Significant access to Structural Funds/ funded action programmes	*Number of significant legislative acts (high 10+, medium 10–5, low 5–0)*	*Probability of future policy expansion*
Free movement	yes/yes	high	medium
Health and safety	yes/yes	high	medium
Employment rights	no/no	low	low
Working conditions	no/no	medium	medium
Worker participation	no/no	low	low
Social dialogue	yes/yes	high	medium
Gender	yes/yes	high	high
Anti-poverty	yes/no	low	low
Anti-racist discrimination	yes/yes	low	low
Public health	no/yes	medium	medium
Elderly	yes/yes	low	low
Disability	yes/yes	low	low
Youth	yes/yes	high	high

As explored in chapter 3, freedom of movement and health and safety policy have deep roots in the historical foundations of the EU and have evolved into substantial fields of legislation, particularly following their attainment of QMV status within the Council during the SEA. Both are significantly integrated into the Structural Funds criteria, have independently funded action programmes, and are supported by observatories, research institutes and interest groups. Moreover, they are firmly entrenched in EU law. Overall, these areas are well established and firmly entrenched within the EU institutions and, as such, one would expect to see continued policy development. However, their success is also an indirect limitation. If these policy areas were to expand substantially, they would begin to raise much more difficult questions, costs and political dynamics. Thus, I would expect both to experience only a medium-level policy expansion.

The labour policy extensions outlined in chapter 4 present a mixture of potential policy developments. With no mention in the early treaties, unanimous voting in the Council, no access to the Structural Funds or a funded action programme, and a low level of legislation, employment rights seem unquestionably set for few future developments. This is accentuated by the fact that the last significant piece of legislation in this area was passed as long ago as 1980. In contrast, working conditions were briefly mentioned in the early treaties and obtained QMV under the SEA. However, due to its poor access to the Structural Funds and the lack of an action programme, I would expect to see only an intermediate level of future policy development. Worker participation did not have a basis in the earlier treaties and did not emerge until the activity of the 1970s and 1980s. It did gain QMV status under the Maastricht Treaty, but without access to the Structural Funds, an action programme and a significant legislative base, there are unlikely to be momentous developments in this area. Finally, although the social dialogue has a deep historical foundation in the EU treaties and institutions (particularly in relation to the Economic and Social Committee), it did not begin to develop significantly until the 1990s. The dialogue has led to a small number of legislative developments, but with the continued difficulty of obtaining agreements between the key social partners (ETUC and UNICE), legal challenges by other trade unions and business organizations to the exclusive nature of the dialogue, and the end of the British opt-out (undermining some of the justification of the social dialogue), it is unlikely to see a policy output beyond this level.

Gender policy has been one of the most successful policy areas. Though mentioned in the Treaty of Rome, it did not begin to develop until the late 1960s. Distinctively, even before its attainment of QMV status in the Maastricht Treaty it had already obtained a high level of policy achievement through the activities of key gender policy supporters and the promotion of gender rights through the ECJ. With this substantial base, access to the Structural Funds, an action programme and a significant legislative base, one would expect to see continued policy development in this area.

Anti-poverty, anti-racist discrimination and public health policy are all recent additions to the EU social policy agenda and have only brief histories in EU policy development (anti-poverty from the 1970s, anti-discrimination and public health from the 1980s). Their position in the Council has generally improved in the 1990s; anti-poverty and public health policy were given QMV status by the Maastricht Treaty. Anti-discrimination policy against racism still requires unanimous voting procedures. Financially, they represent a mixture. Anti-poverty strategies have access to the Structural Funds but lack an action programme; anti-discrimination policy against racism has both, while public health policy does not have access to the Structural Funds, but does have a substantial action programme. The legislative output for anti-poverty and anti-discrimination policy has been low, while public health policy has been medium. Overall, for anti-poverty policy, which was substantially weakened by the rejection of the Fourth Poverty Programme in 1994, and anti-discrimination policy, which still retains the hurdle of UV procedure in the Council, the expectations for future policy development are low. Public health policy is not powerful. However, due to its firm base in the Maastricht and Amsterdam treaties, the growth of European public health concerns and the consensual nature of its policy areas related to disease control, public health policy should continue to see an intermediate level of policy activity.

Policies on the elderly and disabled present very similar dynamics and positions. Both emerged out of the political demands of the 1970s, developed action programmes and were integrated into the Structural Funds in the 1980s and remain constrained by unanimous voting in the Council. This weak treaty and legal base has clearly constrained their legislative output. Despite their reference in Article 13 of the Amsterdam Treaty I would not expect to see significant policy expansion in these areas in the near future. By contrast, traditional youth policy (training, education and employment), with its firm basis in the early treaties, QMV status, action programmes, substantial access to the Structural Funds and significant legislative base, will undoubtedly continue to make headway in its output. On the other hand, non-traditional areas of youth policy show no indication of further development.

The general impression which this 'map' gives of EU social policy is that it has an intermediate position in the history of the EU. Most of its policy areas did not obtain a treaty base and QMV status until the 1990s. Only a few areas, particularly gender issues, have made a significant impact through the ECJ. The current level of its policy development and funding base is low to medium. Its legislative output is medium. Finally, expectations for its future development are primarily low to medium.

Implications for EU social policy

In the preceding chapters I have only hinted at the multitude of debates that surround the development of EU social policy. Every subfield of social policy is filled with fascinating questions and political debates to explore. My intention was never to answer all these questions, but to provide academics and policy practitioners with an accessible foundation which they could use to explore their own particular questions. Nevertheless, despite the introductory nature of this work, the process of mapping EU social policy has given me six main insights into its nature and future.

(1)   *EU social policy is not like national-level social policy.* West European national social policy regimes emerged out of a variety of distinctive, primarily national factors. The emergence and expansion of civil, political and social citizenship rights, strategies for national unification, struggles between capital and labour, religious divisions, gender relations, the impacts of war and so on all played important roles in the formation of particular social policy regimes. The distinctiveness of these regimes and the difficulty in comparing them has been widely recognized. At best, West European welfare states can be divided into broad ideal-typical types (Esping-Andersen, 1990). However, even this remains problematic.

As demonstrated by the EU social policy 'map', EU social policy is distinct from all three of these models. EU social policy lacks the breadth, depth, legitimacy and financial muscle of these ideal types. Further, its influence is remarkably varied, depending on the social policy area and the different dynamics of member-state social policy regimes. An obvious example of the latter dynamic would be the variable influence of EU Works Council's directives on Britain and Sweden. For Britain, with no tradition of works councils, the EU directive brought about a substantial change in British industrial relations (Geyer and Springer, 1998). For Sweden, with a long tradition of worker representation at firm level, the EU directive was meaningless.

(2)   *EU social policy has become increasingly regulatory.* With limited finances (except for the ESF) and implementation capabilities, EU social policy relies on the willingness of member states to finance and carry out many of its policies and focuses on creating a system of policy rules and regulations rather than directly implementing policy outcomes. This regulatory nature has led to a growing importance and reliance on the activities of the ECJ to act as an actor and arena for social policy promotion, and has led to a number of comparisons with the structure of policy formation of the federal government in the USA (Majone, 1996). In the 1990s, the term 'neo-voluntarism' has been increasingly used to define the regulatory nature of EU social policy (Streeck, 1996). The regulatory/neo-voluntarist nature of EU social policy further distinguishes it from the other three ideal types of national social policy regimes. As such, blithe comparisons of the EU's social policy structure with that of the three ideal types often leads to confusing and over-generalized conclusions. It is something new and different!

(3)   *EU social policy exhibits a variety of policy dynamics.* After noting that EU social policy does have a strong regulatory/neo-voluntarist structure, it is essential to remember that its component parts demonstrate a variety of dynamics that cannot be reduced to any

one theory. Federalist hopes and dreams have played a significant role in inspiring social policy developments. How else could Delors justify his vision of a balanced social and economic EU development without the underlying recognition of some element of federalism? Neo-functionalism and the impact of 'spillover' can be seen in a variety of policy areas. The development of the social dimension spilling over from the success of the SEA, the expansion of labour policy from its strict focus on mobility and health and safety, and the extension of social policy into anti-poverty, anti-discrimination and public health are all clear indicators of the spillover dynamic. At the same time, intergovernmentalism has continued to play an essential role in limiting social policy formation, as demonstrated by the 1994 rejection of the Fourth Poverty Programme, the UK's social policy opt-out in the Maastricht Treaty, the continued influence of the member states in the allocation of the ESF, and a multitude of other obvious examples. Clearly, there is no general theory of EU social policy development. The importance of institutions, the multi-level structure of the policy process, the variable relationship between national- and EU-level policy areas, and other factors all combine to create the variable development of the different areas of EU social policy. At a theoretical level, the result is that, as Wayne Sandholtz has argued: 'it is probably pointless to seek a single theory of European integration that can capture its dynamic evolution. ... Rather, we should probably admit that different kinds of theories are appropriate for different pieces of the EU puzzle' (Sandholtz, 1996: 427). This recognition of theoretical complexity is not easy for students of EU policy. The EU policy process is remarkably complex, and tracing the development of policies within that process is difficult enough. Added to that difficulty is the need to compare and contrast different theoretical explanations for those policy developments. It can be done (Geyer, 1996), but it is difficult and leaves the student of EU policy with little confidence in making broader comparisons and conclusions.

(4)   *EU social policy is becoming increasingly interest-group-led.* Emerging mostly out of the 1980s and 1990s, EU social policy interest groups have had a growing influence on European social policy, particularly gender policy. All of the main arenas of social policy have active interest groups that have varying degrees of influence in the policy process. However, these groups remain very dependent on the Commission. This relationship to the Commission is both a strength and a weakness. Most EU social policy groups are funded by the Commission. They gain strength and legitimacy from this at the same time as the Commission creates a political base for its social policy activities. It is very unlikely that the Commission will be able to expand the

level of support for social policy groups in the foreseeable future. Therefore, these groups will need to expand their own economic and political foundations. This will not be easy, and will be particularly difficult
for certain social policy groups which represent the weakest and poor-
est sections of society. Thus, although interest groups are playing a
growing role in the social policy process, one is unlikely to see fully
developed interest group politics as in the USA.

(5) *Mainstreaming EU social policy will likely produce mixed results.* Mainstreaming has proved to be an effective strategy for some
areas of EU social policy. In a period of strong economic constraints,
it offered a cheap way of integrating social issues, particularly gender,
into core EU policy areas. It is also a good strategy for keeping the
spotlight on social policy issues and for bringing social policy actors
into the policy process. However, due to the problems of mainstreaming
competition and overload (Geyer, 1999a) mainstreaming can work
for only a limited number of policy areas. In essence, mainstreaming is
a form of privileging. If social policy groups are able to work together,
they may be able to raise the general profile and impact of social policy.
However, they will also be strongly tempted to maximize their groups'
interests to the detriment of others.

(6) *EU social policy is not significantly replacing or undermining
national-level social policy.* One of the major conclusions of recent
research on West European welfare states and social policy regimes is
the remarkable popularity and resilience of these regimes in the face of
substantial internal and external challenges in the 1980s and 1990s.
Globalization, Europeanization and the growth of postmodern issues
and concerns have all confronted the traditional West European welfare states with a number of challenges and difficulties. These social
policy regimes have adapted to these challenges in a variety of ways,
depending on the particular structure of the regime and specific challenges confronting it. Nevertheless, there is no clear sign pointing to a
collapse of West European social policy regimes, nor any clear indication of their converging around a given model. In short, the evidence
seems to indicate that for the foreseeable future national welfare states
and social policy regimes will retain their influence, size and distinctiveness.

When this realization is combined with the recognition of the weakness and unevenness of EU social policy, demonstrated in the lists at
the beginning of this chapter, two main implications for West European social policy present themselves. First, it is extremely unlikely
that EU social policy will soon replace existing national social policies. During the 1980s, when the forces of globalization were rapidly
emerging and national economic policies were becoming increasingly

difficult to maintain, a branch of Europeanist socialist/social democratic thinking emerged that hoped that the EU might serve as a future
arena for the recapturing of the lost powers of the nation-state. In
theory, in order to combat the growing European and international-
level economic forces, European-level state and social controls would
have to develop to replace fading national ones. As David Martin,
Vice-President of the Socialist Group in the Parliament, wrote: 'Europe's traditional commitment to a high level of social development is
well known. The commitment must now be developed on a European
scale. The development of a *European social dimension* therefore con-
stitutes . . . [a] major item of the left's agenda' (Martin, 1989: 116;
emphasis in original). However, despite the efforts and hopes of
Europeanist social democrats, the EU has failed to develop a social
policy that even begins to rival the most basic of West European social
policy regimes. EU social policy will continue to set minimum standards, encourage member-state and interest group co-operation, promote 'best practice' and respond to specific European social policy
demands. In certain areas, particularly health and safety, vocational
training, mobility and gender policy, for example, the impact of EU
social policies will be quite substantial. In others, such as worker participation, poverty alleviation and anti-discrimination policy, its impact will be negligible. Overall, its regulatory orientation, minimal
financing, weak legitimacy, dependence on the member states, and the
general weakness of social policy promoters at the EU level, confirms
its incapacity to replace national-level social policy.

The second main implication is that EU social policy does not appear to be substantially undermining existing national social policies.
Despite the fears of social dumping, a competition of standards and/or
a competitive dynamic of social deregulation, national welfare states
and social regimes have been notably able to maintain their distinctive
developmental paths (disproving the assumptions of convergence) and
their overall level of provision and social coverage (disproving fears of
overall social policy decline and retrenchment). With its regulatory/
neo-voluntarist orientation and financial and institutional weaknesses,
EU social policy appears to be most similar to the Anglo-American
welfare state model. This, as Wolfgang Streeck argued, could mean
that 'supranational neovoluntarism may help gradually transform national social policy regimes from social-democratic models into more
liberal ones' (Streeck, 1995: 431). This is clearly a concern for West
European social democrats and supporters of the West European social model. However, as just argued, national regimes have remained
sufficiently resilient in the face of global and European dynamics to
maintain their distinctive developments. Furthermore, EU social policy

remains too weak to substantially undermine or rescue the West European welfare state. In essence, instead of viewing the EU as a powerful replacement for or threat to West European welfare states and social regimes, it is best seen as a facilitator for national-level welfare state adjustment to challenges at the international and European level. *Instead of harmonizing national-level social policy regimes, EU social policy may actually encourage them to diversify.*

The next wave of EU social policy research

As argued in my opening chapters, the next wave of EU social policy research should be directed towards the interaction of EU social policy and national social policy regimes. Distinctive national social policy regimes are neither vanishing nor converging. Moreover, EU social policy is in no position to significantly undermine or replace these regimes. The impact of EU social policy will clearly vary depending on the particular policy area and the dynamics of a distinctive member state's social policy regimes. This is a vast new field of comparative policy studies that has significant implications for European and international studies. Given the difficulty and complexity of detailed comparisons between fifteen or more member states, researchers will necessarily drift towards using comparisons of ideal types of regimes. I intend, and also encourage others, to pursue this strategy to build a detailed understanding of the interaction between the EU and member-state policy regimes.

The lists on pp. 204 and 205 outline my specific and general expectations for the future of EU social policy. For the present, EU social policy development will continue to be uneven, but will maintain a low- to medium-level development trajectory. This will obviously depend on a number of key developments, including the overall development of the EU, the success or failure of EMU and the integration of the new member states of Eastern Europe. As shown in earlier chapters, successful EU social policy has often been coterminous with the success of general EU policy developments. If the EU were to experience a significant period of stagnation, I would certainly expect EU social policy to go through a similar process. Likewise, EMU has the potential for greatly complicating the economic burdens and financial bases of national-level welfare states. As recently explored by Paul Teague, the existing monetary and budgetary policy restrictions in the EMU criteria 'would not add up to the complete dismantling of welfare provision, but it could involve large-scale cutbacks [of European social systems]. Europe would probably experience a decisive shift toward an American-type economic system where the social safety net is thin and the private insurance sector plays a key role' (Teague, 1998: 136).

Similarly, with their crippled economies and substantially weaker social policy regimes, the addition of the Eastern European member states will put a substantial strain on the future of EU social policy and on the social policy regimes of some member states. An obvious example would be the economic and social costs of integrating mobile Eastern European workers into the high skill/social protection economies of Western Europe, particularly the German economy (which is already struggling to readapt the workforce of the former communist East Germany). How the EU deals with these major challenges will be an essential element in setting the stage for future EU social policy expansion or stagnation. Other, more specific, factors include: the political composition of key member states; the growth of social policy linkages to the EU legal system and implications of 'soft law'; the success of mainstreaming; the growing influence of the Parliament; and the increasing impact of social policy pressure groups.

Clearly, EU social policy is a diverse and dynamic policy area which is likely to play an increasingly important role in the future of the European social model. However, it is neither the primary solution to nor the cause of the challenges confronting national-level social policy regimes. Like the EU itself, it both undercuts and supports national-level dynamics. In the end, its fate remains uncertain and contingent. However, with effort, we can get an idea of what it looks like, what it is not, and the general direction it appears to be going.

Appendix: Accessing EU Social Policy

My assumption throughout this book has been that readers are well versed in the basic functioning of the European Union, aware of its fundamental institutions, and familiar with its essential policy-making processes. With the revival of the EU in the 1980s and the intellectual and academic resurgence of European integration studies, there is now a significant choice of works in all major aspects of EU institutions, politics and policy. I will make no attempt to select the main works in these areas. The reader can easily browse through the index or their library catalogue to find a wealth of options.

Instead, I would like to mention the growing array of internet websites that offer key information on the EU and its policies. They can act as a gateway to both detailed policy knowledge (essential for the researcher lacking easy access to a European Documentation Centre) and up-to-date developments and press releases (for those living outside the EU or who do not have access to EU oriented newspapers).

http://www/europeanaccess.co.uk
EuropeanAccess provides an excellent overview of policy areas with one of the best collections of links to other EU information sites. The links to social policy organizations are particularly useful. Some of these links are:

European Women's Lobby   http://www.womenlobby.org
European Disability Forum   http://www.edf.unicall.be
Eurolink Age   http://www.eurolinkage.org/euro

European Anti-Poverty Network
http://www.epitelio.org/maineapn.htm
Platform of European Social NGOs   **http://www.platform-ngos.org**

http://europa.eu.int
This is the central site for policy documentation, information on institutions, up-to-date developments and links to other sites. Beginners start here.

http://europa.eu.int/eur-lex
This is a key sub-site of the europa system and offers free access to a mass of EU judicial and legislative information.

http://www.ecu-notes.org
InfoEurope is an EU-funded site that provides up-to-date information on EU social policy and industrial relations plus some links to the sites of EU social policy interest groups.

http://www.lib.berkeley.edu/GSSI/eu.html
This excellent site, entitled European Union Internet Resources, contains an impressive collection of links to 'EU servers in institutions', 'EU documents on the web' and 'Servers of interests in or from EU countries'.

http://www.cec.org.uk
This is the site of the European Commission Representatives in the UK and is a good base for looking into the British–EU relationship.

http://www.eurunion.org
This is the site of the European Union website in the USA and is an excellent base for looking into the USA–EU relationship (also see the site of the USA representatives in the EU, **http://www.useu.be**).

http://www.ecsa.org
The European Communities Studies Association is one of the largest and most active academic organizations for studying the EU and maintains an excellent website with links to a wide variety of other sites.

It is important to note that these are just a few of the existing sites and were correct at the time of this book's going to press (December 1999).

Notes

Preface

1   See Geyer (1992, 1993, 1997, 1997a), Geyer and Ayres (1995), and Geyer and Swank (1997).

Introduction

1   I have copied the metaphor of Sisyphus from the excellent work of Stanley Hoffmann (1995).
2   Examples include Betten (1989), Gold (1993), Leibfried and Pierson (1995), Room et al. (1991), Sykes and Alcock (1998).
3   These include Beck et al. (1998); Brewster and Teague (1989); Cram (1997); Falkner (1998); Hantrais (1995); Nielsen and Szyszczak (1993); Rees (1998); Springer (1992, 1994); and Wise and Gibb (1993).
4   For early theoretical examinations of this crossover, see Almond (1989); Biersteker (1993); Gourevitch (1978); Parry (1993).
5   Classic works in institutionalism and historical institutionalism include March and Olsen (1984, 1989); North (1990); Pierson (1996); Steinmo et al. (1992).
6   For more on the difference between a comparative method and approach, see Cantori and Ziegler (1988); Chilcote (1981).
7   Giandomenico Majone, particularly in his work *Regulating Europe* (1996), is excellent at exploring the intricacies of EU–USA policy similarities. In this book, I do not have the space to fully examine and integrate his work. Nevertheless, his work on EU social policy remains one of the main areas of theoretical innovation in EU social policy.
8   Throughout I use the ECU (European Currency Unit), a weighted basket

of EC currencies which was established in 1979 with the creation of the European Monetary System, as the predominant currency unit. In 1995, 1 ECU was equal to 1.3 US dollars and 0.82 British pounds. With the creation of European Monetary Union in 1999 the ECU was transformed into the Euro. In EU policy, one billion equals one thousand million.

Chapter 1   European Social Policy 1950–1969

1 Paragraphs 159–60, cited in Collins (1975a: 32).
2 Karl Deutsch would later develop the concept of 'transactionalism' (Deutsch, 1957).
3 For an excellent overview and critical review of neo-classical/mainstream economic theory, see Hodgson (1987).
4 As Michael Aglietta argued: 'the neo-classical theory of international relations is nothing other than a theory of the tendential dissolution of this spatial heterogeneity (the existing world of nation-states) and its replacement by the homogeneous space of 'pure' market relations on a world scale' (Aglietta, 1982: 1).
5 As argued by Lipson (1983) and Tsoukalis (1996), intra-industrial trade has a much less disruptive impact than inter-industrial trade. If West European trade growth had involved inter-industry competition, one would have expected to see increasing national specialization as industries collapsed or boomed according to the comparative advantages which they had in their given nation-states. Whole industries would have collapsed and massive social disruption would have been generated. In fact, the opposite occurred. With regulated intra-industrial trade, industries specialized within a particular sector, West European nation-states took on increasingly similar industrial profiles, and massive social dislocations were avoided.
6 It is interesting to note that this is one of the few areas in US government and policy-making where political scientists had a substantial degree of influence. A key example would be the career and influence of Henry Kissinger.
7 This article and many of his other key articles can be found in Hoffmann (1995).

Chapter 2   European Social Policy 1970–1999

1 The text of Delors' speech of October 1989 is in Nelsen and Stubb (1994: 60).
2 Reviews of the development of these two documents include Calingaert (1988); Cameron (1992); Hoffmann (1989); Moravcsik (1991); Sandholtz and Zysman (1989).
3 As a commentator for *The Economist* noted about the White Paper, 'Europe has laboured long to produce a mouse' ('Europe's Smiling Mouse',

The Economist, 7 December 1985: pp.47–8).

4 The reduction of technical barriers provides a good example of the immobilizing effect of the harmonization strategy. According to Lauwaars (1988), from 1964 to 1984 the Council adopted only seven directives a year to remove technical barriers.

5 For more information on this case, see John Pinder (1989); Rasmussen (1989); Weatherill and Beaumont (1995).

6 These areas were: freedom of movement; employment and remuneration; improvement of living and working conditions; social protection; freedom of association and collective bargaining; vocational training; equal treatment for men and women; information, consultation, and participation for workers; health protection and safety at the workplace; protection of children and adolescents, the elderly and the disabled.

7 Identifying supporters and opponents of EU social policy during this period was complicated by the militancy of British opposition. On almost any piece of social policy legislation, a British veto was guaranteed. Hence, if a member state did not like the legislation but did not want to appear 'anti-European', it was much easier to support social policy proposals, since they knew they would never pass the British veto. Hence, the member states and Council could engage in 'cheap talk' (Lange, 1992: 242) on social policy.

8 As the Maastricht Treaty's Protocol on Social Policy stated: 'Acts thus adopted by the Council *and any financial consequences of measures taken in application of [the last indent of Article 118 (3)] shall not be applicable to the United Kingdom*' (emphasis in original).

9 In an unusually open display of dissent, Mrs Vasso Papandreou (the retiring EC Commissioner for Social Affairs) complained: 'We are at the end of 1992, and on the eve of the Single Market, our hopes have come to nothing ... The British presidency has been effective as to its aim which was to take as few [social policy] decisions as possible' (*Agence: Europe*, 5 December 1992).

Chapter 3   Labour Policy: Core Areas

1 General works on EU labour policy include Barnard (1996); Bercusson (1992, 1994); Brewster and Teague (1989); Cox (1963); Davies et al. (1996); Due (1991); Falkner (1998); Grahl and Teague (1989, 1992); Hall (1994); Marsden (1992); Rhodes (1991, 1992, 1995, 1995a); Streeck (1992, 1994); Teague (1989, 1994); Wedderburn (1990, 1991, 1995); Weiss (1992).

2 General works on freedom of movement policy include Dahlberg (1968); Green et al. (1991); Handoll (1995); Hantrais (1995: chapter 9); Ireland (1995); Johnson and O'Keeffe (1994); Nielsen and Szyszczak (1993: chapter 2); Springer (1992: chapter 9); Weatherill and Beaumont (1993).

3 Other key mobility articles include Articles 52–8 on the rights of the self-employed and Articles 59–66 on the rights of individuals to create estab-

lishments and provide services.

4 Broadly interpreted, these categories could substantially constrain movement. However, these derogations were not developed and were later strictly constrained by legal decisions (Barnard, 1996: 157).

5 In a similar fashion the Schengen Agreement, first proposed in 1985, wished to eliminate internal border controls at the same time as creating intensified external border and security co-operation, through the Schengen Information System (Ireland, 1995: 253).

6 Their second-class status is evident in the Commission's proposal to 'ensure that Member States give priority to third-country nationals *permanently and legally* resident in another Member State, when job vacancies cannot be filled by EU nationals or nationals of third countries legally resident in the Member State' (Commission, 1995a: 17; my emphasis).

7 General works on health and safety policy include Eberlie (1990); James (1993); James and Lewis (1986); Neal (1995); Neal and Wright (1992); Neilsen and Szyszczak (1993: chapter 8); Smith et al. (1993); Springer (1992: chapter 8).

8 The Permanent Mines Safety Commission was an early model of corporatist organizations within the EU. Each member state sent two government representatives, one employer and one worker representative. The Commission acted on majority vote.

9 Oddly, at the time this division of DGV was located in Luxembourg rather than Brussels.

10 The first European directive on health and safety issues was adopted under the EuroAtom treaty in 1959 and dealt with the protection of workers and the public from ionizing radiation. Obviously, EuroAtom had a number of health and safety implications, but I have not explored them in this book.

11 The Advisory Committee was responsible for all economic sectors except those covered by arrangements under the ECSC and EuroAtom. The health and safety research performed within the European Foundation was transferred to the newly created European Agency for Health and Safety at Work in 1994.

12 It has been argued that the British were willing to see this area develop since they have historically had a well-developed array of legal protections in this area and were afraid that it might become a competitive disadvantage in relation to other EU member states.

13 Extractive industries and nuclear plants were co-opted from former ECSC and EuroAtom areas.

Chapter 4   Labour Policy: Extensions

1 General works on employment rights and working conditions include Benson (1993); Burrows and Mair (1996); Due et al. (1991); European Foundation (1991); Falkner (1998); Hall (1994); Hepple (1977); Marsden (1992); Meulders et al. (1994); Moussis (1997); Springer (1992).

2　An earlier version of this directive gave the consulted public authorities the ability to prohibit the dismissals. This clause was strongly opposed by the British Conservative government in 1974 and subsequently removed from the text (Hepple, 1977: 118).

3　B. A. Hepple, a leading academic on EU social policy, concluded that 'The directives discussed in this article are likely to be simply the beginning of Community measures in the field of job security' (Hepple, 1977: 126).

4　The three categories were: independent workers – those with uneven or difficult-to-determine hours of work (managing executives, family workers, religious workers); workers connected with industries that work twenty-four hours a day (security and surveillance, hospitals, airport, media); and workers in industries with uneven work times (agriculture, tourism, postal services).

5　UEAPME, an organization of small and medium-sized enterprises, challenged the legality of the EU's making legislation using the social partners and excluding groups like itself. Its first challenge, regarding the Parental Leave Directive, was rejected by the Court of First Instance in 17 June 1998, but it has threatened to challenge other agreements.

6　General works on European worker participation include Blanpain et al. (1983); Brewster and Teague (1989); Clark and Hall (1992); Falkner (1996 and 1998); Geyer (1996); Geyer and Springer (1998); Gold and Hall (1994); Hall (1992, 1994), Hall et al. (1995); Holle (1992); Nielsen and Szyszczak (1993); Rhodes (1995); Streeck (1992).

7　In March 1993 a French Hoover factory chose to close down its operations and transfer its activities to a low-wage and less regulated area in Scotland. To European trade unions, this seemed like a perfect example of the kind of 'social dumping' that a free-market EU was capable of producing.

8　General works on the social dialogue include Abbot (1997); Carley (1993); Dølvik (1997); Falkner (1998); Geyer (1996); Gorges (1996); Hamilton (1983); Henley and Tsakalotos (1992); Marginson and Sisson (1998); McLaughlin (1985); Rhodes (1992); Teague and Grahl (1989).

9　Even in the ESC's own literature, it admits that 'it was regarded as the most unobtrusive of Community institutions' (Economic and Social Committee, 1986: 13–14).

10　From 1989 onwards, the social dialogue produced a number of 'joint opinions'. These are seen as the formal expressions of the social dialogue, but do not carry any legislative weight and are not binding. By early 1996 over fifteen joint opinions had been issued.

11　This was complicated by a declaration attached to Article 118b, which stated that: 'the content of the agreements . . . implies no obligation on the Member States to apply the agreements directly or to work out rules for their transposition, nor any obligation to amend national legislation in force to facilitate their implementation'.

Chapter 5   Gender Policy

1   General works on EU gender policy include Docksey (1987, 1991); Ellis (1998); Elman (1996, 1998); Hantrais (1995); Hoskyns (1996); Lewis (1992); Mazey (1988); Neilson (1998); Ostner and Lewis (1995); Prechal and Burrows (1990); Rees (1998); Rubery (1992); Vogel-Polsky (1985).

2   As noted in Hoskyns (1996: 56), the original text of the article stated that there should also be equal pay for 'work of equal value'. This interpretation could have raised a number of difficult questions over whether different types of work were of a similar value and had much broader implications.

3   For an overview of second wave feminism and its transnational development, see Cowley and Himmelweit (1992); Dahlerup (1986); Haug (1989); Lovenduski (1986).

4   For a detailed review of the Defrenne case, see Burrows and Mair (1996: chapter 2); Hoskyns (1996: chapter 4).

5   During one of the later trials, the advocate for Sabena argued that it was reasonable for an air traveller (assumed to be male) to wish 'to have his whisky served by an attractive woman' (Hoskyns, 1996: 70).

6   After agreeing to the case and briefing the lawyers, Defrenne chose to have no further involvement with the case.

7   Direct effect implies that in the most important areas of EU law, individuals have the right to use EU law at the national level. Treaty provisions which confer rights have both 'vertical' (where an individual is defending him/herself against the state) and 'horizontal' (where an individual is defending him/herself against another individual or firm) effect. In some ways it is the most powerful of the EU's legal provisions. For a further discussion, see Barnard (1996: 28–32).

8   Cited in Hoskyns, 1996: 103.

9   The text of the directive is in Burrows and Mair (1996: 319–23).

10   These networks are listed in Rees (1998: 61).

11   It is interesting to note how far women had come in influencing the EU agenda. As one EU expert noted: 'At the heart of the EEC, there is no doubt that from among the *disadvantaged* groups, it is women who have profited from the most deep analyses' (Vogel-Polsky, 1985: 112; emphasis in original).

12   COM (89) 568 final, pp. 35–8.

13   Positive discrimination was challenged by the *Kalanke v. Bremen* case (Case C-450/93). The ECJ found that the Bremen local government had been too direct in promoting positive discrimination for women. A later case, *Marschall v. Land Nordrhein-Westfalen* (Case C-409/95), confirmed that positive discrimination was acceptable if it was flexibly implemented. Amendments to the Equal Treatment Directive (76/207/EEC) were subsequently proposed to clarify the situation.

14   The mainstreaming strategy had a much more uneven impact on other areas of social policy (see chapter 8).

15   For the first time, a minister – Ulrika Messing, Sweden's Minister for

Women – brought her child (in this case a ten-month-old baby) to the EU meeting, 5 May 1998. The picture of Messing in casual clothing with her baby in a sling was quite a radical change from the usual dark-suited men in ties.

Chapter 6   The Structural Funds and the ESF

1 For basic reviews of the Structural Funds and ESF, see Anderson et al. (1995); Armstrong et al. (1994); Bachtler and Turok (1997); Commission (1998); Harrop (1996); Marks (1992, 1993); Smith and Tsoukalis (1997); Tsoukalis (1997).

2 The Structural Funds have become a remarkably complicated set of funding institutions. At present, an important element of these funds is aid to agriculture and agricultural regions, primarily through the European Agricultural Guidance and Guarantee Fund (EAGGF). For reasons outlined above, I do not explore the obvious social and economic role of the EAGGF in this book.

3 Excerpts from 'The Schuman Declaration' are in Harryvan and van der Harst (1997: 61–3).

4 The ECSC was a leader in promoting standardized, prefabricated housing. It also funded a number of experimental programmes for exploring the use of non-traditional building materials (particularly steel!) in housing construction. See Collins (1975: 91–6).

5 Excerpts from this text can be found in Harryvan and van der Harst (1997: 94).

6 Quota percentages in 1984 were as follows: UK 23.8%, Belgium 1.11%, Denmark 1.06%, France 13.64%, Ireland 5.94%, Italy 35.49%, Luxembourg 0.07%, Netherlands 1.24%, Germany 4.65% and Greece 13.0%.

7 By 1982 the Commission was already receiving over 10,000 applications for ESF projects.

8 The Commission's plans were outlined in Commission (1989b). The relevant legislation for the transformation of the funds was Regulations (EEC) 2052/88 and (EEC) 4253/88.

9 Council Regulation (EEC) 2081/93 redefined Structural Fund tasks and co-ordination. Council Regulation (EEC) 2082/93 contained further provisions. Council Regulation (EEC) 2084/93 dealt with changes to the ESF.

10 The Objective 6 inducements were particularly important in the Swedish referendum, which was quite close (54–46%). However, they were not enough to swing the Norwegians who voted against membership (46–54%).

11 One of the most interesting programmes was the 'Peace and Reconciliation Initiative' for Northern Ireland which allocated nearly 428 million ECU for 1995–9 to promote moves to consolidate peace in the region and promote the regeneration of areas affected by the conflict.

12 Several of my interviewees in the Commission who were working with

the ESF were clearly relieved at the prospect of reduced responsibilities and simplified guidelines.

13 This new employment orientation was so strong that several Commission and Parliament actors commented to me during interviews in late 1997 and early 1998 that if any new social policies were going to be funded in the near future, they had to be linked to employment issues. In a sense, employment has become the 'health and safety' Trojan horse issue for the late 1990s.

Chapter 7   Expansion and Extensions I

1 Response to 1993 EU social policy Green Paper (Commission, 1995: 138).
2 Charter to Combat Racism and Poverty (EAPN, 1997: 79).
3 Commission, 1998: 6.
4 Core works on EU anti-poverty policy include Beck et al. (1998); Berghman (1995); Duffy (1995, 1998); Hantrais (1995: chapter 8); Leibfried and Pierson (1992, 1995); Levitas (1996); Robbins (1990, 1993); Room (1990, 1995, 1995a, 1995b); Room et al. (1990, 1991, 1992); Sykes and Alcock (1998); Yepez del Castillo (1994).
5 Interestingly, according to sources in the Commission, Padraig Flynn was both 'pleased and surprised' that the exclusion wording was left in at all.
6 Eurostat, *Statistics in Focus*, 1997: 6 pointed out that 33 per cent of poor households were composed of retired/elderly, while 35 per cent were working poor. For these groups access to the labour market is not a concern or difficulty.
7 A clear example of the difficulty of funding broader anti-poverty policies was the result of Case 106/96 in the ECJ. In response to the Council rejection of the 1994 anti-poverty programme, the Commission attempted to continue funding some of the earlier anti-poverty and elderly programmes through its own discretionary funds. The British Conservative government (backed by Germany and Denmark) challenged the right of the Commission to allocate these funds without a Decision from the Council in 1996. In mid-May 1998, the ECJ found in favour of Britain and concluded that 'the Commission was not competent to commit the expenditure necessary to fund the projects [and] . . . acted in breach of Article 4(1) of the Treaty'. This unleashed a wave of confusion in the EU institutions since it curtailed the right of the Commission to allocate nearly 200 million ECUs of social funding. In the months following the ECJ decision, the Commission desperately tried to push legislation through the Council that would keep its complicated array of programmes afloat. As this book goes to print, the Commission had cleared nearly all of the funds, but its ability to independently support such programmes was significantly constrained.
8 This weakness in the political will has been re-emphasized by the lack of attention that the British government has shown to the exclusion issue at the EU level. This is somewhat ironic since before the UK Presidency

began, the new Labour government created its own national, Social Exclusion Unit. This was based on similar thinking to the EU's earlier social exclusion thinking, was backed by the Prime Minister Tony Blair, and was focused on just three areas (truancy, homelessness, and poor housing estates). With substantial political backing from Blair and a concentrated focus, this unit has a substantial chance of success. Unfortunately, for the present, the unit has made no attempt to link to the EU level (Geyer et al., 1999).

9   Key works on EU anti-discrimination policy include: Baimbridge et al. (1994); Commission 1997n); Geddes (1995, 1998, 1999); Hall (1995); Handoll (1995); Ireland (1995); Kohli (1998); Layton-Henry (1990); Mitchell and Russell (1995, 1998); Parliament (1985, 1991); Wrench and Solomos (1993).

10   See Geddes (1995: 211) and Parliament (1991). It is also important to note that the strength of these laws varied depending on whether they were positioned within civil and/or criminal proceedings. If a law is located in the criminal code then remedy is far more difficult to secure because of the tougher burden of proof than if there is civil redress available. The UK has civil redress in its 1976 legislation, which targets direct and indirect discrimination. Interestingly, the UK's Commission for Racial Equality was sceptical of EU developments in the field, fearing that they would undermine existing national commitments.

11   As several observers have noted, there have been a number of internal problems with the Migrants Forum. A more effective group has emerged, Starting Line Group, which concentrates more specifically on anti-discrimination policy against racism in the EU (Starting Line Group, 1997, 1998).

12   Key references to public health policy include Abel-Smith et al. (1995); Belcher (1998); Commission (1997i); Fox (1989); McKee (1998); Mossialos et al. (1997); Mossialos and McKee (1997, 1998); Normand and Vaughan (1993); Stein (1996).

13   The breadth of health policy was confirmed by the ECJ in 1996 by its rejection of the British government's arguments that it was limited to those areas mentioned in Article 129. See Case C–180/96R, *United Kingdom v. Commission*.

14   It is important to note that the budgetary allocations for these programmes was generally quite small. For example, for 1996–2000 the health promotion programme was allocated a total budget of 30 million ECU.

15   See n. 13 above.

Chapter 8   Expansion and Extensions II

1   For basic works on the development of elderly policy in the EU, see Anderson et al. (1992); Commission (1990b); Eurolink Age (1993, 1997); Hantrais (1995); Hugman (1994); McGlone and Cronin (1994); Miller (1993); Pacolet (1996); Watson (1988).

2   This was one of the small programmes that was challenged by the UK in the 1996 ECJ case that later threw much of EU social funding into disarray in 1998.

3   Key works on disability and Europe include Albeda (1984); Daunt (1991); Degener and Hendricks (1994); Degener and Koster-Dreese (1995); Doyle (1995); European Disability Forum (1996, 1997); Holloway (1981); Samoy (1992); STAKES (1998); Tomasevski (1995); Waddington (1995, 1997, 1999).

4   One of the reasons for the success of the disabled accessing these funds was the well-developed German system of vocational training for disabled workers. From 1960 to 1973 Germany obtained 42 per cent of all ESF funding for retraining and resettlement, much of it going to projects to help disabled workers (Commission, 1998h: 13).

5   This was closely modelled on United Nations Standard Rules on the Equalization of Opportunities for Persons with Disabilities, adopted by the General Assembly on 27 December 1993.

6   For a review of the debates over the position of the disabled in the treaty developments, see European Disability Forum (1998).

7   The EDF claimed that it was their focused intervention on this issue that got the point inserted in the guidelines.

8   Basic works on EU training and youth policy include: Commission (1989a, 1993a, 1997c); Ducatel (1994); Field (1998); Hantrais (1995: chapter 3); Mallet and Milliat (1997: chapter 8); Meulders et al. (1994); Moschonas (1998); Rainbird (1993); Rees (1998).

9   In 1957, 41 per cent of all coal workers were under thirty years old. By 1964, it was only 28 per cent (Collins, 1975: 56).

10   *EEC Bulletin* (1963), no. 4, paragraph 29.

11   The list appears as table 7.1 in Rees, 1998: 125, which was adapted from the Commission of the European Communities (1993) *EC Education and Training Programmes 1986–1992. Results and Achievements: An Overview*. Luxembourg: Office for Official Publications of the European Communities (COM(93) 151 final), Table 1. Budget details are up to 1992 only. Most of these funds were a 50 per cent contribution matched by the applicants from other sources from their respective member states. A 'mecu' is million ECU. An ECU was worth roughly 80p at the time of writing (1996).

12   For more details, see the sixth, ninth, thirteenth and fifteenth joint opinions of the social partners (Commission, 1996b: 354–66).

References

Abbot, K. (1997) 'The European Trade Union Confederation: Its Organisation and Objectives in Transition', *Journal of Common Market Studies*, 35, 3: 465–81.

Abel-Smith, B. et al. (1995) *Choices in Health Policy: An Agenda for the European Union*. Hants: Dartmouth Publishing.

Abrahamson, P. (1998) 'Combating Poverty and Social Exclusion in Europe' in Beck et al. (eds), 1998:145–76.

Addison, J.T. and Siebert, W.S. (1991) 'The Social Charter of the European Community: Evolution and Controversies', *Industrial and Labor Relations Review*, 44, 4: 597–625.

Adnett, N. (1993) 'The Social Charter: Unnecessary Regulation or Prerequisite for Convergence?', *British Review of Economic Issues,* 15, 36: 63–79.

Adnett, N. (1995) 'Social Dumping and European Economic Integration', *Journal of European Social Policy*, 5, 1: 1–12.

Agence: Europe, 1990–.

Aglietta, M. (1982) 'World Capitalism in the 1980s', *New Left Review*, 134: 5–41.

Albeda, W. (1984) *Disabled People and Employment*. Luxembourg: Commission of the European Communities.

Almond, G. (1989) 'Review Article: The International-National Connection', *British Journal of Political Science*, 19: 237–59.

Andersen, R. (1984) 'Exchange Rate Regimes: How the Dollar Stole Christmas' in Hewlett, S. et al. (eds) *The Global Repercussions of US Monetary and Fiscal Policy*, Cambridge: Ballinger.

Andersen, S.S. and Eliassen, K.A. (1991) 'European Community Lobbying', *European Journal of Political Research*, 20, 2: 173–89.

Anderson, J.J. (1995) 'Structural Funds and the Social Dimension of EU Policy: Springboard or Stumbling Block?' in Leibfried and Pierson (eds), 1995:123–58.

Anderson, R. et al. (1992) *The Coming of Age in Europe: Older People in the European Community*. London: Age Concern.

Armstrong, H. (1985) 'The Reform of the European Community Regional Policy', *Journal of Common Market Studies*, 23: 4.

Armstrong, H. et al. (1994) 'Regional Policy' in Artis, M. and Lee, N. (eds) *The Economics of the European Union: Policy and Analysis*. Oxford: Oxford University Press.

Armstrong, K. and Bulmer, S. (1997) *The Governance of the Single European Market*. Manchester: Manchester University Press.

Armstrong, K. (1998) 'Legal Integration: Theorising the Legal Dimension of European Integration', *Journal of Common Market Studies*, 36, 2: 155–75.

Armstrong, P., Glyn, A. and Harrison, J. (1984) *Capitalism since World War II*. London: Fontana.

Ashford, D.E. (1986) *The Emergence of Welfare States*. Oxford: Blackwell.

Bachtler, J. and Turok, I. (eds) (1997) *The Coherence of EU Regional Policy*. London: Jessica Kingsley.

Baimbridge, M., Burkitt, B. and Macey, M. (1994) 'The Maastricht Treaty: Exacerbating Racism in Europe?', *Ethnic and Racial Studies*, 17: 420–41.

Baldwin-Edwards, M. and Schain, M. (1994) 'The Politics of Immigration Control: Introduction', *West European Politics*, 17, 2: 1–6.

Barnard, C. (1996) *EC Employment Law*. Chichester: Wiley.

Beck, W. et al. (eds) (1998) *The Social Quality of Europe*. Bristol: The Policy Press.

Begg, I. (1996) 'Introduction: Regulation in the European Union', *Journal of European Public Policy*, 3, 4: 525–35.

Begg, I. and Nectoux, F. (1995) 'Social Protection and Economic Union', *Journal of European Social Policy*, 5, 4: 285–302.

Belcher, P. (1998) 'The Role of the European Union in Health Care', *Eurohealth*, 4: 2.

Benson, E. (1993) 'Employment Protection' in Gold (ed.), 1993: 64–84.

Bercusson, B. (1990) 'The European Community's Charter of Fundmental Social Rights of Workers', *The Modern Law Review*, 53: 5.

Bercusson, B. (1992) 'Maastricht: a Fundamental Change in Labour Law', *Industrial Relations Journal*, 23.

Bercusson, B. (1994) 'Social Policy at the Crossroads: European Labour Law after Maastricht' in Dehousse, R. (ed.) *Europe After Maastricht: An Ever Closer Union?* Munich: Beck.

Berghman, J. (1995) 'Social Exclusion in Europe: Policy Context and Analytical Framework' in Room (ed.), 1995b: 10–29.

Berghman, J. (1998) 'Social Protection and Social Quality in Europe' in Beck et al. (eds), 1998: 251–69.

Betten, L. (ed.) (1989) *The Future of European Social Policy*. Boston: Kluwer Law and Taxation Publishers.

Biersteker, Thomas (1993) 'Evolving Perspectives on International Political Economy: Twentieth-Century Contexts and Discontinuities', *International Political Science Review*, 14: 1.

Black, R. (1996) 'Immigration and Social Justice: Towards a Progressive EU

Immigration Policy?', *Transactions of the Institute of British Geographers*, 21: 64–75.

Blanpain, R. et al. (1983) *The Vredeling Proposal: Information and Consulation of Employees in Multinational Enterprises*. Boston: Kluwer.

Block, F. (1977) *The Origins of International Economic Disorder*. Berkeley: University of California Press.

Blondel, J. (1981) *The Discipline of Politics*. London: Butterworth Books.

Boer, M. (1995) 'Moving between Bogus and Bona Fide: The Policing of Inclusion and Exclusion in Europe' in Miles, R. and Thränhardt, D. (eds) *Migration and European Integration: The Dynamics of Inclusion and Exclusion*, London: Pinter Press.

Bretherton, C. and Sperling, L. (1996) 'Women's Networks and the European Union: Towards an Inclusive Approach', *Journal of Common Market Studies*, 34, 4: 487–507.

Brewster, C. and Teague, P. (1989) *European Community Social Policy*. London: Institute of Personnel Management.

Bulmer, S. (1983) 'Domestic Politics and EC Policy-Making', *Journal of Common Market Studies,* 21, 4: 349–63.

Bulmer, S. (1994) 'The Governance of the European Union: A New Institutionalist Approach', *Journal of Public Policy*, 13, 4: 351–80.

Burrows, N. and Mair, J. (1996) *European Social Law*. Chichester: John Wiley and Sons.

Calingaert, M. (1988) *The 1992 Challenge from Europe*, Washington, DC: National Planning Association.

Cameron, D. (1992) 'The 1992 Initiative: Causes and Consequences' in Sbragia (ed.), 1992: 23–75.

Cantori, L. and Ziegler, A. (eds) (1988) *Comparative Politics in the Postbehavioral Era*. Boulder: Lynne Rienner.

Caporaso, J. and Keeler, J. (1995) 'The European Union and Regional Integration Theory' in Mazey, S. and Rhodes, C. (eds) *The State of the European Union*, vol. 3. Boulder: Lynne Rienner.

Carley, M. (1993) 'Social Dialogue' in Gold (ed.), 1993: 105–35.

Cecchini, P. (1988) *The European Challenge 1992*. Aldershot: Wildwood House.

Chilcote, R. (1981) *Theories of Comparative Politics: The Search for a Paradigm*. Boulder: Westview Press.

Church, C.H. and Phinnemore, D. (1994) *European Union and European Community: A Handbook and Commentary on the 1992 Maastricht Treaties*. England: Prentice Hall.

Clark, J. and Hall, M. (1992) 'The Cinderella Directive? Employee Rights to Information about Conditions Applicable to their Contract or Employment Relationship', *Industrial Law Journal*, 21, 2: 106–18.

Cocks, P. (1980) 'Towards a Marxist Theory of European Integration', *International Organization*, 34, 1: 1–40.

Colchester, N. and Buchan, D. (1990) *Europower*. London: The Economist Books.

Collins, D. (1975) *The European Communities: The Social Policy of the First*

Phase. The European Coal and Steel Community 1951–70, vol. 1. London: Martin Robertson & Co.

Collins, D. (1975a) *The European Communities: The Social Policy of the First Phase. The European Economic Community 1958–72*, vol. 2. London: Martin Robertson & Co.

Collins, D. (1985) 'The New Role of the European Social Fund' in Vandamme, J. (ed.) *New Dimensions in European Social Policy*. London: Croom Helm.

Comité des Sages (1996) *For a Europe of Civic and Social Rights*, final report. Brussels.

Commission (1974) *Social Action Programme, Bulletin of the European Communities*, supplement 2/74. Brussels.

Commission (1976) *Report on the Development of the Social Situation in the Communities in 1975*. Brussels.

Commission (1981) *A New Community Action Programme on the Promotion of Equal Opportunities for Women*. Brussels (COM (81) 758).

Commission (1985) 'Guidelines for a Community Policy on Migration', *Bulletin of the European Communities*, supplement 9/85 (COM (85) 48 final).

Commission (1986) *Single European Act: Bulletin of the European Communities*, supplement 2/86.

Commission (1987) *The Regions of the Enlarged Community*. Luxembourg.

Commission (1988) *The Social Dimension of the Internal Market*. Brussels (COM (88) 1148 final).

Commission (1989) *Communication from the Commission Concerning its Action Programme Relating to the Implementation of the Community Charter of Basic Social Rights for Workers*. Brussels (COM (89) 568).

Commission (1989a) *Guide to the European Community Programme in the Fields of Education, Training, and Youth*. Brussels.

Commission (1989b) *Guide to the Reform of the Community's Structural Funds*. Luxembourg.

Commission (1990) *Community Charter of the Fundamental Social Rights of Workers*. Luxembourg.

Commission (1990a) *Equal Opportunities for Men and Women: The Third Medium Term Action Programme 1991–1995*. Brussels (COM (90) 449 final).

Commission (1990b) *Proposal for a Council Decision on Community Actions for the Elderly*. Brussels.

Commission (1991) *First Report on the Application of the Union Charter of the Fundamental Social Rights of Workers*. Brussels.

Commission (1993) *Options for the Union*. Brussels (COM (93) 551) [Green Paper on European social policy].

Commission (1993a) *Guide to the European Community Programmes in the Fields of Education, Training and Youth*. Brussels.

Commission (1994) *Growth, Competitiveness, Employment: The Challenges and Ways Forward into the 21st Century*. Brussels.

Commission (1994a) *European Coal and Steel Community: Redeployment Aid for Workers, Social Europe*, supplement 2. Brussels.

Commission (1994b) *European Social Policy: A Way Forward for the Union*.

Brussels (COM (94) 333) [White Paper].

Commission (1994c) *Men as Carers*. Brussels.

Commission (1994d) *The European Union and the Family: Social Europe.* Luxembourg.

Commission (1994e) *Women's Rights and the Maastricht Treaty on European Union.* Luxembourg.

Commission (1995) *Contributions to the Preparatory Work for the White Paper on European Social Policy: Social Europe.* Luxembourg.

Commission (1995a) 'Medium-Term Social Action Programme 1995–1997', *Social Europe*, 1/95.

Commission (1995b) 'Two Years of Community Social Policy: July 1993– June 1995', *Social Europe*, 3/94.

Commission (1996) 'Action for Employment in Europe: A Confidence Pact', *Bulletin of the EU*, supplement 4/96.

Commission (1996a) *Community Action Programme 'Europe against AIDS'.* Luxembourg.

Commission (1996b) *Community Social Policy: Current Status 1 January 1996.* Luxembourg.

Commission (1996c) *Community Social Policy: Programmes, Networks and Observatories.* Brussels.

Commission (1996d) *First Report on Economic and Social Cohesion 1996.* Brussels.

Commission (1996e) *Fourth Report from the Commission to the Council: The European Parliament and the Economic and Social Committee on the Application of the Community Charter of the Fundamental Social Rights of Workers.* Luxembourg.

Commission (1996f) *How to Create a Gender Balance in Political Decision-Making.* Brussels.

Commission (1996g) *Incorporating Equal Opportunities for Women and Men into All Community Policies and Activities.* Brussels.

Commission (1996h) 'Progress Report on the Implementation of the Medium-Term Social Action Programme 1995–97', *Social Europe*, supplement 4/96.

Commission (1996i) *Social and Economic Inclusion through Regional Development: The Community Economic Development Priority in European Structural Funds Programmes in Great Britain.* Brussels.

Commission (1996j) *Structural Funds and Cohesion Fund 1994–99: Regulations and Commentary.* Luxembourg.

Commission (1996k) 'Work and Childcare: A Guide to Good Practice', *Social Europe*, supplement 5/96.

Commission (1997) *Agenda 2000: For a Stronger and Wider Union.* Brussels (COM (97) 2000).

Commission (1997a) *An Employment Agenda for the Year 2000.* Brussels.

Commission (1997b) *EC Structural Funds: Territorial Employment Pacts: Examples of Good Practice.* Luxembourg.

Commission (1997c) *Education Training & Youth: Guide to Programmes.* Luxembourg.

Commission (1997d) '*Europe Against Cancer' Programme: Smoking Prevention Actions 1996*. Luxembourg.

Commission (1997e) *Gender, Power and Change in Health Institutions of the European Union*. Luxembourg.

Commission (1997f) *Guide to Programmes: Education, Training and Youth*, Brussels.

Commission (1997g) 'Partnership for a New Organization of Work', *Bulletin of the European Union*, supplement 4/97 (COM (97) 128 final).

Commission (1997h) *Partnership for a New Organization of Work: Case Studies*. Brussels: Commission [Green Paper].

Commission (1997i) *Public Health in Europe*. Luxembourg.

Commission (1997j) *Social Dialogue & Social Rights: Developing an Intercultural Outlook*. Luxembourg.

Commission (1997k) *Territorial Employment Pacts: Examples of Good Practice*. Brussels.

Commission (1997l) *The European Employment Strategy. Contributions to and Outcome of the Dublin European Council, 13 and 14 December 1996*. Brussels.

Commission (1997m) *The European Institutions in the Fight against Racism: Selected Texts*. Brussels.

Commission (1997n) *The State of Women's Health in the European Community*. Luxembourg.

Commission (1997o) *The Way Forward: The European Employment Strategy*. Brussels.

Commission (1998) *Communication on the Development of Public Health Policy in the European Community*. Brussels (COM (98) 230).

Commission (1998a) *Employment & European Social Fund: From Guidelines to Action: The National Action Plans for Employment*. Brussels.

Commission (1998b) *Employment & Labour Market: The 1998 Employment Guidelines Council Resolution of 15 December 1997*. Brussels.

Commission (1998c) *European Social Fund: Pathways to Integration*. Brussels.

Commission (1998d) *Progress Report from the Commission on the Follow-up to the Communication: 'Incorporating Equal Opportunities for Women and Men into all Community Policies and Activities'*. Brussels (COM (98) 122 final).

Commission (1998e) *Social Action Programme 1998–2000*. Luxembourg (COM (98) 259 final).

Commission (1998f) *The ADAPT and EMPLOYMENT Community Initiatives*. Brussels.

Commission (1998g) *The ESF in the Member States 1994–1999*. Luxembourg.

Commission (1998h) *The European Social Fund: An Overview of the Programming Period 1994–1997*. Brussels.

Commission (1998i) *An Action Plan against Racism*. Brussels.

Commission (1992–) *Employment & Social Affairs: Forum*.

Commission (1992–) *ESF InfoReviews*.

Corbett, R. et al. (1995) *The European Parliament*. London: Cartermill.

Cowley, H. and Himmelweit, S. (eds) (1992) *Knowing Women*. Cambridge: Polity Press.

Cox, R. (1993) 'Social and Labour Policy in the European Community', *British Journal of Industrial Relations*, 1, 1: 5–22.

Cram, L. (1993) 'Calling the Tune without Paying the Piper? Social Policy Regulation: the Role of the Commission in European Union Social Policy', *Policy and Politics*, 21: 135–46.

Cram, L. (1997) *Policy-Making in the European Union: Conceptual Lenses and the Integration Process*. London: Routledge.

Crespo, E. B. (1989) 'Horizon 1992 and the Left', *Contemporary European Affairs*, 1, 1/2: 29–45.

Cutler, T. et al. (1989) *1992 – The Struggle for Europe: A Critical Evaluation of the European Community*. Oxford: Berg.

Dahlberg, J. (1968) 'The EEC Commission and the Politics of the Free Movement of Labour', *Journal of Common Market Studies*, 6, 310–33.

Dahlerup, D. (ed.) (1986) *The New Women's Movement: Feminism and Political Power in Europe and the USA*. London: Sage.

Daubler, W. (1977) 'The Employee Participation Directive: A Realistic Utopia?' in Kapteyn, P. (ed.) *The Social Policy of the European Communities*. Leyden: A. W. Sijthoff.

Daunt, P. (1991) *Meeting Disability: A European Response*. London: Cassell.

Davies, P., Lyon-Caen, A., Sciarra, S. and Simitis, S. (1996) *European Community Labour Law: Principles and Perspectives*. Oxford: Oxford University Press.

Degener, T. and Hendricks, A. (1994) 'The Evolution of a European Perspective on Disability Legislation', *European Journal of Health Law*, 1: 00.

Degener, T. and Koster-Dreese, Y. (eds) (1995) *Human Rights and Disabled Persons: Essays and Relevant Human Rights Instruments*. Dordrecht: Martin Nijhoff.

Dehousse, R (1993) 'Integration v. Regulation? On the Dynamics of Regulation in the European Community', *Journal of Common Market Studies*, 330, 4: 383–402.

Delors, J. (1985) 'Preface', in Vandamme (ed.), 1985: ix–xvii.

Delors Report (Committee for the Study of Economic and Monetary Union) (1989) *Report on Economic and Monetary Union in the European Community*. Luxembourg: Office for Official Publications of the European Communities.

Deutsch, K. et al. (1957) *Political Community and the North Atlantic Area: International Organization in the Light of Historical Experience*. Princeton, NJ: Princeton University Press.

Docksey, C. (1987) 'The European Community and the Promotion of Equality' in McCrudden, C. (ed.) *Women, Employment and European Equality Law*. London: Eclipse.

Docksey, C. (1991) 'The Principle of Equality between Women and Men as a Fundamental Right under Community Law', *Industrial Law Journal*, 20, 4: 258–80.

Dølvik, J. (1997) 'The ETUC and Development of Social Dialogue and European Negotiations after Maastricht', Working Paper. University of Oslo.

Dowding, K. (1995) 'Model or Metaphor? A Critical Review of the Policy Network Approach', *Political Studies*, 43: 136–58.

Doyle, B. (1995) *Disability, Discrimination and Equal Opportunities: A Comparative Study of the Employment Rights of Disabled People*. London: Mansell.

Ducatel, K. (ed.) (1994) *Employment and Technical Change in Europe: Work Organisation, Skills and Training*. Cheltenham: Edward Elgar.

Due, J., et al. (1991) 'The Social Dimension: Convergence or Diversification of Industrial Relations in the Single European Market?', *Industrial Relations Journal*, 22, 2: 85–102.

Duff, A. (ed.) (1997) *The Treaty of Amsterdam: Text and Commentary*. London: Sweet & Maxwell.

Duffy, K. (1995) *Social Exclusion and Human Dignity in Europe,* Strasbourg: Council of Europe.

Duffy, K. (1998) 'Combating Social Exclusion and Promoting Integration in the European Union', in Oppenhein, C. (ed.) *An Inclusive Society: Strategies for Tackling Poverty,* London: Institute for Public Policy Research.

EAPN (1997) *Racism and Poverty in Europe*. Brussels: EAPN.

EAPN (1996–) *Network News*. Brussels.

Eberlie, R.F. (1990) 'The New Health and Safety Legislation of the European Community', *Industrial Law Journal*, 19: 81–97.

Economic and Social Committee (1986) *The Other European Assembly*. Brussels.

Edwards, G. and Spence, D. (1997) *The European Commission*. London: Cartermill Publishing [second edition].

Egeberg, M. and Trondal, J. (1999) 'Differentiated Integration in Europe', *Journal of Common Market Studies*, 37, 1: 133–42.

Eichengreen, B. and Frieden, J. (eds) (1994) *The Political Economy of European Monetary Unification*. Oxford: Westview Press.

Ellis, E. (1998) *EC Sex Equality Law*. Oxford: Oxford University Press.

Elman, R. A. (eds.) (1996) *Sexual Politics and the European Union: The New Feminist Challenge*. Oxford: Berghahn Press.

Elman, R. A. (1998) 'The EU and Women: Virtual Equality' in Laurent, P. and Maresceau, M. (eds) *The State of the European Union*, vol. 4: *Deepening and Widening,* vol. 4. Boulder: Lynne Rienner.

Ermisch, J. (1991) 'European Integration and External Constraints on Social Policy: Is a Social Charter Necessary?', *National Institute Economic Review*, 136: 93–108.

Esping-Andersen, G. (1990) *The Three Worlds of Welfare Capitalism*. Princeton: Princeton University Press.

Esping-Andersen, G. (ed.) (1996) *Welfare States in Transition: National Adaptations in Global Economies*. London: Sage.

Eurolink Age (1993) *A European Community Health Policy for Older People*. Brussels.

Eurolink Age (1997) *Public Policy Options to Assist Older People*. Brussels.

Eurolink Age (1997–) *The Bulletin*.

European Disability Forum (1996) *Towards Equalisation of Opportunities for Disabled People: Into the Mainstream?* Brussels: EDF.

European Disability Forum (1997) *The European Disability Forum Strategy Document and Work Programme.* Brussels: EDF.

European Disability Forum (1997–) *Equates.*

European Disability Forum (1998) *Guide to the Amsterdam Treaty.* Brussels: EDF.

European Foundation for the Improvement of Living and Working Conditions (1998–) *Communique.*

European Public Health Alliance (19??–) *Update.* Brussels.

European Trade Union Confederation (1995) *Social Rights in Europe.* Brussels.

European Trade Union Confederation (1997) *Framework Agreement on Parental Leave.* Brussels.

European Women's Lobby (1996–) *Newsletter.* Brussels.

European Works Councils Bulletin University of Warwick.

Eurostat (1997) *Basic Statistics of the European Union.* Luxembourg.

Eurostat (1997) *Statistics in Focus.* Luxembourg.

Falkner, G. (1996) 'European Works Councils and the Maastricht Social Agreement: Towards a New Policy Style?', *Journal of European Public Policy*, 3, 2: 192–208.

Falkner, G. (1996a) 'The Maastricht Protocol on Social Policy: Theory and Practice', *Journal of European Social Policy*, 6, 1: 1–16.

Falkner, G. (1998) *EU Social Policy in the 1990s: Towards a Corporatist Policy Community.* London: Routledge.

Featherstone, K. (1988) *Socialist Parties and European Integration: A Comparative History.* Manchester: Manchester University Press.

Ferrera, M. (1996a) 'The Southern Model of Welfare in Social Europe', *Journal of European Social Policy*, 6, 1: 17–37.

Field, J. (1998) *European Dimensions: Education, Training and the European Union.* London: J. Kingsley.

Fitzpatrick, B. (1992) 'Community Social Law after Maastricht', *Industrial Law Journal*, 21, 3: 199–213.

Flora, P. (ed.) (1986) *Growth to Limits*, 2 vols. Berlin: De Gruyter.

Fox, J. (ed.) (1989) *Health Inequalities in European Countries.* Aldershot: Gower.

Galenson, W. (1981) *The International Labor Organization: An American View.* Madison, Wisconsin: University of Wisconsin Press.

Garrett, G. and Weingast, B. (1993) 'Ideas, Interests and Institutions: Constructing the European Community's Internal Market' in Goldstein, J. and Keohane, R. (eds) *Ideas and Foreign Policy: Beliefs, Institutions and Political Change.* London: Cornell University Press.

Garrett, G. and Tsebelis, G. (1996) 'An Institutional Critique of Intergovernmentalism', *International Organisation*, 50, 2: 269–99.

Geddes, A. (1995) 'Immigrant and Ethnic Minorities and the EU's "Democratic Deficit"', *Journal of Common Market Studies*, 33, 2: 197–217.

Geddes, A. (1998) 'The Representation of "Migrants' Interests" in the European Union', *Journal of Ethnic and Migration Studies*, 24, 4: 695–713.

Geddes, A. (1999) *Immigration and European Integration: Towards Fortress Europe?* Manchester: Manchester University Press.

George, S. (1990) *An Awkward Partner: Britain in the European Community*. Oxford: Oxford University Press.

George, V. and Taylor-Gooby, P. (eds) (1996) *European Welfare Policy: Squaring the Welfare Circle,* London: Macmillan.

Geyer, R. (1992) 'Democratic Socialism and the EC: The British Case', *Journal of European Integration*, 16, 1: 5–27.

Geyer, R. (1993) 'Socialism and the EC after Maastricht: From Classic to New-Model European Social Democracy' in Cafruny A. and Rosenthal G. (eds), *The State of the European Community*, vol. 2: *The Maastricht Debates and Beyond*. Boulder: Lynne Rienner.

Geyer, R. (1996) 'EU Social Policy in the 1990s: Does Maastricht Matter?', *Journal of European Integration*, 20, 1: 5–34.

Geyer, R. (1997) 'Traditional Norwegian Social Democracy and the Rejection of the EU: A Troublesome Victory', *Scandinavian Studies*, 69, 3: 322–45.

Geyer, R. (1997a) *The Uncertain Union: British and Norwegian Social Democrats in an Integrating Europe*. Aldershot: Avebury.

Geyer, R. (1998) 'Globalisation and the (Non) Defence of the Welfare State', *West European Politics*, 21, 3: 77–103.

Geyer, R. (1999) 'Can EU Social Policy Save the Social Exclusion Unit and Vice Versa?', *Politics*, 19, 3: 159–64.

Geyer, R. (1999a) 'Whose Mainstream is it Anyway: The Advantages and Contradictions of Mainstreaming EU Gender, Disabled, and Elderly Policy', manuscript.

Geyer, R. and Ayres, J. (1995) 'Rethinking Conventional Wisdom: Political Opposition to Integration in Denmark and Canada', *Journal of Commonwealth and Comparative Politics*, 33, 3: 377–99.

Geyer, R. and Springer, B. (1998) 'EU Social Policy after Maastricht: The Works Council Directive and the British Opt-Out' in Laurent, P. and Maresceau, M. (eds) *The State of the European Union*, vol. 4. *Deepening and Widening*. 207–25. Boulder: Lynne Rienner.

Geyer, R. and Swank, D. (1997) 'Rejecting the European Union: Norwegian Social Democratic Opposition to the EU in the 1990s', *Party Politics*, 3, 4: 549–62.

Geyer, R., Ingebritsen, C. and Moses, J. (eds) (2000) *Globalization, Europeanization, and the End of Scandinavian Social Democracy*. London: Macmillan.

Giavazzi, F. and Giovannini, A. (1989) *Limiting Exchange Rate Flexibility: The European Monetary System*. Cambridge, MA: MIT Press.

Gilpin, R. (1987) *The Political Economy of International Relations*. Princeton: Princeton University Press.

Glöckler, G. et al. (1998) *Guide to EU Policies*. London: Blackstone Press Ltd.

Goetschy, J. (1991) '1992 and the Social Dimension: Normative Frames, Social Actors and Content', *Economic and Industrial Democracy*, 19: 259–75.

Goetschy, J. (1994) 'European Social Policy after Maastricht', *Economic and Industrial Democracy*, 15: 477–85.

Gold, M. (ed.) (1993) *The Social Dimension: Employment Policy in the European Community*. London: Macmillan.

Gold, M. and Hall, M. (1994) 'Statutory European Works Councils: The Final Countdown?', *Industrial Relations*, 25, 3: 177–86.

Golding, P. (ed.) (1986) *Excluding the Poor*. London: Child Poverty Action Group.

Gomien, D. et al. (1996) *Law and Practice of the European Convention on Human Rights and the European Social Charter*. Strasbourg: Council of Europe Publishers.

Gorges, M. (1996) *Euro-Corporatism?: Interest Intermediation in the European Community*. New York: University Press of America.

Gough, I. (1979) *The Political Economy of the Welfare State*. London: Macmillan.

Gourevitch, P. (1978) 'The Second Image Reversed: The International Sources of Domestic Politics', *International Organization*, 32, 4: 881–912.

Grahl, J. and Teague, P. (1989) 'The Cost of Neo-Liberal Europe', *New Left Review*, 174: 33–52.

Grahl, J. and Teague, P. (1992) 'Integration Theory and European Labour Markets', *British Journal of Industrial Relations*, 30, 4: 515–27.

Green, N., Hartley, T. and Usher, J. (1991) *The Legal Foundations of the Single European Market*. Oxford: Oxford University Press.

Greenwood, J. (1997) *Representing Interests in the European Union*. London: Macmillan.

Greenwood, J. and Aspinwall, M. (eds) (1998) *Collective Action in the European Union: Interests and the New Politics of Associability*. London: Routledge.

Greenwood, J., Grote, J. and Ronit, K. (eds) (1992) *Organised Interests and the European Community*. London: Sage.

Greve, B. (1996) 'Indications of Social Policy Convergence in Europe', *Social Policy and Administration,* 30, 4: 348–67.

Grieco, J. (1988) 'Anarchy and the Limits of Cooperation: A Realist Critique of the Newest Liberal Institutionalism', *International Organization*, 42, 3: 485–508.

Groom, A.J.R. (1994) 'Neofunctionalism: A Case of Mistaken Identity' in Nelsen and Stubb (eds), 1994: 111–25.

Grosser, A. (1982) *The Western Alliance*. New York: Vintage.

Haahr, J.H. (1993) *Looking to Europe: The EC Policies of the British Labour Party and the Danish Social Democrats*. Aarhus: Aarhus University Press.

Haas, E. (1958) *The Uniting of Europe: Political, Social and Economic Forces, 1950–1957*. Stanford: Stanford University Press.

Haas, E. (1964) *Beyond the Nation-State: Functionalism and International Organisation*. Stanford: Stanford University Press.

Haas, E. (1970) 'The Study of Regional Integration: Reflections on the Joys and Anguish of Pre-Theorising', *International Organisation*, 4: 607–46.

Hall, M. (1992) 'Behind the European Works Councils Directive: The European Commission's Legislative Strategy', *British Journal of Industrial Relations*, 30, 4: 547–65.

Hall, M. (1994) 'Industrial Relations and the Social Dimension of European Integration: Before and after Maastricht' in Hyman, R. and Ferner, A. (eds) *New Frontiers in European Industrial Relations*. Oxford: Blackwell.

Hall, M. et al. (1995) *European Works Councils: Planning for the Directive*. Warwick: Industrial Relations Research Unit.

Hall, P. (1989) *The Political Power of Economic Ideas*. Princeton, NJ: Princeton University Press.

Hall, S. (1995) *Nationality, Migration Rights and Citizenship of the Union*. Dordrecht: Martinus Nijhoff.

Hamilton, G. (1983) *The Vredeling Proposal and Multinational Trade Unionism*, Occasional Paper no. 11. Washington, DC: Centre for Multinational Studies.

Handoll, A. (1995) *Free Movement of Persons in the EU*. Chichester: Wiley.

Hannequart, A. (ed.) (1992) *Economic & Social Cohesion in Europe: A New Objective for Integration*. London: Routledge.

Hantrais, L. (1995) *Social Policy in the European Union*. London: Macmillan.

Hardy, S. et al. (eds) (1995) *An Enlarged Europe: Regions in Competition?* London: Jessica Kingsley Publishers Ltd.

Harrison, R.J. (1974) *Europe in Question*. London: George Allen & Unwin.

Harrop, J. (1996) *Structural Funding and Employment in the European Union: Financing the Path to Integration*. Cheltenham: Edward Elgar.

Harryvan, A. and van der Harst, J. (eds) (1997) *Documents on European Union*. London: Macmillan.

Haug, F. (1989) 'Lessons from the Women's Movement in Europe', *Feminist Review*, 31: 107–16.

Heater, D. (1992) *The Idea of European Unity*. University of Leicester.

Henley, A. and Tsakalotos, E. (1992) 'Corporatism and the European Labour Market after 1992', *British Journal of Industrial Relations*, 30, 4: 567–86.

Hepple, B. and Byre, A. (1989) 'EEC Labour Law in the United Kingdom: A New Approach', *Industrial Law Journal*, 18: 129–43.

Hepple, B.A. (1977) 'Community Measures for the Protection of Workers against Dismissal' in Kapteyn, P. (ed.) *The Social Policy of the European Communities*. Leyden: Sijthoff.

Hill, M. (1996) *Social Policy: A Comparative Analysis*. Hemel Hempstead: Prentice Hall/Harvester Wheatsheaf.

Hirst, P. and Thompson, G. (1996) *Globalization in Question*. Cambridge: Polity Press.

Hix, S. (1994) 'The Study of the European Community: The Challenge to Comparative Politics', *West European Politics*, 17, 1: 1–30.

Hodgson, G. (1987) *Economics and Institutions: A Manifesto for a Modern Institutional Economics*. Philadelphia: University of Philadelphia Press.

Hoffmann, S. (1989) 'The European Community and 1992', *Foreign Affairs*, 68, 4: 27–47.

Hoffmann, S. (1995) *The European Sisyphus: Essays on Europe 1964–1994.* Oxford: Westview Press.

Holle, C. (1992) 'Workers' Participation and EC Legislation', *Bulletin of Comparative Labour Relations*, 23: 19–34.

Holloway, J. (1981) *Social Policy Harmonisation in the European Community.* Gower: Farnborough.

Hooghe, L. (1998) 'EU Cohesion Policy and Competing Models of European Capitalism', *Journal of Common Market Studies*, 36, 4: 457–77.

Hoskyns, C. (1996) *Integrating Gender: Women, Law and Politics in the European Union.* London: Verso.

Hugman, R. (1994) *Ageing and the Care of Older People in Europe.* London: Macmillan Press Ltd.

Hurst, R. (1995) 'Choice and Empowerment: Lessons from Europe', *Disability and Society*, 10, 4: 529–35.

Ireland, P.R. (1995) 'Migration, Free Movement, and Immigrant Integration in the EU: A Bifurcated Policy Response' in Leibfried and Pierson (eds), 1995: 231–67.

James, P. (1993) 'Occupational Health and Safety' in Gold (ed.), 1993: 135–53.

James, P. and Lewis, D. (1986) 'Health and Safety at Work' in Lewis, R. (ed.) *Labour Law in Britain.* Oxford: Blackwell.

James, S. (1998) 'Labour Markets and Social Policy in Europe: The Case of the European Union' in Sykes and Alcock (eds), 1998: 29–55.

Johnson and O'Keeffe (1994) 'From Discrimination to Obstacles to Free Movement: Recent Developments concerning the Free Movement of Workers', *Common Market Law Review*, 31: 1313–47.

Jowell, T. (1998) 'Developing EU Public Health Policy', *EuroHealth*.

Kassim, H. (1994) 'Policy Networks, Networks and European Union Policy Making: A Sceptical View', *West European Politics*, 17, 4: 15–27.

Kempson, E. et al. (1994) *Hard Times.* London: Policy Studies Institute.

Kenen, G. (1984) 'Introduction' in Hewlett, S. et al. (eds) *The Global Repercussions of US Monetary and Fiscal Policy.* Cambridge: Ballinger.

Keohane, R. and Hoffmann, S. (1991) (eds) *The New European Community: Decision-Making and Institutional Change.* Boulder: Westview.

Keohane, R. and Nye, J. (1977) *Power and Interdependence: World Politics in Transition.* Boston: Little, Brown.

Kohler-Koch, B. (1996) 'Catching up with Change: The Transformation of Governance in the European Union', *Journal of European Public Policy*, 3, 3: 359–80.

Kohli, J. (1998) ' "Race": An Emergent Policy Area in the European Union' in Sykes and Alcock (eds), 1998: 171–91.

Krasner, S. (1983) *International Regimes.* Ithaca, NY: Cornell University Press.

Kuper, B.O. (1994) 'The Green and White Papers of the European Union: The Apparent Goal of Reduced Social Benefits', *Journal of European Social Policy*, 4, 2: 129–37.

Lange, P. (1992) 'The Politics of the Social Dimension' in Sbragia (ed.), 1992: 225–57.

Lange, P. (1993) 'Maastricht and the Social Protocol: Why Did They Do It?', *Politics and Society*, 21: 1, 5–36.

Lauwaars, R. (1988) 'The Model Directive on Technical Harmonization' in Beiber, R. et al. (eds) *1992 One European Market?* Baden-Baden: Nomos.

Lavalette, M. and Pratt, A. (eds) (1997) *Social Policy: A Conceptual and Theoretical Introduction*. London: Sage.

Layton-Henry, Z. (1990) *The Political Rights of Migrant Workers in Western Europe*. London: Sage.

Lefebvre, M. C. (1998) 'Taking Account of Equal Opportunities for Men and Women in ESF Support Measures' in ESF Workshop Reports, 26–8 May. Birmingham: ESF Congress.

Leibfried, S. (1993) 'Towards a European Welfare State?' in Jones, C. (ed.) *New Perspectives on the Welfare State in Europe*. London: Routledge.

Leibfried, S. and Pierson, P. (1992) 'Prospects for Social Europe', *Politics and Society*, 20, 3: 333–66.

Leibfried, S. and Pierson, P. (1995) 'Semi-Sovereign Welfare States: Social Policy in a Multitiered Europe' in Leibfried and Pierson (eds), 1995: 43–7.

Leibfried, S. and Pierson, P. (eds) (1995) *European Social Policy: Between Fragmentation and Integration*. Washington, DC: Brookings Institution.

Levi-Sandri, L. (1968) 'Free Movement of Workers in the European Community', *Bulletin of the European Communities*, 11.

Levitas, R. (1996) 'The Concept of Social Exclusion and the New Durkheimian Hegemony', *Critical Social Policy*, 16: 5–20.

Lewis, J. (1992) 'Gender and the Development of Welfare Regimes', *Journal of European Social Policy*, 2, 3: 159–73.

Lindberg, L. and Scheingold, S. (1970) *Europe's Would-Be Polity: Patterns of Change in the European Community*. Englewood Cliffs, NJ: Prentice Hall.

Lindberg, L. and Scheingold, S. (eds) (1971) *Regional Integration: Theory and Research*. Cambridge, MA: Harvard University Press.

Lingle, C. (1991) 'The EC Social Charter, Social Democracy and Post-1992 Europe', *West European Politics*, 14, 1: 129–39.

Lipson, C. (1983) 'The Transformation of Trade: The Sources and Effects of Regime Change' in Krasner, S. (ed.) *International Regimes*. Ithaca, NY: Cornell University Press.

Lodge, J. (1978) 'Towards a Human Union: EEC Social Policy and European Integration', *British Review of International Studies*, 4: 107–34.

Lodge, J. and Herman, V. (1980) 'The Economic and Social Committee and EEC Decision Making', *International Organisation*, 34, 2: 265–84.

Lovenduski, J. (1986) *Women and European Politics*. Brighton: Wheatsheaf Books.

Majone, G. (1992) 'Regulatory Federalism in the European Union', *Government and Policy*, 10: 299–316.

Majone, G. (1993) 'The European Community: Between Social Policy and Social Regulation', *Journal of Common Market Studies*, 31, 2: 153–69.

Majone, G. (1996) *Regulating Europe*. London: Routledge.

Mallet, A. and Milliat, M. (1997) *Introduction à l'Europe Sociale*. Rennes: ESNP.

March, J. and Olsen, J. (1984) 'The New Institutionalism: Organization Factors in Political Life', *American Political Science Review*, 78, 3: 734–49.

March, J. and Olsen, J. (1989), *Rediscovering Institutions*. New York: Free Press.

Marginson, P. and Sisson, K. (1998) 'European Collective Bargaining: A Virtual Prospect?', *Journal of Common Market Studies*, 36, 4: 505–28.

Marglin, S. and Schor, J. (eds) (1991) *The Golden Age of Capitalism*. Oxford: Clarendon Press.

Marks, G. (1992) 'Structural Policy in the European Community' in Sbragia (ed.), 1992: 191–225.

Marks, G. (1993) 'Structural Policy and Multi-Level Governance in the European Community' in Cafruny, A. and Rosenthal, G. (eds) *The State of the European Community*. New York: Lynne Rienner.

Marks, G., Scharpf, F.W., Schmitter, P.C. and Streeck, W. (eds) (1996) *Governance in the European Union*. London: Sage.

Marks, G., Hooghe, L. and Blank, K. (1996a) 'European Integration from the 1980s: State-Centric v. Multi-Level Governance', *Journal of Common Market Studies*, 34, 3: 341–77.

Marsden, D. (1992) 'European Integration and the Integration of European Labour Markets', *Labour: Review of Labour Economics and Industrial Relations*, 6, 1: 3–35.

Marshall, T.H. (1950) *Citizenship and Social Class*. Cambridge: Cambridge University Press.

Marshall, T.H. (1964) *Class, Citizenship and Social Development*, Garden City, NY: Doubleday.

Marshall, T.H. (1975) *Social Policy in the 20th Century*. London: Hutchinson.

Martin, David (1989) 'A Left Agenda for Europe', *Contemporary European Affairs*, 1, 1/2: 109–28.

Mazey, S. (1988) 'European Community Action on Behalf of Women: The Limits of Legislation', *Journal of Common Market Studies*, 68: 63–84.

Mazey, S. and Richardson, J. (eds) (1993) *Lobbying in the European Community*. Oxford: Oxford University Press.

McCrudden, C. (ed.) (1987) *Women, Employment and European Equality Law*. London: Eclipse.

McGlone, F. and Cronin, N. (1994) *A Crisis in Care? The Future of Family and State Care for Older People in the European Union*. London: Family Policies Study Centre.

McGowan, F. and Wallace, H. (1996) 'Towards a European Regulatory State', *Journal of European Public Policy*, 3, 4: 560–76.

McKee, M. (1998) 'An Agenda for Public Health Research in Europe', *European Journal of Public Health*, 8: 3–7.

McLaughlin, D. (1985) 'The Involvement of the Social Partners at the European Level' in Vandamme (ed.), 1985: 155–75.

Meulders, D. et al. (1994) *Atypical Employment in the EC*. Aldershot:

Dartmouth Publishing Company.

Meulders, D. and Plasman, R. (1997) 'European Economic Policies and Social Quality' in Beck et al. (eds), 1998: 19–41.

Miller, G. (1993) *The Future of Social Security in Europe in the Context of Economic and Monetary Union*. Report to the European Commission, Brussels: Observatoire Social Européen.

Mitchell, M. and Russell, D. (1995) 'National Identity, Immigration and Citizenship in the New Europe' in Jenkins, B. and Sofos, S. (eds) *Nation and Identity in Contemporary Europe*. London: Routledge.

Mitchell, M. and Russell, D. (1998) 'Immigration, Citizenship, and Social Exclusion in the New Europe', in Sykes and Alcock (eds), 1998: 75–95.

Mitrany, D. (1966) *A Working Peace System*. Chicago: Quadrangle.

Moravcsik, A. (1991) 'Negotiating the Single European Act: National Interests and Conventional Statecraft in the European Community', *International Organisation*, 45: 19–56.

Moravcsik, A. (1993) 'Preferences and Power in the European Community: A Liberal Intergovernmentalist Approach', *Journal of Common Market Studies*, 31, 4: 473–524.

Moschonas, A. (1998) *Education and Training in the European Union*. Aldershot: Ashgate.

Mosley, H. (1990) 'The Social Dimension of European Integration', *International Labour Relations Review*, 129, 2: 147–64.

Mossialos, E. et al. (1997) 'Health Care and the Single Market', *European Journal of Public Health*, 7: 235–7.

Mossialos, E. and McKee, M. (1997) 'The European Union and Health: Past, Present and Future' in Harrison, E. Anthony (ed.) *Health Care UK*. London: Kings Fund.

Mossialos, E. and McKee, M. (1998) 'The Amsterdam Treaty and the Future of European Health Policy', *Journal of Health Policy*, 3: 65–7.

Moussis, M. (1997) *Handbook of Social Europe: Guide to Community Legislation and Programmes*. Rixensart: European Study Service.

Mutimer, D. (1989) '1992 and the Political Integration of Europe: Neofunctionalism Reconsidered', *Journal of European Integration*, 13: 75–101.

Neal, A. (1995) 'Promoting Occupational Safety and Health in the European Union' in Neal and Foyn (eds), 1995.

Neal, A. and Foyn, S. (eds) (1995) *Developing the Social Dimension in an Enlarged European Union*. Oslo: Scandinavian University Press.

Neal, A. and Wright, F. (1992) *The European Communities' Health and Safety Legislation*. London: Chapman Hall.

Neilson, J. (1998) 'Equal Opportunities for Women in the European Union: Success or Failure?', *Journal of European Social Policy*, 8, 1: 64–79.

Nelsen, B. and Stubb, A. (eds) (1994) *The European Union: Readings on the Theory and Practice of European Integration*. Boulder: Lynne Rienner.

Neville Brown, L. and Kennedy, T. (1995) *The Court of Justice of the European Communities*. London: Sweet & Maxwell [fourth edition].

Nielsen, R. and Szyszczak, E. (1993) *The Social Dimension of the European*

Community. Copenhagen: Handelschjskolens Forlag [second edition].

Normand, C. and Vaughan, J. (eds) (1993) *Europe without Frontiers: The Implication for Health*. London: John Wiley.

North, D. (1990) *Institutions, Institutional Change, and Economic Performance*. Cambridge: Cambridge University Press.

O'Neill, M. (1996) *The Politics of European Integration: A Reader*. London: Routledge.

Orloff, A.S. (1992) 'Gender and the Social Rights of Citizenship: The Comparative Analysis of Gender Relations and Welfare States', *American Sociological Review*, 58, 3: 303–28.

Ostner, I. and Lewis, J. (1995) 'Gender and the Evolution of European Social Policies' in Leibfried and Pierson (eds), 1995: 159–94.

Pacolet, J. (ed.) (1996) *Social Protection and the European Economic and Monetary Union*. Aldershot: Avebury.

Parliament (1969) *Fundamental Problems of European Community Policy*. Brussels, 3 November.

Parliament (1985) *Committee of Inquiry into the Rise of Fascism and Racism in Europe: Report of the Finding of the Inquiry*. Luxembourg.

Parliament (1991) *Committee of Inquiry into Racism and Xenophobia: Report of the Finding of the Inquiry*. Luxembourg.

Parliament (1995) *Confronting the Fortress: Black and Migrant Women in the European Community*. Brussels.

Parliament (1998) *Working Document on the European Union Health Policy on the Eve of the Millennium*. Luxembourg.

Parry, G. (1993) 'The Interweaving of Foreign and Domestic Policy-Making', *Government and Opposition*, 28, 2: 143–51.

Parry, R. (1995) 'Redefining the Welfare State' in Hayward, J. and Page, E. (eds) *Governing the New Europe*. Cambridge: Polity Press.

Pelling, H. (1992) *A History of British Trade Unionism*. London: Penguin Books.

Pentland, C. (1973) *International Theory and European Integration*. New York: Free Press.

Peters, B. (1992) 'Bureaucratic Politics and the Institutions of the European Community', in Sbragia (ed.), 1992: 75–23.

Peters, B. (1994) 'Agenda-Setting in the European Community', *Journal of European Public Policy*, 1, 1; 9–26.

Peterson, J. (1995) 'Decision-Making in the European Union: Towards a Framework for Analysis', *Journal of European Public Policy*, 2, 1: 69–93.

Peterson, J. (1995a) 'Policy Networks and European Union Policy Making: A Reply to Kassim', *West European Politics*, 18, 2: 389–407.

Pierson, C. (1991) *Beyond the Welfare State*. Cambridge: Polity Press.

Pierson, P. (1996) 'The Path to European Integration: A Historical Institutionalist Analysis', *Comparative Political Studies*, 29, 2: 123–63.

Pierson, P. and Leibfried, S. (1995) 'The Dynamics of Social Policy Integration' in Leibfried and Pierson (eds), 1995: 432–67.

Pierson, P. and Leibfried, S. (1995a) 'Multitiered Institutions and the Making of Social Policy' in Leibfried and Pierson (eds), 1995: 1–40.

Pinder, J. (1989) 'The Single Market: A Step Towards European Union' in Lodge, J. (ed.) *The European Community and the Challenge of the Future.* New York: St. Martin's Press.

Platform of the European Social NGOs (1988) *The European Social Fund: Investing in People.* Brussels.

Ploeg, F. (1990) 'International Interdependence and Policy Coordination in Economies with Real and Nominal Wage Rigidity' in Courakis, A. and Taylor, M. (eds) *Private Behaviour and Government Policy in Interdependent Economies.* Oxford: Clarendon Press.

Pochet, P. et al. (1994) 'European Digest', *Journal of European Social Policy*, 4, 3: 230–41.

Polanyi, K. (1957) *The Great Transformation: The Political and Economic Origins of Our Time.* Boston: Beacon.

Pollack, M. (1995) 'Creeping Competence: The Expanding Agenda of the European Community', *Journal of Public Policy*, 14: 97–143.

Pollack, M. (1996) 'The New Institutionalism and EC Governance: The Promise and Limits of Institutional Analysis', *Governance*, 9, 4: 429–58.

Prechal, S. and Burrows, N. (1990) *Gender Discrimination Law of the European Community.* Aldershot: Dartmouth.

Puchala, D. (1972) 'Of Blind Men, Elephants and International Integration', *Journal of Common Market Studies*, 10: 267–85.

Putnam, R.D. (1988) 'Diplomacy and Domestic Politics', *International Organisation*, 42: 427–61.

Rainbird, H. (1993) 'Vocational Education and Training' in Gold (ed.), 1993: 184–202.

Rasmussen, H. (1989) *The European Community Constitution: Summaries of Leading EC Court Cases.* Copenhagen: Handelschjskolens Forlag.

Rees, T. (1998) *Mainstreaming Equality in the European Union: Education, Training and Labour Market Policies.* London: Routledge.

Rhodes, M. (1991) 'The Social Dimension of the Single European Market: National Versus Transnational Regulation', *European Journal of Political Research*, 19, 2/3: 245–80.

Rhodes, M. (1992) 'The Future of the "Social Dimension": Labour Market Regulation in Post-1992 Europe', *Journal of Common Market Studies*, 30, 1: 23–51.

Rhodes, M. (1995) 'A Regulatory Conundrum: Industrial Relations and the Social Dimension' in Leibfried and Pierson (eds), 1995: 78–123.

Rhodes, M. (1995a) 'Subversive Liberalism: Market Integration, Globalisation and the European Welfare State', *Journal of European Public Policy*, 2, 3: 384–406.

Rhodes, M. (1996) 'Globalisation and West European Welfare States: A Critical Review of Recent Debates', *Journal of European Social Policy*, 6, 4: 305–27.

Richard, I. (1985) 'Community Action on Economic and Social Relance' in Vandamme (ed.), 1985: 199–206.

Rifflet, R. (1985) 'Evaluation of the Community Policy' in Vandamme (ed.), 1985: 17–39.

Riker, W.H. (1964) *Federalism: Origin, Operation, Significance*. Boston: Little, Brown.

Robbins, D. (1990) *Marginalisation and Social Exclusion* (Report to the European Commission). Brussels.

Robbins, D. (1993) *Towards a Europe of Solidarity: Combatting Social Exclusion*, V/6171/93. Brussels: European Commission.

Room, G. (1995) 'Poverty and Social Exclusion: The New European Agenda for Policy and Research' in Room (ed.), 1995b: 1–10.

Room, G. (1995a) 'Poverty in Europe: Competing Paradigms of Analysis', *Policy and Politics*, 23, 2: 103–13.

Room, G. (ed.) (1995b) *Beyond the Threshold: The Measurement and Analysis of Social Exclusion*. Bristol: The Policy Press.

Room, G. et al. (1990) *'New Poverty' in the European Community*. London: Macmillan.

Room, G. et al. (1991) *National Policies to Combat Social Exclusion* (First Annual Report of the EC Observatory on Policies to Combat Social Exclusion). Brussels: European Commission.

Room, G. et al. (1992) *National Policies to Combat Social Exclusion* (Second Annual Report of the EC Observatory on Policies to Combat Social Exclusion). Brussels: European Commission.

Ross, G. (1995) *Jacques Delors and European Integration*. Cambridge: Polity Press.

Ross, G. (1995a) 'Assessing the Delors Era and Social Policy' in Leibfried and Pierson (eds), 1995: 357–89.

Rothstein, B. (1992) 'Labor-Market Institutions and Working-Class Strength' in Steinmo et al. (eds), 1992: 33–57.

Rubery, J. (1992) 'Pay, Gender, and the Social Dimension to Europe', *British Journal of Industrial Relations*, 30: 4.

Ruggie, J. (1982) 'International Regimes, Transactions, and Change: Embedded Liberalism in the Postwar Economic Order', *International Organization*, 36, 2: 379–415.

Salmon, T. and Nicoll, W. (eds) (1997) *Building European Union: A Documentary History and Analysis*. Manchester: Manchester University Press.

Samoy, E. (1992) *Sheltered Employment in the European Community*. Luxembourg: Commission of the European Communities.

Sandholtz, W. (1993) 'Choosing Union: Monetary Politics and Maastricht', *International Organization*, 47: 1–39.

Sandholtz, W. (1996) 'Membership Matters: Limits of the Functional Approach to European Institutions', *Journal of Common Market Studies*, 34, 3: 403–29.

Sandholtz, W. and Zysman, J. (1989) '1992: Recasting the European Bargain', *World Politics*, 42, 1: 95–128.

Sbragia, A. (ed.) (1992) *Euro-Politics: Institutions and Policymaking in the 'New' European Community*. Washington, DC: Brookings Institution.

Scharpf, F. (1994) 'Community and Autonomy: Multi-Level Policy-Making in the European Union', *Journal of European Public Policy*, 1, 2: 219–39.

Scharpf, F. (1996) 'Negative and Positive Integration in the Political Economy of European Welfare States' in Marks et al. (eds), 1996: 15–40.

Schmitt, H. (1962) *The Path to European Union: From the Marshall Plan to the Common Market*. Baton Rouge: Louisiana State University Press.

Schmitter, P. (1996) 'Examining the Present Euro-Polity with the Help of Past Theories' in Marks et al. (eds), 1996: 1–14.

Schwarzmantel, J. (1991) *Socialism and the Idea of the Nation*. London: Harvester/Wheatsheaf.

Seche, J.-C. (1977) 'Free Movement of Workers under Community Law' in Kapteyn, P. (ed.) *The Social Policy of the European Communities*. Leyden: Sijthoff.

Shanks, M. (1977) *European Social Policy Today and Tomorrow*. Oxford: Pergamon Press.

Sheldrake, J. (1991) *Industrial Relations and Politics in Britain 1880–1989*. London: Pinter.

Shonfield, A. (1980) *Modern Capitalism*. London: Oxford University Press.

Sisson, K. (1989) 'Personnel Management in Perspective' in Sisson, K. (ed.) *Personnel Management in Britain*. Oxford: Blackwell.

Smith, A. and Tsoukalis, L. (eds) (1997) *The Impact of Community Policies on Economic and Social Cohesion*. Bruges: College of Europe/ Sussex European Institute.

Smith, D. and Ray, J. (eds) (1993) *The 1992 Project and the Future of Integration in Europe*. New York: Sharpe.

Smith, G. et al. (1993) *Health and Safety: The New Legal Framework*. London: Butterworths.

Spicker, P. (1997) 'Exclusion', *Journal of Common Market Studies*, 35, 1: 133–43.

Springer, B. (1992) *The Social Dimension of 1992: Europe Faces a New EC*, London: Praeger.

Springer, B. (1994) *The European Union and its Citizens: The Social Agenda*. London: Greenwood Press.

Stabenov, W. (1977) 'The European Social Fund' in Kapteyn, P. (ed.) *The Social Policy of the European Communities*. Leyden: Sijthoff.

STAKES National Research and Development Centre for Welfare and Health (1998) *The Promise of the Information Society: Good Practice in Using the Information Society for the Benefit of Older People and Disabled People*. Helsinki: STAKES.

Starting Line Group (1997) *Briefing Note on the Treaty of Amsterdam, Racial Discrimination and Third Country Nationals*. Brussels: Starting Line Group.

Starting Line Group (1998) *Proposals for Legislative Measures to Combat Racism and the Promotion of Equal Rights*. Brussels: Starting Line Group.

Stein, H. (1996) 'Public Health and Public Health Research at European Union Level', *Eurohealth*, 2, 2: 23–4.

Steinmo, S. et al. (eds) (1992) *Structuring Politics: Historical Institutionalism in Comparative Analysis*. Cambridge: Cambridge University Press.

Stewart, M. (1984) *The Age of Interdependence: Economic Policy in a Shrinking World*. Cambridge, MA: MIT Press.

Streeck, W. (1992) 'National Diversity, Regime Competition and Institutional Deadlock: Problems in Forming a European Industrial Relations System', *Journal of Public Policy*, 12, 4: 301–30.

Streeck, W. (1994) 'European Social Policy after Maastricht: The "Social Dialogue" and "Subsidiarity" ', *Economic and Industrial Democracy*, 14: 151–77.

Streeck, W. (1995) 'From Market Making to State Building? Reflections on the Political Economy European Social Policy' in Leibfried and Pierson (eds), 1995: 389–432.

Streeck, W. (1996) 'Neo-Voluntarism: A New European Social Policy Regime?' in Marks et al. (eds), 1996: 64–95.

Streeck, W. and Schmitter, P. (1991) 'From National Corporatism to Transnational Pluralism', *Politics and Society*, 19, 2: 133–64.

Swank, D. (1998) 'Funding the Welfare State: Globalization and the Taxation of Business in Advanced Market Economies', *Political Studies*, 46, 4: 671–93.

Swank, D. and Hicks, A. (1992) 'Politics and the Structural Dependence of the State in Democratic Capitalist Nations', *American Political Science Review*, 86: 38–54.

Sydow, H. (1988) 'The Basic Strategies of the Commission's White Paper' in Bieber, R. et al. (eds), *1992 One European Market?* Baden-Baden: Nomos.

Sykes, R. (1998) 'Studying European Social Policy: Issues and Perspectives' in Sykes and Alcock (eds), 1998: 7–27.

Sykes, R. (1998a) 'The Future of Social Policy in Europe?' in Sykes and Alcock (eds), 1998: 251–65.

Sykes, R. and Alcock, P. (eds) (1998) *Developments in European Social Policy: Convergence and Diversity*. Bristol: The Policy Press.

Taylor, P. (1975) 'The Politics of the European Communities: The Confederal Phase', *World Politics*, April: 336–60.

Taylor, P. (1983) *The Limits of European Integration*. Beckenham: Croom Helm.

Taylor, P. (1984) 'The Nation-State in the European Communities: Superficial Realities and Underlying Uncertainties', *International Journal*, 39: 577–98.

Taylor, P. (1991) 'The European Community and the State: Assumptions, Theories and Propositions', *Review of International Studies*, 17: 109–25.

Taylor-Gooby, P. (1991) *Social Change, Social Welfare and Social Science*. London: Harvester Wheatsheaf.

Taylor-Gooby, P. (1991a) 'Welfare State Regimes and Welfare Citizenship', *Journal of European Social Policy*, 1, 2: 93–105.

Taylor-Gooby, P. (1997) 'European Welfare Futures: The Views of Key Influentials in Six European Countries on Likely Developments in Social Policy', *Social Policy and Administration*, 31, 1: 1–19.

Teague, P. (1989) 'Constitution or Regime?: The Social Dimension of the 1992 Project', *British Journal of Industrial Relations*, 27, 3: 310–30.

Teague, P. (1994) 'Coordination or Decentralisation?: EC Social Policy and European Industrial Relations' in Lodge, J. (ed.) *The EC and the Challenge of the Future.* London: Pinter.

Teague, P. (1998) 'Monetary Union and Social Europe', *Journal of European Social Policy,* 8, 2: 117–37.

Teague, P. and Grahl, J. (1989) 'European Community Labour Market Policy: Present Scope and Future Direction', *Journal of European Integration,* 13.

Teague, P. and Grahl, J. (1991) 'The European Community and the State: Assumptions, Theories and Propositions', *Review of International Studies,* 17: 109–25.

Teague, P. and Grahl, J. (1992) *Industrial Relations and European Integration,* London: Lawrence and Wishart.

Thelen, K. and Steinmo, S. (1992) 'Historical Institutionalism in Comparative Politics' in Steinmo et al. (eds), 1992: 1–33.

Titmuss, R. (1974) *Social Policy.* London: Allen and Unwin.

Titmuss, R. (1976) *Commitment to Welfare.* London: Allen and Unwin.

Tomasevski, K. (1995) 'The Right to Health for People with Disabilities' in Degener and Koster-Dreese (eds), 1995: 131–47.

Townsend, P. (1992) *Hard Times: The Prospects for European Social Policy,* Eleanor Rathbone Memorial Lecture no. 35. Liverpool: Liverpool University Press.

Tranholm-Mikkelsen, J. (1991) 'Neo-Functionalism: Obstinate or Obsolete? A Reappraisal in the Light of the New Dynamism of the European Community', *Millennium,* 20, 1: 1–22.

Traxler, F. and Schmitter, P. (1995) 'The Emerging Euro-Polity and Organised Interests', *European Journal of International Relations,* 1, 2: 191–218.

Tsoukalis, L. (1997) *The New European Economy: The Politics and Economics of Integration.* London: Oxford University Press.

Tyszkiewicz, Z. (1989) 'Employers' View of the Community Charter of Basic Social Rights for Workers', *Social Europe,* 1, 90: 22–4.

UNICE (1996) 'Social Policy, Employment and the 1996 Intergovernmental Conference speech', by Z.J.A. Tyszkiewicz, typescript.

Vandamme, J. (1985) 'Introduction', 'From European Social Policy to L'Espace Social Europeen', and 'Reinforcing the Community by a New Social Policy' in Vandamme (ed.) 1985: 1–6; 7–17; 191–9.

Vandamme, J. (ed.) (1985) *New Dimensions in European Social Policy.* London: Croom Helm.

Venturi, P. (1988) *1992: The European Social Dimension.* Brussels: Commission of the European Communities.

Vobruba, G. (1998) 'Social Policy for Europe' in Beck et al. (eds), 1998: 119–39.

Vogel-Polsky, E. (1985) 'New Social Needs: The Problems of Women' in Vandamme (ed.), 1985: 95–115.

Waddington, L. (1995) *Disability, Employment and the European Community.* London: Blackstone.

Waddington, L. (1997) 'The European Community and Disability Discrimination: Time to Address the Deficit of Powers?', *Disability and Society,* 12, 3: 465–79.

Waddington, L. (1999) 'The European Community's Response to Disability' in Jones, A. and Basser Marks, L.A. (eds) *Disability, Divers-ability and Legal Change*. Deventer: Kluwer.

Watson, P. (1988) 'Social Security and the European Communities' in Whyte, G. (ed.) *Sex Equality, Community Rights and Irish Social Welfare Law*. Dublin: Irish Centre for European Law, Trinity College.

Watson, P. (1990) 'Social Security Rights of Migrant Workers' in xxx (ed.) *Mobility of People in the European Community*. Dublin: Irish Centre for European Law, Trinity College.

Watson, P. (1993) 'Social Policy after Maastricht', *Common Market Law Review*, 30: 481–513.

Weatherill, S. and Beaumont, P. (1995) *EC Law: The Essential Guide to the Legal Workings of the European Community*. London: Penguin.

Wedderburn, L. (1990) *The Social Charter, European Company and Employment Rights*. London: The Institute of Employment Rights.

Wedderburn, L. (1991) *Employment Rights in Britain and Europe*. London: Lawrence and Wishart.

Wedderburn, L. (1995) *Labour Law and Freedom*. London: Lawrence and Wishart.

Weiss, M. (1992) 'The Significance of Maastricht for European Community Social Policy', *International Journal of Comparative Labour Law and Industrial Relations*, 8: 3–14.

Wendon, B. (1998) 'The Commission and European Union Social Policy' in Sykes and Alcock (eds), 1998: 55–75.

Wessels, W. (1997) 'An Ever Closer Fusion? A Dynamic Macropolitical View on Integration Processes', *Journal of Common Market Studies*, 35, 2: 267–99.

Wheare, K. (1953) *Federal Government*. London: Oxford University Press.

Whiteford, E. (1993) 'Social Policy after Maastricht', *European Law Review*, 18, 3: 202–22.

Willis, F.R. (1968) *France, Germany and the New Europe 1945–1967*. London: Oxford University Press.

Wise, M. and Gibb, R. (1993) *Single Market to Social Europe*. London: Longman.

Women of Europe (1991–) *Newsletter*.

Wrench, J. and Solomos, J. (1993) *Racism and Migration in Western Europe*. Oxford: Berg.

Wyatt, D. (1977) 'The Social Security Rights of Migrant Workers and their Families', in Kapteyn, P. (ed.) *The Social Policy of the European Communities*. Leyden: Sijthoff.

Yepez del Castillo, I. (1994) 'A Comparative Approach to Social Exclusion: Lessons From France and Belgium', *International Labour Review*, 133, 5–6: 613–34.

Youth Forum (1996–), *Opinion Jeunesse*.

Index